Conquered Populations in Early Islam

Edinburgh Studies in Classical Islamic History and Culture
Series Editor: Carole Hillenbrand

A particular feature of medieval Islamic civilisation was its wide horizons. In this respect it differed profoundly from medieval Europe, which from the point of view of geography, ethnicity and population was much smaller and narrower in its scope and in its mindset. The Muslims fell heir not only to the Graeco-Roman world of the Mediterranean, but also to that of the ancient Near East, to the empires of Assyria, Babylon and the Persians – and beyond that, they were in frequent contact with India and China to the east and with black Africa to the south. This intellectual openness can be sensed in many interrelated fields of Muslim thought: philosophy and theology, medicine and pharmacology, algebra and geometry, astronomy and astrology, geography and the literature of marvels, ethnology and sociology. It also impacted powerfully on trade and on the networks that made it possible. Books in this series reflect this openness and cover a wide range of topics, periods and geographical areas.

Titles in the series include:

Arabian Drugs in Early Medieval Mediterranean Medicine
Zohar Amar and Efraim Lev

The Abbasid Caliphate of Cairo, 1261–1517: Out of the Shadows
Mustafa Banister

The Medieval Western Maghrib: Cities, Patronage and Power
Amira K. Bennison

Keeping the Peace in Premodern Islam: Diplomacy under the Mamluk Sultanate, 1250–1517
Malika Dekkiche

Queens, Concubines and Eunuchs in Medieval Islam
Taef El-Azhari

The Kharijites in Early Islamic Historical Tradition: Heroes and Villains
Hannah-Lena Hagemann

Medieval Damascus: Plurality and Diversity in an Arabic Library – The Ashrafiya Library Catalogue
Konrad Hirschler

A Monument to Medieval Syrian Book Culture: The Library of Ibn ʿAbd al-Hādī
Konrad Hirschler

The Popularisation of Sufism in Ayyubid and Mamluk Egypt: State and Society, 1173–1325
Nathan Hofer

Defining Anthropomorphism: The Challenge of Islamic Traditionalism
Livnat Holtzman

Making Mongol History: Rashid al-Din and the Jamiʿ al-Tawarikh
Stefan Kamola

Lyrics of Life: Saʿdi on Love, Cosmopolitanism and Care of the Self
Fatemeh Keshavarz

Art, Allegory and The Rise of Shiism In Iran, 1487–1565
Chad Kia

A History of the True Balsam of Matarea
Marcus Milwright

Ruling from a Red Canopy: Political Authority in the Medieval Islamic World, From Anatolia to South Asia
Colin P. Mitchell

Islam, Christianity and the Realms of the Miraculous: A Comparative Exploration
Ian Richard Netton

Conquered Populations in Early Islam: Non-Arabs, Slaves and the Sons of Slave Mothers
Elizabeth Urban

edinburghuniversitypress.com/series/escihc

Conquered Populations in Early Islam

Non-Arabs, Slaves and the Sons of Slave Mothers

Elizabeth Urban

EDINBURGH
University Press

Dedicated to the memory of Cricket

Edinburgh University Press is one of the leading university presses in the UK. We publish academic books and journals in our selected subject areas across the humanities and social sciences, combining cutting-edge scholarship with high editorial and production values to produce academic works of lasting importance. For more information visit our website: edinburghuniversitypress.com

Edinburgh University Press Ltd
The Tun – Holyrood Road
12 (2f) Jackson's Entry
Edinburgh EH8 8PJ

First published in hardback by Edinburgh University Press 2020

Typeset in 11/15 Adobe Garamond by
Servis Filmsetting Ltd, Stockport, Cheshire

A CIP record for this book is available from the British Library

ISBN 978 1 4744 2321 2 (hardback)
ISBN 978 1 4744 9179 2 (paperback)
ISBN 978 1 4744 2322 9 (webready PDF)
ISBN 978 1 4744 2323 6 (epub)

Contents

List of Tables and Figures vi
Acknowledgements vii
Notes on the Text x

1 Introduction: Why Muslims of Slave Origins Matter 1
2 Insiders with an Asterisk: *Mawālī* and Enslaved Women in the Quran 19
3 Abū Bakra, Freedman of God 48
4 Enslaved Prostitutes in Early Islamic History 77
5 Concubines and their Sons: The Changing Political Notion of Arabness 106
6 Singers and Scribes: The Limits of Language and Power 140
7 Conclusions 176

Bibliography 188
Index 211

Tables and Figures

Tables

5.1 Generational scheme derived from Ibn Saʿd's *Ṭabaqāt* 110
5.2 Database categories 110
5.3 Sample database entry 110
6.1 Chronological change in scribal practice according to identity 156
6.2 Scribal identities according to place (numbers and percentages) 158
6.3 Scribal practice according to occupation (numbers and percentages) 160

Figures

5.1 Percentage of children born of *umm walad*s (UWs) 112
5.2 Average number of free wives (FWs) and *umm walad*s (UWs) per man 113
5.3 Birth rates of free wives (FWs) vs *umm walads* (UWs) 115
5.4 Percentage of children born to *umm walad*s (UWs) according to tribe 116
5.5 Adjusted numbers of free wives and *umm walad*s according to tribe 117
6.1 Changing percentages of scribal practice according to identity 157
6.2 Percentage of scribal identities according to place 159

Acknowledgements

This monograph has grown from the green seed of my 2012 doctoral dissertation at the University of Chicago. As such, I can only begin by acksnowledging my dissertation advisor, Fred Donner. He is a brilliant professor and gracious mentor, and he has continued to advocate for me and perform the often-thankless, behind-the-scenes work of supporting an advisee. Likewise, my other teachers at the University of Chicago guided the initial stages of this research and equipped me with the language skills I needed to conduct it successfully. These supporters include (in alphabetical order) Orit Bashkin, Ahmed El Shamsy, Kay Heikkenen, Frank Lewis, Farouk Mustafa (*allāh yarḥamhu*), Wadad Kadi, Walter Kaegi, Tahera Qutbuddin, Michael Sells, Donald Whitcomb and John Woods. I also benefited greatly from dialogues with my fellow University of Chicago graduate students, whether it was in class, at Arabic circle or over lunch.

Many conversations and conference panels have helped shape the monograph into its current form. I have profited greatly from discussions with other scholars about historical 'sites of memory', and about the narrative strategies that Arabic-Islamic authors employ in their writings. In this regard, Antoine Borrut deserves special thanks for his stimulating scholarship and his professional mentorship. I also thank Sarah Bowen Savant, Tayeb El-Hibri, Ari Hagler, Gershon Lewenthal and Scott Savran for their contributions and insights. I have also enjoyed thought-provoking exchanges with Michael Bates on early Islamic coinage and on strategies for de-centring the Rashidun and Umayyad caliphates, and also with Luke Yarbrough on non-Muslim scribes in the Umayyad bureaucracy. Beyond the field of early Islamic historiography,

I have also learned much from scholars who specialise in enslavement and unfreedom. My initiator into this field is Matthew Gordon, who also invited me to participate in the illuminating Binghamton Conference on Medieval Unfreedoms in 2018. I have also engaged in fruitful conversations with Kurt Franz, Kathryn Hain, Younus Mirza, Karen Moukheiber, Lisa Nielson, Craig Perry, Dwight Reynolds, Majied Robinson and Noel Mellick Voltz.

Throughout the process of researching and writing this book, I have received much scholarly support. First, I have received gracious invitations to contribute parts of my research to edited volumes, special issues and handbooks. Many thanks to Paul Cobb for inviting me to participate in the festschrift for Fred Donner; to Myriam Wissa for the *Scribal Practices* edited volume; to Matthew Gordon and Kathryn Hain for the *Concubines and Courtesans* edited volume; to Mohamad Rihan for the *Hawliyat* special issue dedicated to Aziz El Azmeh; and to Murad Idris for the *Oxford Handbook of Comparative Political Theory*. Thanks also to the anonymous peer reviewers of my research, including this monograph – they have helped me become a better scholar. (Although of course, any mistakes that remain in my work are my own.)

Second, I am thankful for the institutional backing I have received while conducting my research. Joseph Lumbard supported me during my first post-graduate job, as a visiting assistant professor in the Near Eastern and Judaic Studies department at Brandeis University. Subsequently, the History faculty at Williams College was incredibly gracious and inclusive during my Mellon post-doctoral fellowship; thanks particularly to Magnús Bernhardsson for his mentorship. Finally, my home institution, West Chester University of Pennsylvania (WCUPA), has enabled me to complete the monograph. Many thanks are due to my colleagues in the History department for their friendship, encouragement and advice on how to balance a heavy teaching load with an ambitious research plan. Particularly, I thank Lisa Kirschenbaum for sharing her experience and expertise in crafting a successful book proposal. Additionally, the College of Arts and Humanities at WCUPA granted me a 2018 Research and Creative Activities Grant that allowed me to complete the research for Chapter 5 of this monograph.

I am incredibly grateful for all the academic and institutional support I have received, but my deepest thanks go to my family and friends. My parents and siblings have read many drafts of my work in order to ensure that it is accessible to non-specialists. Writing workshops with Rebecca Makas, Amy Anderson and Kristine Ervin have helped keep me on task. Hayley Brown always pushes me to think more deeply and articulate my ideas more clearly. In addition to being a fantastic friend, Tanya Treptow has brought me several early Islamic history books from her travels to Egypt. Special thanks go to Jennifer London for her undying enthusiasm, patience and generosity. Finally, my husband, Glenn McDorman, has been a boundless source of love and support. Not only is he a fantastic scholar and teacher, but he also makes sure that I remember to eat and sleep when I am deep inside my writing bubble.

There are so many more people I could name – my editors, my students and others I may have inadvertently neglected to mention. While writing can at times feel like a solitary affair, the creation of scholarship is truly collaborative, and I could not have succeeded without these many sources of support.

Notes on the Text

Throughout this book, I have written dates in a dual Hijra/Common Era (AH/CE) format. For example, the date of Abū Bakra's death is rendered 52/672; likewise, the scholar Muḥammad ibn Saʿd is described as working in the third/ninth century.

When transliterating Arabic words, I have used the Library of Congress system, with a few small modifications (in particular, I render the *tā marbūṭa* as '*a*' rather than '*ah*,', and I render the feminine *nisba* ending as '*iyya*' rather than '*īyah*'). The specialist reader will be able to discern the original Arabic spelling of terms; the non-specialist reader can simply disregard diacritical markings. For place names with a standard English usage (such as Mecca and Medina), I have used the English spelling instead of the transliterated Arabic.

With the exception of a few key Arabic terms that I have left untranslated, I have translated all Arabic texts cited in this monograph into English. Unless otherwise stated, all translations in this monograph are my own, including Quranic translations.

1

Introduction: Why Muslims of Slave Origins Matter

This book traces the journey of new Muslims in the first and second centuries AH (seventh and eighth centuries CE), as they joined the nascent Islamic community and articulated their identities within it. It focuses particularly on Muslims of slave origins, who belonged to the Islamic religious community but whose slave backgrounds linked them to the outside world and rendered them somehow alien. By analysing how these liminal Muslims resolved the tension between belonging and otherness, this book reveals the shifting boundaries of the early Islamic community. Particularly, it illuminates how Islam transformed from a small and relatively egalitarian piety movement in Western Arabia into the official doctrine of a Near Eastern empire that tried to uphold a hierarchical distinction between the conquerors and the conquered.

This monograph concentrates on three groups that inhabited a grey area between insider and outsider in early Islamic history: 1) the *mawālī* (singular: *mawlā*) – freed slaves, captives and other conquered people who became subordinate members of conquerors' households, often glossed as 'non-Arab Muslims'; 2) enslaved women (*jawārī*) who acted as prostitutes, concubines and courtesans in the Islamic community; and 3) 'mixed-breed' or 'half-blood' (*hajīn*) children born to enslaved mothers and free Arab-Muslim fathers. Each of these groups is worthy of its own individual study, but taken together as three different types of unfree or liminal Muslims, they intersect in illuminating ways. For example, it appears that enslaved men and women played an active role in negotiating the boundaries of the earliest community under Muḥammad (*c.* 610–632 CE). However, later rulers such as 'Abd al-Malik (r. 65–86/685–705) instituted a stronger socio-political hierarchy that rendered enslaved and freed persons subalterns whose ties to the non-Arab, non-Muslim world needed to be controlled. In this hierarchical, imperial setting, enslaved people could gain power by mastering Arabic, but they had to use their linguistic expertise in ways that pleased their masters. Additionally, it appears that the children of enslaved mothers resolved their liminal position by re-defining themselves as full 'Arabs' by the mid-second/eighth century; they were only able to do so by excluding the *mawālī* as 'non-Arabs'. Moreover, one can only understand how these children of enslaved mothers transformed from liminal 'half-breeds' into full 'Arabs' by analysing the position of the enslaved mothers themselves. Thus, by examining these groups together as three facets of the same prism, this monograph sheds light on the expansion of the young Islamic community and its accommodation of diverse peoples.

It is difficult to paint a comprehensive picture of enslaved and freed persons in the Islamic sources – they are everywhere, from anonymous servants and nameless mothers to famous bureaucrats and consorts of prophets. In order to make sense of this overwhelming material, this book analyses multiple types of Arabic-Islamic sources, using multiple scales of enquiry. For instance, on a small scale, it analyses specific verses of the Quran and individual biographies from sources such as al-Balādhurī's *Ansāb al-Ashrāf* (Genealogies of the Notables) and Ibn ʿAsākir's *Tārīkh Madīnat Dimashq* (History of Damascus). To get a large-scale picture of demographic patterns and institutional changes, it presents quantitative analyses of sources such as Ibn Saʿd's *Al-Tabaqāt al-Kubrā* (Greatest Generations) and al-Jahshiyārī's *Kitāb al-Wuzarā' wa-al-Kuttāb* (Book of Viziers and Scribes). To compensate for the difficulties of the Arabic-Islamic source material, this book also employs a range of historical methodologies. For instance, it analyses oral chains of transmission to pinpoint more accurately when and where particular prophetic traditions were circulating. It uses literary analysis to show how different authors, working in different genres, wrote about early Islamic history in ways that fit their wider ideological visions. Throughout, it uses feminist historical analysis to attempt to recover the experiences of women and subalterns, as well as their interpretations of normative texts. By using these varied sources and techniques, this monograph paints a pointillist image of early Islamic history, made up of a dozen little bright spots of insight.

Historical Background

Following recent trends in the scholarship, this monograph divides early Islamic history into two general periods: a period of Islamic Origins in the first/seventh century, and a period of Imperial Elaboration in the second/eighth century. While there is no hard-and-fast boundary between these two periods, it appears that the first period was more open and ecumenical, while the second was more hierarchical and imperial. The earliest decades of Islamic history were more fluid in terms of integrating enslaved members, or as Patricia Crone says, the earliest community was 'open to reshuffling' identity categories.[1] As the empire spread and became increasingly centralised, identity categories hardened, and in particular the boundary between the subaltern conquered populations and the free conquerors became more rigid. However, the boundaries were never completely solid; there was always tension between more inclusive and more exclusive interpretations of who belonged to the *umma*.

The first period of Islamic Origins – which has also been called the 'Believers' Movement' and 'Paleo-Islam'[2] – centres on the first-/seventh-century Hijaz, in Western Arabia. It includes the career of the Prophet Muḥammad and his immediate successors, the so-called 'Rightly Guided' caliphs (11–40/632–661). This period also witnessed the first wave of Islamic conquests outside Arabia, as well as the devastating First Fitna, or Civil War (35–40/656–661), which was eventually won by the Umayyad family. Arabic-Islamic source materials write extensively about this period as a Golden Age of piety and the triumph of God's message. However, the problem with most of these Arabic-Islamic source materials is that they are late; most were written in the second to fourth/eighth to tenth centuries, a century or more after the events they purport to describe. These sources have also been written by particular authors with particular agendas, shaped into salvation histories and moralising tales. Since the mid-twentieth century, scholars of early Islamic history have become critical – indeed sceptical – of these late literary sources and the vision of early Islam that they present.[3] By instead relying on a few extant documents, inscriptions and non-Arabic writings from this period, historians have radically revised their interpretations of Islamic Origins.[4]

Several works of revisionist scholarship have informed the underlying assumptions of this monograph. First, following scholars such as Fred Donner and Aziz Al-Azmeh, I view the Quran itself as an authentic source from the first/seventh century, and I attempt to reconstruct it as a 'polyvalent communicative act' between Muḥammad and his followers.[5] I take it as axiomatic that these first decades of Islamic history were not an ossified golden age, but a period of dynamism, creativity and adaptability. I heed Al-Azmeh's call to analyse 'Paleo-Islam' on its own terms, rather than 'looking backwards' at this period from the viewpoint of the Classical Islamic tradition elaborated in the second to fourth/eighth to tenth centuries in imperial centres such as Damascus and Baghdad.[6] I also accept Donner's thesis that the earliest adherents of Muhammad's message did not call themselves 'Muslims' or think of themselves as constituting an entirely new religion; rather, they called themselves 'Believers' and represented an ecumenical reform movement that could include all kinds of righteous, pious monotheists. In addition, I accept Peter Webb's recent thesis that the earliest Believers did not view themselves as 'Arabs', but rather the notion of 'Arabs' as an elite class of Muslim conquerors only emerged in the Umayyad period.[7] The first three chapters of this book contribute to this field of Islamic Origins, using the text of the Quran and close analysis of later literary sources to understand how enslaved persons belonged to the nascent Believers' Movement in the Hijaz.

The second period, Imperial Elaboration, covers the Umayyad caliphate (r. 41–132/661–749) and the first decades of the Abbasid caliphate (r. 132–656/749–1258).[8] During this period, caliphs and governors grappled with the practical realities of governing a vast empire, including the need to define the relationship between religion and politics. The first Umayyad caliph, Muʿāwiya (r. 41–60/661–80) appears to have been a brilliant administrator; he adopted many trappings of the Byzantine Empire, including minting Byzantine-style coins, introducing some Roman laws, and nominating his own son as heir apparent in typical imperial fashion.[9] However, the Great Fitna, or second Civil War (60–73/680–692), revealed deep-seated, unresolved debates about the nature of Islamic rule and the structure of the Islamic polity. After defeating his rival ʿAbdallāh Ibn al-Zubayr and resolving the

Great Fitna, the fifth Umayyad caliph, ʿAbd al-Malik (r. 65–86/685–705), instituted imperial reforms that consolidated the Umayyads' control over the empire. The period of ʿAbd al-Malik and his successors (known collectively as the Marwanids) was a period of internal contraction, as the caliph attempted to control more tightly who could belong to the imperial elite. ʿAbd al-Malik was apparently trying to gain greater control not only over the conquered populations, but also over the growing Islamic community itself.

First, ʿAbd al-Malik and his children increasingly defined the empire as explicitly Islamic, as opposed to ecumenical or generally monotheistic. For example, in Jerusalem ʿAbd al-Malik built the Dome of the Rock, which contains several anti-Trinitarian inscriptions; he also issued new coins that contained the so-called 'double *shahāda*', which professes faith not only in God but also in Muḥammad as God's messenger.[10] Other scholars have noted that Christian soldiers and bureaucrats had played a prominent role in early Umayyad history but appear to have lost their place of prominence under the Marwanids.[11] Milka Levy-Rubin has also argued that the earliest conquerors dealt with the conquered populations in relatively flexible, ad hoc ways, while the Marwanids began adopting more systematic, hierarchical and restrictive methods (familiar from other Late Antique empires such as the Byzantines and Sasanians) for differentiating the conquerors from the conquered.[12]

Second, ʿAbd al-Malik and the socio-political elites of his day increasingly defined the empire as Arab. Most famously, ʿAbd al-Malik and his sons adopted Arabic as the official language of the bureaucracy, and they had Greek/Byzantine and Persian/Sasanian government registers translated into Arabic.[13] Recently, Peter Webb has argued that Muslim elites began using the term 'Arab' in the Umayyad period in order to differentiate themselves from the conquered populations. Before then, the elites had seen themselves as 'Muhājirūn' (Emigrants), that is, those who emigrated to garrison towns such as Basra, Kufa and Fustat in order to conduct the conquests. In the Umayyad period, as members of the Muslim elite settled down to civilian jobs and stopped emigrating and conquering, they needed a new way to differentiate themselves from the subalterns. 'Arab' – as the Quran's description of its own language and as a marker of linguistic purity and transcendence – seemed like a good choice. The final two chapters of this monograph address this field of Imperial Elaboration. I suggest that the Umayyad caliphs came to rely increasingly on concubinage as a reproductive practice, in order to consolidate political power in the Umayyad family alone. I also argue that, as the Marwanid government became increasingly centralised and autocratic, slaves and subalterns could access a certain degree of political power through their proximity to the caliph. Finally, I provisionally suggest that enslaved and unfree groups might have influenced the Marwanid desire to more rigidly define 'Islam'.

Slavery and Unfreedom

This monograph takes enslaved and freed persons as its main historical subjects.[14] Thus, it is important to understand the basic parameters of early Islamic forms of slavery. It is particularly important that non-specialist audiences realise that the model of modern trans-Atlantic slavery does not accurately describe pre-modern Islamic slavery – early Islamic forms of slavery more closely resembled those of the ancient and Late Antique Roman world. Kurt Franz has recently identified four features of normative Islamic slavery, derived from the Quran and hadith: 1) slaves are 'deemed in many respects to be humans and not mere chattels'; 2) slaves' inferiority is legal, not ontological, making emancipation easy or even expected; 3) domestic slavery is the norm, and masters and slaves 'relate to each other personally in a familiar household framework'; 4) and masters are repeatedly encouraged to be kind to slaves and to manumit them.[15] It is also worth emphasising that several Quranic verses allow men to have licit sexual intercourse with 'those their right hands possess (*mā malakat aymānuhum*)', the common Quranic euphemism for slaves.[16] While the master had sexual access to the female slaves in his household, the same exhortations towards kindness and manumission presumably still applied in this case.

Islamic law did not substantially change any of these features of slavery, although it added more details about categories and regulations. [17] For example, lawyers extrapolated from a single Quranic verse that all slaves who commit crimes should only be given half the punishment that a free person would receive. Lawyers clarified that female slaves must only cover their genitals and buttocks when in the company of strangers, while free females must cover most of their bodies.[18] Lawyers decreed that no Muslim or Arab could be reduced from a state of freedom to a state of slavery.[19] (Muslims could still be slaves, if they were born into slavery or if they converted to Islam after their enslavement.) Lawyers were also particularly interested in matters of inheritance and manumission, including the institutions of *kitāba* (contractual manumission) and *tadbīr* (automatic manumission upon the death of the master). For the purposes of this book, however, the two most crucial legal categories are the *umm walad* (slave-mother) and the *mawlā* (freedman). Neither of these legal concepts appears to have direct roots in the Quran; rather, they appear to have precedent in Near Eastern and Roman law, and they represent Islamic lawyers' attempts to accommodate the many captives and slaves who entered Islamic society as a result of the conquests.[20]

As for the *umm walad*, classical Sunni law gives a female slave some limited rights if she bears a child that her master acknowledges as his own. By doing so, she becomes an *umm walad*, or 'mother of a child'. According to Sunni law, the *umm walad* could never be sold, and she was automatically freed upon the death of her master. Additionally, her child was considered freeborn and fully legitimate.[21] (Conversely, Imami-Shii lawyers reserved none of these rights for the *umm walad*, who was treated like a normal slave who could be sold or inherited by her master's heirs.) In some Sunni law schools, the *umm walad* was also exempted from menial labour, and she was often expected to be veiled or secluded, like a free wife. Ultimately, classical Sunni lawyers considered concubinage a perfectly legitimate form of sexual relationship and means of producing children,[22] and motherhood also placed concubines on the path to manumission.

As for post-manumission status, classical Sunni law insists that all freed persons maintain a tie of patronage with their former master.[23] The legal term for this form of clientage is *walā'*, and both client and patron are called *mawlā* (pl. *mawālī*).[24] There was much debate and discrepancy among early Islamic lawyers regarding *walā'*, but by the third/ninth century classical lawyers considered *walā'* to be a form of kinship that permanently tied the freed person to the former master's family.[25] The patron was responsible for protecting his client and paying the fine for any crime that his client might commit; in return for this protection, the patron had a right to inherit some of his client's estate.[26] Thus, even after manumission, the freed slave was in some ways legally subordinated to his master.

Classical Islamic law is immensely informative, but it is important to realise that such legal material does not encapsulate the institution of slavery. It tells us little about the experiences of the earliest slaves in the *umma*, the different occupations slaves held, the actual practice of buying and selling slaves, the kinds of social relationships slaves built or the ways that slaves could exercise political power. In fact, Islamic law seems in many cases to be completely divorced from, or uninterested in, contemporary social practice. Many scholars have analysed this gap between theory and practice.[27] For instance, as Kurt Franz reminds us, Islamic lawyers write nothing about agricultural slavery or serfdom, military slavery or corvée labour – all of which existed in Islamic history. Likewise, Jonathan Brockopp has highlighted the divide between the theory and practice of concubinage: early Maliki jurists showed no interest in the contemporary Abbasid practice of using *umm walad*s to produce heirs to the throne.[28] Jamal Juda has also shown that *mawālī* provided all kinds of service for their former masters, including acting as business agents, messengers, water-carriers, scribes, personal bodyguards and many other activities not stipulated in Islamic law.[29] Moreover, the classical Islamic law books provide no information on the *qayna* (pl. *qiyān*), that is, the courtesan or 'singing girl'. Instead, scholars learn about the *qiyān* from the medieval Arabic-Islamic authors who devoted many literary anthologies, poetry collections and essays to them.[30] Thus, while I certainly do not advocate a disregard for legal sources, this monograph focuses instead on narrative historical texts, biographies and genealogical literature in order to unpack the experiences of early Islamic enslaved and freed persons.

In order to avoid over-emphasising normative legal definitions of slavery, this monograph suggests that the concept of 'unfreedom' is useful in studying Muslims of slave origins.[31] Unfreedom highlights the personal, relational nature of enslavement, servitude and other forms of coercion; one is 'unfree' in relation to another person or entity. Unfreedom allows scholars to analyse those social bonds that limit personal freedom but also provide 'social life',[32] bonds that embed people in unequal but mutually beneficial social networks. Put otherwise, unfreedom allows us to see the relationship between conquerors and conquered as reciprocal, if unequal.[33] It allows scholars to analyse how the enslaved or freed person was expected to show loyalty to the master in return for receiving welfare, support and patronage. In many early Islamic contexts, it seems that the enslaved or freed person was assumed to have the master's interests at heart; the enslaved or freed person was expected to practice 'inter-agency', that is, to make individual choices that served the greater needs of the master's household.[34] Enslaved persons may not have been fully equal to adult members of the natal family, but they were certainly not outsiders. They likely adopted the language, values, beliefs and social networks of their patrons. They were assimilated into the household, or they were at least on the path towards assimilation. The sources provide plenty of evidence of slaves and *mawālī* in this familiar household context.

Unfreedom also provides a flexible framework for understanding forms of subjugation that do not fall under the legal rubric of 'slavery' per se (as *mawālī* and the children of enslaved mothers were not technically slaves). The freedman was legally free, but socially he inhabited something like a state of extended adolescence – he could make many of his own decisions, but he was ultimately dependent on his patron's support and curried his patron's favour. Unfreedom presents itself as more of a fluid continuum than an artificially stark dichotomy; instead of viewing slavery and freedom as mutually incompatible opposites, unfreedom offers more of a sliding scale.[35] Using this framework also allows scholars to analyse various manifestations of unfreedom. For instance, scholars can use this concept to parse the difference between *mawālī* and other subordinated or subaltern groups, such as serfs and *dhimmī*s. Finally, unfreedom provides value-neutral language for analysing the costs and benefits of being enslaved or manumitted, for examining the ways subalterns exercised agency and the ways their agency was limited, and for interrogating the ways enslaved and freed persons were subordinated but also active participants in society.[36] While the Arabic-Islamic sources do not use the term 'unfreedom' to describe historical actors, I suggest that the term is nevertheless useful in interrogating the position of groups such as concubines, courtesans, *mawālī* and the children of enslaved mothers.

Book Layout

The book proceeds roughly chronologically, with the first three chapters treating the period of Islamic Origins, and the final two chapters focusing on the period of Imperial Elaboration. Chapter Two analyses two Quranic passages that express the liminal position of believing slaves. The first passage, 33:4–6, assures believers of unknown parentage that they fully belong to the *umma* as 'brothers in religion', but it also indicates that such believers lack deeper social bonds to other members of the *umma*. I argue that the key term *mawālī* in this passage refers to the bonds of support that cement all believers, but that such bonds do not necessarily entail full social equality. The second passage, 24:32–33, discourages men from forcing their slave women into prostitution, but it also indicates that believing slave women are unable to attain certain morality standards. I argue that the key term '*taḥaṣṣun*' in this passage places the master–concubine relationship somewhere between licit and illicit sexual activity for the slave woman. These two Quranic passages illustrate the tension of a first-/seventh-century community struggling to define the relationship between spiritual equality and social hierarchy.

Both Chapters Three and Four build upon these ambiguous Quranic foundations to further elucidate first-/seventh-century Islamic history, as well as to show how later Muslims re-worked early Islamic history to fit their own ideological needs. Chapter Three investigates an early Muslim freedman named Abū Bakra (d. 52/672) who appears in exegeses of Q 33:5. While Abū Bakra is not a particularly famous or prominent member of early Islamic history, he is important as a micro-historical case study precisely because his identity is so contested. I argue that during his lifetime in the first/seventh century, Abū Bakra was identified primarily as a 'freedman of God' (*ṭalīq allāh*), an anomalous phrase that highlighted his belonging to the *umma*. However, in the subsequent centuries, this inclusive designation lost its meaning, so that later authors sought to place Abū Bakra into the more familiar social categories of Arab and *mawlā*. Historians such as al-Balādhurī use Abū Bakra's *mawlā* identity to illustrate the values of piety, humility and political neutrality; conversely, hadith compilers such as al-Bukhārī present Abū Bakra as an Arab in order to highlight literalistic legal standards for determining identity. Thus, Abū Bakra's story helps us discern that seemingly straightforward identifiers such as *mawlā* and Arab are deeply intertwined in the wider narratives different authors hoped to tell about the trajectory of early Islamic history.

Chapter Four analyses a group analogous to the early Islamic *mawālī*, namely enslaved prostitutes. Just as Abū Bakra invoked Q 33:5 to articulate his place in the early Islamic *umma*, so two prostitutes of the first/seventh century seem to have invoked Q 24:33 to seek justice and inclusion in the earliest *umma*. But by the third/ninth century, Quranic exegetes had downplayed or even forgotten the stories of these two prostitutes; they instead told symbolic tales of Muʿādha, a reformed harlot who stopped working as a prostitute when she converted to Islam. While exegetes tell this uplifting story of a 'good' prostitute, narrative historians instead focus on the figures of 'bad' prostitutes who enjoyed fornicating. Unpacking such dichotomous portrayals of female sexuality allows scholars to recover more nuanced and complex visions of the status of enslaved women in the earliest *umma*.

Chapters Five and Six move away from the history of the earliest *umma* in the first/seventh century, and into the Umayyad empire of the second/eighth century. Chapters Five and Six each study a dyad of male and female Muslims of slave origins, in order to elucidate how gender and slavery shaped Umayyad politics. Chapter Five examines Umayyad-era concubines (*umm walads*) and their sons. Concubines raised questions in the Umayyad period about the role of genetic lineage in determining who belonged to the *umma*, who counted as an 'Arab' and who deserved the right to hold the caliphate. In order to be embraced as full insiders, concubines' children first had to demonstrate that they were true Muslims, loyal to the Islamic empire and knowledgeable in religious lore. Later, in order to gain political power as caliphs, the children of concubines had to re-define themselves as full 'Arabs'. To do so, they dismissed their mothers as essentially inconsequential, and they justified this move by invoking paradigmatic examples of slave mothers from the Islamic religious tradition. Thus, slave women indirectly changed the face of Umayyad politics, challenging the elite 'Arab' class to define its doctrine of lineage more clearly, and impelling the articulation of new political ideologies.

Chapter Six turns away from mothers and their sons, and towards two subaltern groups who used their Arabic language mastery to gain political power in the Umayyad empire: the *qiyān* (courtesans) and the *kuttāb* (scribes). Both groups reveal the complex intersection of language mastery, cultural identity, unfreedom and political power in the Umayyad period. Both groups indicate that the increasing centralisation of the Marwanid ruling household (r. 64–132/684–749) provided increased opportunities for educated unfree persons to exercise political power. While these groups could be powerful, they were always in a precarious position, for they had to use their linguistic mastery in ways that pleased their imperial masters. For instance, the late-Umayyad courtesan Ḥabāba used her poetic and musical talents to gain a powerful position in the harem; yet, she was unable to secure the more lasting, systematised forms of power that later Abbasid concubine-queens would exercise. Likewise, Umayyad-era scribes could influence Arabic prose style and act as the 'eyes and ears' of the caliph, but they could just as easily be cast out as scapegoats.

The Conclusion chapter, in addition to reflecting on the main ideas of the monographs, suggests potential avenues for future research. In particular, it suggests that scholars should continue to study the *mawālī* through the lens of unfreedom, rather than through the lens of 'non-Arab' ethnicity. Many questions remain about the relationship between individual *mawālī* and the collective known as 'the *mawālī*' or 'the society of *mawālī*' (*ma'shar al-mawālī*).[37] The lens of unfreedom may also help scholars discern subtle differences between various conquered groups, such as peasants, vassals, *ahl al-dhimma* and *mawālī*. Finally, it is worth considering the relationship between unfree groups and the emergence of 'Islam' as the official name of Muhammad's religion.

Ultimately, Muslims of slave origins provide a valuable window onto Islamic history because their identities are complex and contested. They reveal debates about who can belong to the faith, who can belong to the social elite and who can wield political power. They also reveal debates about the meanings of seemingly straightforward terms, such as 'Arab'. They show that the meanings of these terms are neither simple nor obvious, but are re-negotiated as new members enter the Islamic community. For example, Muslims of slave origins raise tensions between more closed, lineage-based definitions of Arabness and more open, language-and-culture-based definitions. Rather than attempting to resolve these tensions, this monograph hopes to analyse what these tensions show us about the contested boundaries of the nascent *umma*.

Notes

1. Patricia Crone, *Roman, Provincial and Islamic Law*, 89.
2. Fred Donner has coined the term 'Believers' Movement', and Aziz Al-Azmeh has coined the term 'paleo-Islam'. I will discuss these scholars' contributions below. See Fred Donner, *Muhammad and the Believers;* and Aziz Al-Azmeh, *The Emergence of Islam in Late Antiquity*.

3. For definitions and examples of the different approaches to early Islamic history, see Fred Donner, *Narratives of Islamic Origins*, 1–31.
4. The most famous example of revisionist scholarship that completely scandalised and galvanised the field is Patricia Crone and Michael Cook, *Hagarism*. This book relied only on non-Arabic, non-Islamic sources to re-construct early Islamic history. While many of their findings have now been rejected, the practice of reading contemporary non-Arabic, non-Islamic texts remains a mainstay of the field of early Islamic history. See particularly Hoyland, *Seeing Islam as Others Saw It*.
5. Aziz Al-Azmeh, *The Emergence of Islam in Late Antiquity*. Al-Azmeh also writes that 'the paleo-Islamic Qur'ān was a process of communication in action' (*ibid.*, 444) and he urges scholars to read it '*in statu nascendi* and in its pre-canonical forms' (*ibid.*, 448). Angelika Neuwirth likewise argues that scholars can recover the pre-canonical Quran as a communicative process (Angelika Neuwirth, 'Qur'an and History – A Disputed Relationship', 1–18.)
6. Al-Azmeh, *Emergence*, 358. While I take Al-Azmeh's point, I am not entirely sure how the term 'Paleo-Islam' avoids the assumption of inevitability, as it still invokes the later term 'Islam'. That is, replacing the English term 'early' with the Greek term meaning 'early' (*paleo*) does not appear to resolve the problem of prefiguring a linear development into Islam. Avoiding the term 'Islam' altogether is why Donner uses the term 'Believers Movement', although Al-Azmeh argues that Donner's analysis focuses too much on piety and belief (see *Emergence*, 403–407). Al-Azmeh himself suggests that 'Muḥammadanism' is an accurate term to describe Paleo-Islam, but perhaps he avoids continuing to use the term because of the Orientalist baggage associated with it.
7. Whenever possible, I attempt to use the terms 'Believers' and 'Arabians' when I speak of this period. It proves exceedingly difficult to avoid the term 'Islam' altogether – as I use the term 'Islamic origins' to describe this period. I hope it is clear that when I speak of 'early Islam' or 'Islamic origins', I am not trying to posit that Islam emerged fully formed in its classical iteration.
8. Traditionally, Arabic-Islamic sources (and many modern scholars) present the 'Abbasid Revolution' of 132/749 as a true revolution that swept away the wicked Umayyad dynasty and instituted a new age of righteousness. However, many other recent scholars do not see such a sharp break between the late Umayyad and early Abbasid periods. As Paul Cobb says, 'there is little in 'Abbāsid statecraft that is not recognizably Marwānid'. Rather, the Abbasids simply did a better job of symbolically portraying themselves as cosmopolitan Muslim rulers, rather

than exclusively Arab ones (Paul Cobb, 'The Empire in Syria', 268). For other recent reconsiderations of the 'Abbasid Revolution', see Borrut, *Entre mémoire et pouvoir,* Chapter 7; El-Hibri, 'The Redemption of Umayyad Memory by the Abbasids', 241–265; Al-Azmeh, *Emergence*, 499.

9. In doing so, Muʿāwiya was drawing upon a great Late Antique heritage of monarchy and imperial legitimacy. These Late Antique symbols were not 'foreign' borrowings or influences, but the very language in which Muʿāwiya and his Umayyad family were steeped, the ancient and familiar heritage of Syria and Iraq. On the resonances between Late Antique and early Islamic symbols of rule, see particularly Al-Azmeh, *Emergence*, especially Chapters 1 and 8.
10. Donner, *Muhammad and the Believers*, 195–208.
11. On the contested role of Christians in the Umayyad government, see Borrut and Donner, eds, *Christians and Others in the Umayyad State*, especially the chapters by Muriel Debié ('Christians in the Service of the Caliph: Through the Looking Glass of Communal Identities',) and Luke Yarbrough ('Did ʿUmar b. ʿAbd al-ʿAzīz Issue an Edict Concerning Non-Muslim Officials?').
12. Milka Levy-Rubin, *Non-Muslims in the Early Islamic Empire: From Empire to Co-Existence*.
13. Recent scholarship indicates that this 'Arabisation' was neither as swift nor as complete as has previously been assumed. Allison Vacca has concisely summarised some of this promising scholarship in her 'Conference Report: Navigating Language in the Early Islamic World (The Marco Institute for Medieval and Renaissance Studies, The University of Tennessee, Knoxville, 6–7 April 2018)', *Al-Usur al-Wusta*, 26 (2018), https://islamichistorycommons.org/mem/wp-content/uploads/sites/55/2018/11/UW-26-Vacca.pdf, accessed 12 March 2019.
14. I generally prefer terms such as 'enslaved person', 'enslaved woman' or 'enslaved Muslim' to the word 'slave' throughout this monograph, although sometimes I use the word 'slave' for readability. As Kecia Ali notes, the term 'enslaved person . . . highlights that enslavement is not a natural state but something that is actively done to one human being by another'. Kecia Ali, 'Review of Matthew S. Gordon and Kathryn Hain, eds., *Concubines and Courtesans: Women and Slavery in Islamic History*', *Al-Usur al-Wusta*, 26 (2018), https://islamichistorycommons.org/mem/wp-content/uploads/sites/55/2018/11/UW-26-Ali.pdf, accessed 12 March 2019.
15. Kurt Franz, 'Slavery in Islam: Legal Norms and Social Practice', 53–54. This excellent survey of legal norms and social practice engages deeply with previ-

ous scholarship on the topic of slavery in the Islamic world, and it should be required reading for anyone interested in studying Islamic slavery.

16. Q 23:6 and 70:30, which both say: '[Successful will be the Believers who abstain from sexual activity] except with their wives or "those their right hands possess", in which case they are free from blame' (*illā 'alā azwājihim aw mā malakat aymānuhum fa-innahum ghayru malūmīn*). See also Q 33:50–52. Female slave owners did not enjoy similar rights over their male slaves.
17. Jonathan Brockopp has shown that the Quran and Islamic law use different vocabularies of slavery. For instance, the Quran uses 'that which your right hands possess' (*mā malakat aymānukum*) to refer to slaves, while law uses the term *'abd* (plural *'abīd*). The Quran uses *taḥrīr* and *fakk* to refer to manumission, while law uses *'itq* (Jonathan Brockopp, *Early Mālikī Law*, 128–131).
18. On this, see Baber Johansen, 'The Valorization of the Human Body in Muslim Sunni Law'.
19. The prohibition against enslaving Arabs is apparently prescriptive, not descriptive. As Chase Robinson indicates, 'we know that Arabs were sometimes enslaved' (Chase Robinson, 'Slavery in the Conquest Period', 158). I suggest in this monograph that *muwalladāt*, or women born into slavery in Arabian cities, should perhaps be viewed as 'Arab slaves'. In any case, because of these normative prohibitions against enslaving Arab-Muslims, many slaves in the Islamic polity were brought in through conquest or trade in outlying regions such as East Africa, Eastern Europe and Central Asia. Accordingly, slavery in some historical contexts appears to have taken on racial overtones not condoned in Islamic law. While the law forbids the enslavement of Arabs, it does not imply that certain groups, such as Black Africans or Turks, should be conflated with 'slaves', as often seems to have happened. See on the association of blackness with slavery particularly Bernard Lewis, *Race and Slavery in the Middle East*.
20. Jonathan Brockopp has well established that the *umm walad* category has no clear roots in the Quran or the hadith, but instead developed relatively late, probably in response to the Islamic conquests (Brockopp, *Early Mālikī Law,* Chapter 3). Likewise, Patricia Crone has argued that the legal features of classical *walā'* have no roots in pre-Islamic Arabian practice, but were instead borrowed indirectly from Roman law in Syria (Crone, *Roman, Provincial and Islamic Law*).
21. This definition has been simplified for clarity, for the specifics of *umm walad* status depend on the legal school. On debates about the status of the *umm*

walad, see most recently Younus Mirza, 'Remembering the *Umm al-Walad*', 297–323.

22. Such protections for concubine-mothers have deep roots, going back to Hammurabi's code. See Crone, *Roman Provincial and Islamic Law,* p. 87, fn. 130.
23. Imami lawyers once again diverge from the Sunnis here. For Imamis, only slaves manumitted by an act of individual volition on the part of their masters become the master's *mawlā*. See Crone, *Roman, Provincial and Islamic Law,* 77–84.
24. In this monograph, I almost always use the word *mawlā* to refer to the client, freedman or 'lower' *mawlā* – not the patron, master or 'higher' *mawlā*.
25. On the debates about the parameters of *walā'*, including its pre-classical form as a vestige of slavery rather than a metaphorical kinship tie, see Crone, *Roman, Provincial and Islamic Law.*
26. On the characteristics of classical Islamic *walā'*, see Crone, *Roman, Provincial and Islamic Law,* Chapter 3. On pre-classical *walā'*, see *ibid.*, Chapter 4; and Ulrike Mitter, *Das frühislamische Patronat.*
27. Kurt Franz suggests that forms of unfreedom that diverge from the normative, domestic model of Islamic slavery should not be considered 'slavery' at all. For example, he suggests that the Zanj should be considered unfree agricultural labourers (more like serfs than slaves), and the Mamluks should be considered a caste of military overlords, not military 'slaves'. Hannah Barker likewise shows that slave-merchants ignored the instructions of religious, public morals (*ḥisba*) manuals and instead followed medical slave-buying manuals. Hannah Barker, 'Purchasing a Slave in Fourteenth-Century Cairo'. Both Franz and Barker essentially argue that the rules of Islamic law were more humane and protective towards slaves than these other practices, and thus slave-buyers and slave-users ignored Islamic law because it did not serve their exploitative aims.
28. Brockopp, *Early Mālikī Law,* 205. As far as I know, there has only been one study of case law, rather than legal theory, in the case of the *umm walad*: Ehud Toledano has used Ottoman Cairene police records to recover the story of a late-Ottoman *umm walad* called Şemsigul (Ehud Toledano, 'The Other Face of Harem Bondage: Abuse and Redress', Chapter 2 in *Slavery and Abolition in the Ottoman Middle East*).
29. See Jamal Juda, 'The Economic Status of the *Mawālī* in Early Islam', Chapter 7 in *Patronate and Patronage in Early and Classical Islam*, edited by Monique Bernards and John Nawas. Juda convincingly explodes the notion, propounded by Patricia Crone and especially Daniel Pipes, that all *mawālī* shared a single,

low status. As Juda indicates, shared legal status does not necessarily imply shared social status.

30. For a brief review of the *qiyān* in both primary and secondary source literature, see Urban, 'Gender and Slavery in Islamic Political Thought', in *Oxford Handbook of Comparative Political Theory* (forthcoming). See also Chapter 6 of the current monograph for a deeper discussion of the *qiyān*.
31. The notion of unfreedom has been most often deployed in studies of ancient Greek and Roman slavery. See, for example, M. I. Finley, 'Between Slavery and Freedom'; and Léonie J. Archer, ed., *Slavery and Other Forms of Unfree Labour*. Scholars of medieval European society have also adopted the term to describe phenomena such as serfdom and fealty. See, for example, Alice Rio, 'Freedom and Unfreedom in Early Medieval Francia' and 'Self-sale and Voluntary Entry into Unfreedom, 300–1100'; and Alice Taylor, '*Homo Ligius* and Unfreedom in Medieval Scotland'.
32. I am here inverting Orlando Patterson's famous concept of 'social death'; see Patterson, *Slavery and Social Death*, Introduction and Chapter 2.
33. As Alice Taylor says, 'one could have certain freedoms in a state of unfreedom; equally, there was unfreedom inherent in the dependence that was a necessary part of free status' ('*Homo Ligius*', 110).
34. On the concept of loyalty undergirding the master–slave or patron–client relationship, see P. G. Forand, 'The Relation of the Slave and Client to the Master or Patron in Medieval Islam'; Roy Mottahedeh, *Loyalty and Leadership in an Early Islamic Society*; Reuven Amitai, 'The Mamlūk Institution'; and Ehud Toledano, *As If Silent and Absent: Bonds of Enslavement in the Islamic Middle East.*
35. As many people working in many different fields expressed at the Binghamton Medieval Unfreedoms conference in October 2018, the idea of total and complete 'freedom' would have been a terrifying idea for most pre-modern peoples – it evokes an image of living alone, on a desert island, without any home, family or protection. In many monotheistic traditions, 'freedom' is also an unappealing theological concept, as God is the only truly free agent, while humankind's goal is to submit as God's worshipful 'slaves'. Salvation comes precisely through slavery to God, while freedom implies damnation.
36. I also find unfreedom a helpful concept for pushing back against the language of Patricia Crone, whose *Slaves on Horses* is foundational for understanding *mawālī* military contingents in Umayyad society, but who is too dogmatic when she describes *mawlā* status as a 'humiliation', *mawālī* as inherently 'despised', the conquerors as hoping to completely distance themselves from the conquered

societies and the conquered populations as adding nothing particularly valuable to Islamic society. Her analysis of the Umayyad *mawālī* concludes by noting the 'moral failing' of the Islamic experiment, which is a provocative but dubious claim. See Crone, *Slaves on Horses*, 51–57.

37. Al-Jāḥiẓ uses this phrase, *maʿshar al-mawālī*, in his 'Al-Risāla fī al-Nābita' (*Rasāʾil al-Jāḥiẓ*, 2:17).

2

Insiders with an Asterisk: *Mawālī* and Enslaved Women in the Quran

This book begins with the Quran because it is the earliest and most authentic document that scholars possess for understanding how new believers found a place within the *umma*.[1] While the Quran is an anchor for any enquiry into early Islamic history,[2] it does not provide a definitive blueprint for Islamic society – it is a polyvalent and at times inscrutable text. Attempting to reconstruct the Quranic worldview requires a careful comparison of many concepts and vocabularies, scattered across many verses.[3] Such an analysis allows scholars to glimpse the range of beliefs and practices that were meaningful for the earliest Muslims, as well as to uncover a series of questions with which the nascent *umma* grappled. One of these questions was the place of slaves, foreigners and other outsiders in the new *umma*.

Accordingly, this chapter investigates two Quranic passages that express the liminal position of enslaved believers, or believers with slave origins. The first passage, Q 33:4–6, explicates the role of genealogy in building the *umma*. While this passage assures believers of unknown parentage that they fully belong to the *umma* as 'brothers in religion', it also indicates that believers have closer social ties with their own relatives than they do with such outsiders. I argue that the key term *mawālī* in this passage refers to the bonds of support that cement all believers, but that such bonds do not necessarily entail full social equality. The second passage, Q 24:32–33, speaks of the role of sexual ethics in building the *umma*. While this passage encourages believers to marry virtuous slaves and discourages men from forcing their slave women into prostitution, it also indicates that believing slave women are unable to attain certain morality standards. I argue that the key term '*taḥaṣṣun*' in this passage refers to the enslaved concubine's relationship with her own master, and that it places the master–concubine relationship somewhere between licit and illicit sexual activity for the enslaved woman.

These two passages are certainly not the only ones in the Quran that treat belonging, slavery or the structure of the *umma*.[4] However, they are especially rich because they so clearly express the Quranic tension between spiritual equality and social hierarchy, between the desire for inclusivity and the need for order. These two passages are seemingly disparate and have not been analysed together, but they share many conceptual resonances. Both passages are ambiguous: they indicate that outsiders and slaves can join the *umma*, but that they might not belong quite as fully as free believers. Both passages have a more inclusive reading that focuses on the cohesion of the entire religious community, and a more exclusive reading that highlights the differences among believers. And both passages capture the struggle in the first/seventh century to create a functional faith community that adhered to high moral standards but also dealt practically with everyday social realities. When these two passages are analysed in tandem, they help elucidate how believing slaves impelled the nascent *umma* to clarify its criteria for belonging.

Q 33:4–6 'They Are Your Brothers in Religion and Your *Mawālī*'

The term *mawālī* (singular, *mawlā*) is crucial for understanding the place of outsiders in the Quranic worldview. A common translation of the term *mawālī* in the Quran is 'clients',[5] but I suggest that the Quranic term is much more capacious: it designates the bonds of help, support and kindness that unite all believers into a functional faith community.[6] Verse 33:5 seems to use the term *mawālī* in this inclusive sense when it describes rootless believers as 'your brothers in religion and your *mawālī*'.[7] However, the wider context of the passage Q 33:4–6 also raises the possibility that such outsiders are not socially equal to other believers, and it is therefore easy to see how some parties understood the term '*mawālī*' to designate a specific, subordinate subset of believers. In this passage, the Quran lays the foundation for both the importance and the ambivalence of the term *mawālī* throughout Islamic history.

Arabic philology is key to unlocking this reading of the Quranic term *mawālī* (and its singular, *mawlā*). *Mawālī* comes from the tri-consonantal

Arabic root *w-l-y*, which indicates bonds of mutual support shared among any coherent community.[8] The Quran uses many permutations of this root in addition to *mawlā*, including the verb *tawallā* ('to turn towards or away'), and the noun *walī* ('friend').[9] Many of these permutations are found in parallel contexts, in close proximity to one another, or even as synonyms. For instance, the Quran describes God as 'such a good *mawlā* and such a good helper' (Q 22:78) and 'sufficient as a *walī* and sufficient as a helper' (Q 4:45). Likewise, Q 47:11 states that 'the unbelievers will have no *mawlā*', while Q 42:8 says that 'the unjust will have no *walī* or helper'.[10] In addition to describing God as the ultimate patron or source of protection, the Quran also uses words from the root w-l-y to describe human relationships. Specifically, w-l-y vocabularies imply military support, treating others kindly and maintaining family ties.[11] It is in the light of this broader semantic network that I understand *mawālī* in the Quran to connote that all believers are one another's friends and supporters.

The Quran is particularly explicit about the relationship between biological kinship, religious belief and these bonds of social support. It erases the seemingly inherent connection between biological kinship and social bonds, and instead posits religious belief as the font of social cohesion. The Quran several times encourages believers to break their ties with their unbelieving relatives, as in Q 9:23: 'Do not take your fathers and brothers as friends (*awliyā'*) if they love unbelief more than belief. Whoever of you turns to them in support (*yatawallāhum*) is among the unjust.'[12] Instead, people with shared beliefs and morals are one another's true friends. For example, Q 8:72 states. 'Indeed, those who believed and emigrated and strove with their property and their persons in God's path, and those who sheltered and helped – these are the *awliyā'* of one another.'[13] This phrasing is resonant with the early Islamic document known as the 'Constitution of Medina', which declares, 'The believers are the *mawālī* of one another, to the exclusion of other people.'[14] On the other hand, Q 5:51 describes the Jews and Christians as the *awliyā'* of each other, while Q 6:129 indicates that God has 'made the unjust to befriend (*nuwallī*) one another'.[15] Ultimately, these *w-l-y* words indicate that the *umma* is not merely a community of faith, but a community joined together by mutual action; believers work together to achieve security, stability and eventually victory in their message.

This semantic and conceptual background undergirds Q 33:4–6, a pivotal passage for understanding the complexities of the Quran's worldview. The verses read (emphasis added):

> 33:4. God has not given man two hearts in his body. Nor has He made your wives whom you have divorced by declaring them to be 'like the back of your mothers' [actually] your mothers. Nor has He made your adopted sons [actually] your sons. This is what you say with your mouths, but God speaks the truth, and He shows the right path.
>
> 33:5. Call them by [the names of] their fathers: that is more just before God. **But if you do not know their fathers, then [they are] your brothers in religion and your *mawālī*.** There is no blame upon you if you make a mistake, but [there is blame] if the heart intends [wrong]. God is forgiving and merciful.
>
> 33:6. The Prophet is closer (*awlā*) to the believers than their own selves, and his wives are their mothers. Blood relatives are closer (*awlā*) to one another in the Book of God than believers and emigrants; but you should treat your friends (*awliyā'*) well, for this is decreed in the Book.

Traditionally, scholars and exegetes have understood these verses to be speaking about adoption and inheritance laws.[16] However, disregarding these later interpretations for the time being, I argue that this passage answers some questions that new believers of slave origins may have had concerning their status within the community. Slaves, foundlings, foreigners or other rootless outsiders might have doubted that they could be included in the *umma,* for the Quran sets up genealogy as one of the truths of God's creation: 'He has made for [humankind] relation by blood and relation by marriage' (Q 25:54). Apparently, pre-Islamic Arabians had used the language of genealogy fairly loosely.[17] According to Q 33:4–5, pre-Islamic husbands had divorced their wives by uttering the formula, 'You are to me like the back of my mother', while adoptive fathers had used the language of genealogy to authenticate and authorise their relationships with their adopted sons.[18] Here, the Quran abolishes such inaccurate use of language. Verse Q 33:4 dictates that the language of genealogy should be used only to reflect biological reality (for God 'speaks the Truth'), rather than to perform a utilitarian social function (for that is 'what you say with your mouths').[19] In particular, believers must know the identity of their blood relatives so that they may contract licit marriages. Quran Q 4:23 forbids believers from marrying their own children, parents, siblings, aunts/uncles, nieces/nephews, parents-in-law, children-in-law, step-children or two sisters at the same time. In order to follow these prohibitions, believers must know their genealogies.[20]

As a result, believers who did not know their genealogies might have faced the dire problem of being unable to follow God's law, and thus being excluded from the *umma* entirely. Verse Q 33:5 immediately alleviates these worries by stating, 'If you do not know their fathers, then [they are] your brothers in religion and your *mawālī*.' That is, even believers with unknown genealogies can belong to the *umma* and enjoy the social bonds of help and support that all believers share as one another's *mawālī*. An early Muslim named Abū Bakra – the focus of the next chapter – apparently invoked this phrase in reference to himself, claiming: 'I am one of those whose fathers is unknown, so I am your brother in religion and your *mawlā*.'[21] While later exegetes understood him to be claiming to be a *mawlā* (client) of the Prophet Muḥammad, I suggest that he was instead invoking this phrase in its original Quranic meaning, as an affirmation of his belonging to the community. Abū Bakra was celebrating his identity as a believer, not as a client or freedman.

The Quran quickly complicates this inclusive vision of the *umma*, however, for the next verse indicates that all social bonds within the *umma* are not created equal. Verse 33:6 declares that 'the Prophet is closer (*awlā*) to the believers than [they are] to themselves', and that 'blood relatives are closer (*awlā*) to one another . . . than believers and emigrants'. The first of these statements re-affirms that belief in the Prophet's mission, and not genealogy, is the foundational criterion for belonging to the Islamic community.[22] The primary allegiance of all believers is to the Prophet, and in return they will receive the most effective aid from him. As all believers are fundamentally equal in this respect, this 'Prophet is closer' statement has fundamentally egalitarian message. It appears similar to the Shii concept of *walāya*, wherein all Shia are equal in their shared allegiance to the Imam.[23]

The second statement, 'blood relatives are closer', is more explicitly hierarchical. It finds a parallel in Q 8:75, which states: 'Those who then believe, and emigrate, and strive alongside you, they are of you (*fa-ūlā'ika minkum*).

But blood relatives are closer to one another in the Book of God . . .' Many exegetes understand 'closer' in Q 8:75 to refer to inheritance specifically, but based on my analysis of the root *w-l-y*, I argue that it refers to social bonds more generally.[24] Verses 33:6 and 8:75 are some of the Quran's most highly articulated statements about the relationship between belief and society; all believers share some social bonds by dint of their belief, but some believers share tighter social bonds than others. The Quran thus charts the transition away from a situation where every believer was essentially an unconnected outsider who broke their social bonds to join a radical faith community, and towards a situation where some believers were unconnected outsiders while others had family connections within the *umma*. The social differentiation that is re-inscribed into the *umma* here using the term *awlā* does not necessarily entail the forms of subordination and dependency that would later become associated with the word *mawlā*. However, for those parties who advocated such subordination, this verse could provide a plausible scriptural justification.

Q 24:32–33: 'And Do Not Force Your Slave Women into Prostitution if They Desire Chastity'

The previous Quranic passage could hypothetically apply to both males and females: male and female believers are '*mawālī*' in faith, and both male and female blood relatives are 'closer' than strangers.[25] However, in terms of deciding who belongs to the *umma* and how outsiders should be included in it, the context of Q 33:4–6 implies a male audience – it speaks specifically about 'sons' and 'brothers'. The Quran raises slightly different issues for enslaved women than it does for enslaved men, in that it focuses on sexual ethics rather than genealogy. On the one hand, the Quran explicitly states that enslaved women can be believers, and it allows believing men to marry believing or righteous slave women. On the other hand, the Quran allows believing slave owners apparently unlimited sexual access to their own enslaved concubines. Here, I argue that a key term for understanding the Quran's ambivalent treatment of believing slave women is *taḥaṣṣun*, which I understand to mean something like, 'Trying to emulate the sexual ethics of free women'. The Quran seems to place the enslaved concubine into this liminal position of *taḥaṣṣun*, potentially treating even her sexual relationship with her own master as falling somewhere between chastity and unchastity. While the term *taḥaṣṣun* (unlike *mawālī*) is not a prominent or contested term in early Islamic history, the concept of slave women's chastity and the nature of the master–concubine relationship would remain salient issues for centuries.

My reading of *taḥaṣṣun* as a liminal sexual position builds on other scholars' work on slavery and sexual ethics in the Quran.[26] The Quran often exhorts believers to remain chaste, although it provides slightly different rules for (all) men, free women and enslaved women. For a man, chastity explicitly means to avoid sex with anyone other than his own wives and enslaved concubines.[27] For a free woman, chastity means sex only with her husband – women are not allowed sexual access to their own slaves as concubines. As for slaves, the Quran explicitly states that believers can marry believing slaves (whether male or female), although a person may not marry his *own* slave.[28] Married slave women are expected to remain faithful to their husbands; the husband's right to enjoy exclusive sexual access to his wife trumps the slave master's right to have sex with his female slaves.[29] However, apparently recognising the limited agency of enslaved women, Q 4:25 states that any married slave woman who commits adultery deserves half the punishment of a free woman. Finally, most exegetes and scholars consider that an unmarried slave woman could never be 'chaste' (*muḥṣina*).[30] It is this final assumption that I contest in this chapter – I find that the Quran does not completely despair of enslaved women's chastity, but rather places it in the liminal position of *taḥaṣṣun*.

Philology is once again pivotal for unpacking the term *taḥaṣṣun;* however, unlike the term *mawālī* analysed above, there is only a single attestation of the term *taḥaṣṣun* in the entire Quran. It is certainly related to other terms from the Arabic root *ḥ-ṣ-n,* which literally means to guard or protect, and figuratively refers to sexual chastity. However, *taḥaṣṣun* seems to have a different meaning than the more common terms *iḥṣān* (chasity) and *muḥṣin(a)* (chaste). Harald Motzki has greatly elucidated the meaning of the latter terms in his attempt to solve the puzzling verse Q 4:24,[31] but even this exceedingly rigorous and careful scholar simply glosses the term *taḥaṣṣun* as 'having the same signification as *iḥṣān*'.[32] Motzki follows most classical exegetes in this reading, but I find no textual evidence within the Quran itself to support such a statement, and the basic rules of Arabic grammar indicate that the words should not mean the same thing.[33] *Iḥṣān* and *muḥṣina* come from the strongly active, transitive form IV of the root *ḥ-ṣ-n*; they mean to actively protect and shelter one's chastity. On the other hand, *taḥaṣṣun* comes from the more reflexive form V, which can also have the connotation of wanting or pretending to be something.[34] Words of form V often do not have a direct object, and they fall somewhere in between the active and passive voice in the English language.[35] Accordingly, the meaning of *taḥaṣṣun* would be something like 'to try to be chaste', or 'to have an internal comportment of chastity'.[36] The term seems to acknowledge that full chastity might not be a realistic goal for an enslaved woman, but that she should nevertheless *try* to be chaste. Her intentions and efforts are valuable, even if she never achieves her aim.

Two other Arabic terms are important for my analysis of this passage below: *fatayāt* (young, unmarried, righteous slave women) and *bighā'* (illicit sex). Most scholars have viewed *fatayāt* simply as meaning 'female slaves', and they treat it as a synonym for the most common Quranic term for slave, 'what your right hands possess' (*mā malakat aymānukum*).[37] However, other contexts from the Quran indicate that *fatayāt* is not quite the same thing as *mā malakat aymānukum*. The other uses of *fatā/fatāh* in the Quran can indeed connote enslavement, but they also connote youth and monotheistic righteousness. For instance, Q 21:60 describes Abraham as a *fatā*, likely meaning a young, morally upright man; Q 12:30 describes Joseph as a *fatā*, meaning a young, morally upright and also sexually appealing slave. While the Quran does not explicate either Abraham's or Joseph's marital status at the time they are called *fatā*, they seem to be unmarried. As for the female term *fatayāt*, the Quran uses it only one other time, in verse 4:25:

> If any of you do not have the means with which to marry chaste believing women (*al-muḥṣināt al-mu'mināt*), then [they may marry] their slaves from among their young believing women (*mā malakat aymānuhum min al-fatāyāt al-mu'mināt*) . . .

This verse has led many exegetes and scholars to assert that slave women cannot be considered chaste, for it contrasts the terms *muḥṣināt* (chaste women) and *fatayāt*.[38] However, if the word *fatayāt* here is understood not simply to mean a slave, but more specifically a *young* slave, it colours the picture slightly differently.[39] It implies that, if a believer cannot afford to marry a free woman, then the only kind of enslaved woman he should marry is a young one. Youth here might indicate that the slave has never been married – is perhaps even a virgin – or at least has not lived long enough to be corrupted by pre-Islamic notions of sexual ethics. Far from implying that the slave women in question are *not* chaste, it seems to instruct believing men to try to marry young and 'unsullied' believing slave women (*fatayāt*) insofar as that is possible.

As for *bighā'*, many translators render it as 'prostitution', which is a plausible reading of the term in the context of Q 24:32. Yet, its meaning is not straightforward, given that this is once again the only attestation of the term in the Quran. When placed in the context of its wider Arabic root, it seems that *bighā'* may mean 'illicit sex' more generally, as opposed to the specific practice of prostitution. A related term, *baghy*, or 'transgressing the bounds', is used several times in constructions such as this one in Q 7:33: 'Say: The things which my Lord has forbidden are: shameful acts (*fawāḥish*), whether open or secret, sins (*ithm*), and transgressions (*baghy*) without right.'[40] The fact that *baghy* is found in close proximity to *fawāḥish*, which has a sexual connotation, indicates that *baghy* might also have such a connotation. Even more strikingly, the active participle, *baghiyy* (prostitute/whore), occurs twice in the Quran, both times in Sura 19 (Mary). When Mary receives the annunciation that she is pregnant with Jesus, she asks: 'How can I have a son, given that no man has touched me and I am no whore (*baghiyyan*)?' (Q 19:20). Later, when her family discovers her pregnancy, they chide her, 'O sister of Aaron! Your father was no philanderer and your mother was no whore (*baghiyyan*)!' (Q 19:28). The term *baghiyy* here resembles the English word 'whore', in that it does not necessarily entail prostitution per se, but is a slander word implying that a woman has had sex outside marriage. Accordingly, the word *bighā'* in Q 24:33 might refer to any kind of pre- or extra-marital sexual activity.[41]

This conceptual and semantic background undergirds the seminal passage, Q 24:32–33, which I argue is the Quran's most explicit statement about the enslaved concubine's chastity. The immediately preceding verses, Q 24:30–31, instruct believing men and women to 'lower their gaze and guard their chastity'.[42] Verses 32 and 33 continue (emphasis added):

> 24:32. Marry the single among you, or the virtuous among your male and female slaves (*al-ṣāliḥina min ʿibādikum wa-imāʾikum*). If they are impoverished, God will enrich them from His grace, for God is all encompassing, all knowing.
>
> 24:33 And let those who cannot make a marriage keep chaste until God enriches them from His grace. Those of your slaves who seek a contract of gradual manumission (*kitāba*), make the contract with them if you know any good in them, and give them some of the wealth of God which He has given you. **And do not force your young, righteous slave women (*fatayāt*) into illicit sexual activity (*bighāʾ*) if they want to try to emulate the sexual ethics of free women (*taḥaṣṣun*), seeking the ephemeral goods of this worldly life; whoever forces them, after their forcing God will surely be forgiving and merciful.**

The entire passage raises a host of complex issues, including chastity within marriage, affording the dowry for that marriage and slavery/manumission. Based on the context of the wider passage, it seems that the final sentence of Q 24:33 might not be about the morality of prostitution, but about the role of prostitution as it relates to money (money to pay for marriage, or to pay for manumission). The sentence might imply that masters should not use the proceeds of prostitution to pay for their marriage dowries. Alternatively, because the verse also mentions the writ of manumission (*kitāba*), the sentence might mean that masters should not let enslaved women use the proceeds of prostitution to purchase their own freedom.[43] Finally, it is possible that the final sentence of Q 24:33 hearkens back to 24:32 and the first sentence of 24:33, in which case it would imply that a righteous (*ṣāliḥa*), unmarried slave woman should remain chaste until she gets married. It is the latter possibility that this chapter explores in more detail.

Like the passage Q 33:4–6 analysed above, I argue that this verse answers some questions that liminal believers may have had about their status within the community. An enslaved woman might have wondered whether she could truly belong to the *umma*, for the Quran sets up chastity as an important marker of belief and righteousness. For instance, Q 23:1–8 lists a series of attributes of the 'successful' believers, which includes upholding the prayer and alms, avoiding frivolity, keeping their word and guarding their chastity. Similarly, Q 33:35 promises that God will reward all men and women who submit to God and believe, who are devout, honest, humble, patient, charitable and selfless, and who guard their chastity. That is, chastity ranks among prayer and almsgiving as one of the main attestations of true belief. It is difficult to recover the sexual ethics of the pre-Islamic period, but it seems safe to assume that enslaved women had little sexual agency and were generally not considered 'chaste'.[44] Moreover, the Quran itself explicitly allows a master to have sexual access to 'those his right hands possess', in verses such as 23:6, and 70:30,[45] but there is no explicit parallel to these verses from the enslaved woman's perspective. That is, while concubinage is licit from the male owner's perspective, it is unclear from the enslaved woman's perspective.

As a result, an enslaved woman – particularly an unmarried concubine – might have wondered whether she could adhere to the believers' expected standards of chastity and morality. And if she could not, she might have found herself unable to belong to the *umma* in any meaningful sense. I argue that verse 24:33 alleviates these worries by indicating that an enslaved woman may take more control over her own sexuality. Based on my semantic analysis above, there are two fairly divergent, but equally plausible, readings of this verse that shed new light on the sexual ethics of enslaved women. First, less controversially, this verse may simply indicate that an enslaved woman may refuse to work as a prostitute. She would still be her master's concubine and would not be entitled to refuse the advances of her own master. In this case, the word *taḥaṣṣun* would describe the concubine's sexual relationship with her own master – that is, it would mean something like, 'Do not force your slave women to prostitution, if they desire to abstain from sex with everyone except you.' From her perspective, concubinage itself would fall somewhere between chastity and unchastity. This situation would create something of an ethical double standard between men, who are explicitly allowed to have chastity (*iḥsān*) within the confines of marriage and concubinage, and enslaved women, whose best moral state would be *taḥaṣṣun*.

The second, more radical, reading of this verse would provide an unmarried believing slave woman the prerogative to refuse sex even with her own master. In this reading, *bighā'* would mean 'extra-marital sex' and not merely prostitution, and *taḥaṣṣun* would mean trying to avoid any sexual activity outside the confines of legal marriage. This reading would not necessarily contradict the Quranic passages that allow male masters to practice concubinage with their female slaves (such as Q 23:6 and 70:30), as those passages consider chastity from the male master's perspective. Here in Q 24:33, the issue at stake seems to be whether or not concubinage counts as chastity from the enslaved female's perspective. In this reading, a man may still have sex with his '*mā malakat al-aymān*', meaning generally slaves, but he may not have unlimited sex with his *fatayāt,* meaning a specific subset of young, unmarried, believing, righteous slaves. (This would correspond well with the only other usage of the term *fatayāt,* wherein the Quran encourages believing men to marry them, not to have concubinal sex with them.) This reading would provide a stronger sense that belief – and the sexual ethics that go along with belief – trumps or at least challenges male slave-owners' prerogatives. Even if this is the case, however, the verse still uses the term *taḥaṣṣun* and not the more forceful *iḥṣān* to describe the concubine's position. The softened vocabulary seems to imply that refusing her master's advances is difficult (if not impossible) for an enslaved woman, and it provides her some moral leeway for her in case her master continues to force himself on her. It implies that an enslaved woman may in the end have no power to enact her own chastity, but that she can at least have correct intention and a moral attitude. It is the effort itself that counts as *taḥaṣṣun* for the enslaved concubine. While more radically empowering for the concubine in some ways, this reading still effectively places the master–concubine relationship in the grey area of *taḥaṣṣun* for the enslaved woman.

In either case – the more conventional or the more radical reading of the passage – the word *taḥaṣṣun* seems to pertain to the enslaved woman's sexual relationship with her own master, and it puts her in a liminal ethical position. While all other Muslims, male or female, are held to the standard of *iḥṣān,* the enslaved woman is only held to the standard of *taḥaṣṣun.* This liminal status has a more inclusive reading, and a more exclusionary one. On the inclusive side, it is clear that an enslaved woman can be a believer, and that belief gives her some control over her sexuality. (An enslaved woman can still be compelled to *marry* whomever her master wishes, so the issue here is not the enslaved woman's complete agency to choose her sexual partners. But she can at least demand to have only chaste sexual relations.) Additionally, these lowered moral expectations can be read charitably, as a theological mercy for enslaved women. According to verse 2:286, God does not charge the believers to do what they are not capable of doing; thus, God does not charge enslaved women to become full *muḥṣināt* because they would likely fail, and such a moral failing could send them to hell. In order to help the believing slave woman achieve paradise, the Quran lowers its moral expectations.

On the more exclusive side, these lowered moral expectations can be read less charitably, as giving in to exploitative social practices and power dynamics instead of changing them. One potential upshot of the Quran's focus on attaining the afterlife (as in the Bible and other scriptures) is that it seems to condone the continuation of unjust practices on Earth. It puts the burden on the enslaved woman to 'try to be chaste', instead of demanding that society change such that enslaved women are able to be fully chaste. Moreover, it seems clear that unmarried slave women are still unable to embody their faith quite as fully as any other believer – even married slave women are all at least hypothetically able to follow God's command to remain chaste. And if chastity, like prayer and charity, is a marker of truly belonging to the *umma,* then unmarried slave women are also unable to belong to the *umma* quite as fully as any other believer. In the end, it appears that chastity for the enslaved woman is not black and white in the Quran, but a murky grey *taḥaṣṣun.*

Finally, it is worth considering the resonances, and the ruptures, between this Quranic view and the early Christian view of slavery and sexuality. Jennifer Glancy has noted the polyvalence of the Greek term *porneia,* used by Paul in several of his epistles. This term can mean sexual irregularity more broadly, or prostitution more specifically; the exact parameters of *porneia* are unclear and open to interpretation.[46] The Quranic terms *bighā'* and *zinā* appear to have a similar polyvalence. Paul urges his readers to shun *porneia,* and he instructs Christian men to 'obtain their own vessel' (that is, woman) for licit sexual activity. As Glancy shows, this 'vessel' may have been understood to be either a wife or a slave – for first-century CE society assumed that masters may have sex with their slaves, who were 'morally neutral sexual outlets'.[47] Likewise, the Quran considers under the rubric of 'chastity' a man's sexual relations with his wives and concubines. However, Paul remains pointedly silent on the question of whether such master–slave sexual relationships counted as *porneia* for the enslaved woman herself. Glancy wonders whether Paul's silence 'indicates he believes slaves who are sexually involved with their owners are therefore alienated from the Christian body', or, on the other hand, that 'the forced sexual activity of slaves was beyond moral judgment'.[48] That is, Paul's silence leaves open the question of whether enslaved women could truly belong to a group of Christians whose 'bodies are members of Christ', and whose bodies were 'not for *porneia*, but for the Lord'.

In contrast to Paul's silence, I argue that the Quran makes a more positive statement that enslaved women can indeed belong to the community of believers whose membership is marked by their sexual ethics – they may not belong *fully*, but they belong at least partially. Moreover, in the early Christian Roman context, slaves could not contract legal marriages, while the Quran clearly allows both male and female slaves the ability to marry, and thus to fully embody their community's sexual ethics. Accordingly, it seems that the Quran takes up similar questions to those raised by early Christianity, and it exhibits many of the same polyvalences and uncertainties, yet it resolves the matter of the slave woman's sexual ethics slightly more concretely than does Paul.

The Disconnect between Exegesis and History

In the light of this co-textual analysis of Q 33:4–6 and 24:30–33, it is worth returning to the traditional Muslim exegeses of these passages, to analyse their concerns and to consider how and why they fail to raise the tensions this chapter has highlighted.[49] The exegetes almost universally say that God revealed Q 33:4–5 regarding the Prophet Muḥammad's adopted son Zayd, who had previously been called Zayd ibn Muḥammad but was re-named Zayd ibn Ḥāritha following the command to 'call them by [the names of] their fathers'.[50] As for the statement in Q 33:6 that 'relatives are closer to one another', exegetes almost universally treat it as an abrogation of the 'brotherhood' (*mu'ākhāh*) agreement that Muḥammad had instituted between the Medinan Helpers and Meccan Emigrants shortly after the *hijra*. The metaphorical 'brothers' of this tiny core of believers inherited from and bequeathed to one another for a short while, but, after enough blood relatives had joined the *umma*, the old kinship-based inheritance practices were re-instituted.[51] As for the final sentence of Q 24:33, exegetes understand that this verse forbids the practice of forced slave prostitution, and that it absolves enslaved women if their masters nevertheless prostitute them. These exegeses provide several examples of Medinese women who escaped forced prostitution in this way.[52]

From the perspective of a historian attempting to reconstruct first-/seventh-century history, these exegeses prove largely disappointing. First, on the level of grammar and vocabulary, exegetes sometimes interpret the text inconsistently in order to fit their own frameworks. For instance, they essentially ignore the conditional phrase, 'If you do not know their fathers', when associating Q 33:5 with Zayd ibn Ḥāritha. This conditional phrase should exclude Zayd, for his father was known to be the Kalbī tribesman Ḥāritha ibn Shuraḥīl. The early exegete Muqātil ibn Sulaymān acknowledges this problem when he explains, 'Even if they had not known a father for Zayd to be traced back to, he still would have been your brother in religion and your *mawlā*.'[53] The exegetes' association of Q 33:6 with inheritance laws is also problematic because of their inconsistent understanding of the word *awlā* ('closer'). Regarding blood relatives, they say that *awlā* refers to inheritance; yet, this very same verse also describes Muḥammad as *awlā*, and the exegetes do not indicate that Muḥammad inherited from or bequeathed to his believers.[54] Finally, while there is no inherent problem in associating Q 24:33 with a ban on slave prostitution, the exegetes raise inconsistencies and logical loopholes that they do not resolve when explaining this verse.[55] Shii exegetes solve these problems by arguing that Q 24:33 had been abrogated by Q 4:25, but the Sunni exegetes generally do not even recognise the internal inconsistencies in their own thinking about enslaved women's sexual ethics. Moreover, as I will discuss further in Chapter 4, most of these exegeses provide unhistorical, symbolic examples of women who escaped prostitution as a result of the revelation of this verse.[56]

The usual interpretations also effectively shatter the semantic and conceptual coherence of these passages. Very few exegetes treat Q 33:4–6 as a coherent unit; most treat 33:4–5 separately from 33:6, while others treat verses 4, 5 and 6 separately.[57] As for Q 24:33, most exegetes treat each clause of the verse separately, not considering the entire verse as a unit (much less the wider passage).[58] This trend is not surprising – for medieval exegetes tended to break down their analyses into small units, while moderns have moved towards analysing entire passages, Suras or even the entire Quran as a whole. However, it does mean that the medieval exegetes do not engage with the wider themes of these passages. For example, the tension I find in the term *mawālī* comes from comparing the many versions of the root *w-l-y* found across verses 33:5 and 33:6. Similarly, the tension I notice in the meaning of 24:33 comes from noting the other uses of terms referring to chastity and slavery in the Quran. That is, I have not chosen my analytical units based on scholarly convention, oral tradition or a theory about the chronological order of revelation, but on semantic and conceptual coherence.

More importantly from my historian's point of view, the exegetes mostly fail to consider what these verses might say about Islamic history, or the exegetes' own societies, cultures or polities.[59] For instance, al-Ṭabarī (d. 310/923), whose historical accounts of the Umayyad era and Abbasid revolution are full of *mawālī*, makes no attempt to connect those *mawālī* with this Quranic passage in his *tafsīr* of 33:5. The exegeses of 33:4–6 provide essentially no details about the changing meaning of the word *mawālī*, or insights into how outsiders were incorporated into the *umma* in different historical contexts. Instead, exegetes are interested in legal details, such as what happens if a man inadvertently refers to someone as 'sonny' or 'pops', or what happens when a man actually claims someone as his biological son. For instance, al-Zamakhsharī goes into great detail:

> If the 'claimed' one is of unknown paternity and is younger in years than the one claiming him as a son, then his paternity is set thereupon. If [the claimed son] is a slave of his, then he must be immediately manumitted along with the setting of his paternity. If he does not look at all like him, then the paternity is not set, but he is still freed according to Abū Ḥanīfa; but according to the two Sahibs [Abū Yūsuf and al-Shaybānī], he is not freed. As for one whose paternity is known, then his paternity is not set by [such a claim], but if he is a slave he is still freed.[60]

Many exegetes are also interested in naming practices. They suggest that if a man does not know someone's full name, he should address them as 'O brother' or 'O cousin', to avoid accidentally misattributing their paternity. Exegetes also give suggestions on how to name a slave or freedman of unknown paternity. Suggestions are to call such a slave 'Ibn Muslim' or 'Ibn ʿAbdallāh', or simply to call them 'the *mawlā* of so-and-so', using the *mawlā* tie as a replacement for their missing genealogy. (It seems that Muslims generally followed such advice, for it is fairly easy to spot *mawālī* in the sources because they have such generic names as 'Muḥammad ibn ʿAbdallāh' or 'ʿAbdallāh ibn Muslim'.) Finally, most sources – and Shii sources in particular – care more about the elative term *awlā* ('closer') in Q 33:6 than they do about the related terms *mawālī* or *awliyā'*. For example, al-Qummī finds that 'blood relatives' in Q 33:6 means the Imams, and 'closer' means more deserving of command (*al-amr*). I suggest that the exegetes show little concern for the meaning of the terms *mawālī* and *awliyā'* because they are no longer concerned with the incorporation of outsiders into the *umma*, but rather with the delineation of the *umma*'s internal boundaries and legal structures.[61]

Likewise, pre-modern *tafsīrs* of Q 24:33 never treat the issue of the *qiyān* (enslaved courtesans, sometimes likened to high-class prostitutes), who are prominent figures in Abbasid-era historical and literary works.[62] They do not consider how the Quranic text might apply to the sex trade in Islamic history or society,[63] or engage with the possibility that prostitutes might struggle with economic hardship or limited personal agency.[64] Instead, they are interested in philosophical questions, such as what constitutes true compulsion (*ikrāh*), as opposed to lesser forms of pressure or intimidation. In answering this question, they draw parallels to Q 16:106, which expresses forgiveness for people who deny their faith under duress. For example, al-Zamakhsharī explains that compulsion means, 'One who is compelled on pain of death, or fears injury or loss of limb, as from a violent blow.'[65] That is, economic hardship or social pressure is not enough to constitute true compulsion. The exegetes are also much concerned with the grammatical function of the phrase 'if they desire chastity'. They are generally perplexed by this clause, and some of them ask rhetorically: 'How can a woman be described as "compelled" to prostitution if she *doesn't* desire chastity?' To solve this problem, the exegetes generally agree that 'if' (Arabic *in*) is not a true conditional here, but that its meaning is more akin to the Arabic word *idhā*, 'if-and-when'. As al-Bayḍāwī explains, '*In* is preferred to *idhā* here because the desire for chastity among slave women is like a unique aberration.'[66] Exegetes seem to think that the only woman who would work as a prostitute is one who *enjoys* fornicating, or exhibits an 'unusual perversion' as al-Zamakhsharī puts it.[67] There are also a few sectarian issues here, particularly the Sunni exegetes who view 'prostitution' here as a veiled reference to the Shii practice of *mutʿa* marriage, and the Shii tendency to view Q 24:33 as abrogated by 4:25. In short, these are legal and grammatical minutiae that do not attempt to reckon with the continued practices of prostitution and sexual exploitation in the exegetes' own societies.

Ultimately, exegetes divide their interpretations into two main parts: haggadic stories (*asbāb al-nuzūl*) that are relegated to the distant past of the Quranic revelation and sundered from current events, and halakhic legal details that consider the grammatical issues and juridical particulars of certain parts of scripture.[68] On the one hand, this gap between exegesis and social history is simply a matter of genre. Exegetes have their own conventions, and their focus tends to be on theological, legal and sectarian issues rather than social or historical ones. On the other hand, I suggest that the exegetes of the third/ninth century (and later) had a vested interest in sundering their exegeses from history. The exegetes might have missed the tensions raised in these passages because they almost universally come down on the side of hierarchy. No matter their sectarian affiliation or theological school, these authors represent the class of literate, free, male, slave-holding Muslims in urban centres such as Baghdad. They would almost certainly clamour against my more radical reading of Q 24:33, not because it is textually unsupportable, but because they have a personal stake in upholding the unlimited right of the master to his concubines. They see the world from the perspective of an insider hoping to bolster his position vis-à-vis other Muslims, not from the perspective of an outsider hoping to join the *umma* in the first place. They worry about debates and identity groups *within* the Islamic community, rather than wondering about new converts' sense of belonging.

Conclusion

The medieval exegetes' viewpoints are not the only valid ones – they do not have a monopoly on the Quran's meaning. Accordingly, this chapter has attempted to view the Quran from the perspective of enslaved persons and other outsiders hoping to join the community, and to consider the questions they might have had about their status within the community. In doing so, it highlights the tensions within the Quranic text as it seeks to create a community that balances faith, justice, morality and order. The Quran does not resolve these tensions, but it does grapple with them. Particularly, for rootless outsiders without a known genealogy, the Quran affirms that all believers belong to society as one another's '*mawālī*', but it also indicates that not all believers have access to equal social support. For enslaved women, the Quran certainly discourages masters from prostituting their believing slaves, and it might even more radically discourage slave owners from using their believing slaves as concubines. However, from the enslaved woman's perspective, it also places the master–concubine relationship into the liminal position of *taḥaṣṣun*.

In the coming chapters of this book, I seek to re-connect these Quranic verses with tensions and debates unfolding in early Islamic history. I suggest that the Quran is deeply connected to Islamic history, in that it lays the groundwork for debates surrounding the early Islamic *mawālī* and enslaved women, including both the struggle of some elites to define and subordinate these groups, and these groups' own struggles to articulate their identity and sense of belonging. Particularly, the next two chapters will argue that the earliest *umma* in first-/seventh-century Arabia leaned towards a more inclusive resolution of these tensions. If they never achieved perfect equality, they seem to have been trying to build a society where the salient social bonds grew out of faith and moral probity, and where people were differentiated primarily by their degrees of piety. Thus, this earliest community manumitted slaves without any bonds of subordination, and they actively intervened to stop situations of forced prostitution (or perhaps even forced concubinage). However, these more egalitarian strands can only be found by digging carefully through works of Islamic scholarship, for by the time such works were codified in the second/eighth and third/ninth centuries, the tide had turned in the other direction. Scholars from this later period justify hierarchy and assume the existence of unequal social categories. But ultimately both historical trends, the egalitarian and the hierarchical, trace their way back to the tensions latent within the Quranic text itself.

Notes

1. This book does not begin with the pre-Islamic period for two reasons. One, Arabic sources for the pre-Islamic period were generally written by authors in the Islamic era. That is, these sources are illuminating for the elaboration of Arab identity in the Umayyad and Abbasid periods, but difficult to use for

understanding pre-Islamic values. See Rina Drory, 'The Abbasid Construction of the Jahiliyya: Cultural Authority in the Making', *Studia Islamica*, 83 (1996): 33–49. Second, and more importantly, this book focuses on the elaboration of Islam per se – how slaves and outsiders joined the *umma* – rather than on Islam's historical connections to pre-Islamic laws and customs. Many other scholars have traced such connections, including but not limited to Patricia Crone, *Roman, Provincial and Islamic Law* on legal connections; Mohamad Rihan, *The Politics and Culture of an Umayyad Tribe: Conflict and Factionalism in the Early Islamic Period* (London: Tauris, 2014) on tribal connections; and Thomas Sizgorich, *Violence and Belief in Late Antiquity: Militant Devotion in Christianity and Islam* (Philadelphia: University of Pennsylvania Press, 2014) on ideological connections. Such studies are illuminating and greatly help contextualise early Islamic history, but pre-Islamic Arabia is simply not the focus of my research.

2. Scholars still hotly debate the history of the Quranic text, including its authorship and its codification. Until the mid-twentieth century, scholars tended to accept the traditional Muslim account that caliph ʿUthmān (r. 23–35/644–656) codified the Quran and gave it its final, canonical shape. Scholars such as Richard Bell, Rudi Paret and Theodor Nöldeke mostly concerned themselves with trying to refine the traditional dating of the order of revelations. However, John Wansbrough's *Quranic Studies* revolutionised the field, for he suggested that the Quran, as it has come down to us today, is the result of a centuries-long compilation process led by scholars in third-/ninth-century Iraq. Wansbrough was *not* arguing that the Quran was wholly invented in that context or that it contains no authentic first-/seventh-century materials, but that its repetitive and elliptical style is a result of a compilation of many different regional versions of the text in a highly sectarian milieu. Since then, some scholars have been quite sceptical of the Quran's historicity, while others maintain the basic integrity of the Quranic text. For current debates in the field of Qur'anic studies, see the chapters in Angelika Neuwirth, Nicolai Sinai and Michael Marx, eds. *The Qur'ān in Context*; Gabriel Said Reynolds, ed. *New Perspectives on the Qur'an*; and Angelika Neuwirth and Michael Anthony Sells, eds, *Qur'ānic Studies Today*.
3. This technique is called 'reading the Quran through the Quran'. It deliberately avoids using other types of sources, such as Quranic exegesis (*tafsīr*) and biography of the Prophet (*sīra*), to understand the Quran. Scholars generally agree that these later types of sources are unhelpful for recovering the Quran's original meaning. As F. E. Peters says, 'the suspicion is strong that medieval Muslim scholars were re-creating the "occasion [of revelation]" by working

backwards out of the Qur'anic verses themselves, an exercise at which a modern non-Muslim might be equally adept' (Peters, 'The Quest of the Historical Muhammad', 301). Patricia Crone puts it more bluntly, in her signature incisive style: 'The exegetes had no better knowledge of what this sura meant than we have today' (Crone, *Meccan Trade and the Rise of Islam*, 210). While I argue that the *tafsīrs* can be valuable historical sources for early Islamic history, and will analyse them more carefully in later chapters, I agree that it is crucial to begin with an internal, co-textual analysis of the Quran itself.

4. See, for instance, Kecia Ali, *Marriage and Slavery in Early Islam*; Brockopp, *Early Māliki Law*; Ingrid Mattson, 'A Believing Slave Is Better than an Unbeliever'; Harald Motzki, 'Wal-Muḥṣanātu Mina N-Nisā'i'; and F. M. Denny, 'The Meaning of Ummah in the Qur'ān'.
5. For modern scholars, see, for instance, Günther, 'Clients and Clientage', *EQ*; David S. Powers, *Muhammad is Not the Father of Any of Your Men*, 62–63; and Ella Landau-Tasseron, 'Adoption, Acknowledgment of Paternity, and False Genealogical Claims', 171–173. For Quran translations, Pickthall and Arberry translate the term in Q 33:5 as 'clients', while others translate it as 'those entrusted to you' (Sahih International), 'friends' (Shakir) and 'protéges' (Abdel Haleem). For a side-by-side comparison of more than forty English translations of the Quran, see http://www.islamawakened.com/quran/33/5/default.htm (last accessed 12 March 2019). Finally, many medieval exegetes suggest that *mawālī* here simply means 'freedmen'; see, for instance, al-Ṭabarī, *Tafsīr al-Ṭabarī: Jāmiʿ Al-Bayān ʿan Taʾwīl Āy Al-Qurʾān* (hereafter *Jāmiʿ al-Bayān*), 19:12; and Fakhr al-Dīn al-Rāzī, *Al-Tafsīr al-Kabīr*, 25:193.
6. While I rely only on the Quran to construct the meaning of *walāʾ*, Patricia Crone has likewise found that pre-Islamic poetry almost always uses the term *mawālī* 'in connection with the theme of mutual help, frequently military, but sometimes also material or moral'. Crone, *Roman, Provincial and Islamic Law,* 55.
7. Medieval exegetes generally understand the verb in this passage to be 'call them' your brothers in religion and *mawālī*, rather than 'they are' your brothers in religion and your *mawālī*. For example, al-Zamakhsharī explains that if you do not know someone's lineage, you should call them 'O my brother', or 'O my *mawlā*', and he outlines what should happen if someone accidentally calls their non-relative 'sonny' or 'pops' (Al-Zamakhsharī, *Al-Kashshāf*, 3:506–507). Likewise, Fakhr al-Dīn al-Rāzī explains that this means you should call them 'brother of so-and-so' if they are free, or '*mawlā* of so-and-so' if they are a freed

slave. (Fakhr al-Dīn al-Rāzī, *Al-Tafsīr al-Kabīr,* 25:193). The Quran is slightly ambiguous here, for it does not provide an explicit verb for this phrase; the exegetes apparently apply the force of the verb in the immediately preceding clause, '*call them* by the names of their fathers'. However, the usual vocalisation of this phrase is '*fa-ikhwān**u**kum fī al-dīn wa-mawal**ī**kum*', in the nominative case, which implies that the meaning is that 'they are' your brothers in religion and *mawālī*. (If the meaning were 'call them' your brothers in religion, one would expect the vocalisation to be '*fa-ikhwān**a**kum fī al-dīn wa-mawāl**iya**kum*', in the objective case.) Most modern translations render the phrase here as 'they are' your brothers in religion and *māwālī,* which is the stronger reading in my view.

8. *W-l-y* is one of the many Arabic roots that can mean one thing and its opposite. In the Quran, it can mean to turn *towards* in support, or conversely, to turn *away from* and revoke support. For the sense of turning towards, see, for example, Q 60:13: 'Do not turn in friendship and support (*lā tatawallaw*) toward a people with whom God is angry.' For the sense of turning away, see Q 64:6: '. . . They disbelieved and withdrew their support (*kafarū wa-tawallaw*) . . .' In either case, the root pertains to social bonds – building them with believers, or breaking them with unbelievers.
9. For a quick reference to this root in the Quran, consult El-Said Badawi and M. A. Abdel Haleem, *Arabic-English Dictionary of Qur'anic Usage*, 1,047–1,049. For a deeper analysis, see Elizabeth Urban, 'The Foundations of Islamic Society as Expressed by the Qur'anic Term *Mawlā*'.
10. God is commonly described as a *mawlā* or *walī*; for just a few examples, see Q 2:120, 4:45, 13:11, 29:22, 33:17, 42:31 and 48:22. Alternatively, those who refuse the protection of God are sometimes described as having Satan, hell, jinn or other evil things as their *mawlā* or *walī*. For instance, Q 57:15 says, '. . .Your refuge is the fire, it is your *mawlā* – what an evil outcome!'; and Q 7:30 says: '. . . they took satans as *awliyā'* instead of God . . .' See also Q 4:76, 7:27, 19:45, 22:4 and 22:13, among others.
11. See Q 2:83, 3:36, 2:205, 3: 8:15, 9:76, 47:22 and 48:22. For more examples and a deeper discussion of these types of support, see Urban, 'The Foundations of Islamic Society'.
12. For a similar sentiment, see also Q 3:150 and 9:51.
13. The same idea is conveyed in Q 9:71, which states that 'the male and female believers are the *awliyā'* of one another'.
14. Muḥammad ibn Isḥāq, *Sīrat Rasūl Allāh*, ed. Ferdinand Wüstenfeld, 342. For

an in-depth analysis of this document and its many textual variants, see Michael Lecker, *The 'Constitution of Medina': Muhammad's First Legal Document*. See also R. B. Serjeant, 'The "Constitution of Medina"' and 'The *Sunnah Jami'ah*, Pacts with the Yathrib Jews, and the *Tahrim* of Yathrib'; Moshe Gil, 'The Constitution of Medina: A Reconsideration'; F. M. Denny, '*Umma* in the Constitution of Medina'; Uri Rubin, 'The 'Constitution of Medina': Some Notes'; and Said Amir Arjomand, 'The Constitution of Medina: A Sociolegal Interpretation of Muhammad's Acts of Foundation of the *Umma*'.

15. See also Q 2:257, 3:28, 5:80, 45:19, 60:1, 60:9, 60:13 and 62:6, among others.
16. I will discuss these exegeses in further detail below.
17. For example, Arabian tribes shifted their genealogical histories to accord with political realities; whenever two tribes allied with each other, they would 'discover' a common ancestor. There is an extensive literature on the use of fictive kinship to solidify tribal ties in Arabia from ancient times to the present day. For some perceptive recent studies, see Edouard Conte, 'Agnatic Illusions'; Daniel Martin Varisco, 'Metaphors and Sacred History'; and Zoltán Szombathy, *The Roots of Arabic Genealogy*, and the sources cited therein.
18. Another famous example of this phenomenon is the pre-Islamic poet and folk hero ʿAntara ibn Shaddād. ʿAntara had been raised as a slave, but when he distinguished himself in battle, his mother's master claimed ʿAntara as his own son. A similar thing happened to an early Muslim named Abū Bakra, the subject of the next chapter.
19. It thus strikes me as somewhat ironic that the classical jurists would come to understand *walā'* patronage as a form of agnatic kinship, that is, as a form of *nasab*. The Quran seems to speak explicitly against treating human-constructed relationships as akin to God-given genealogy. See Crone, *Roman, Provincial and Islamic Law,* 37, 40 and 83, where she notes the strangeness of treating *walā'* as *nasab,* and shows that the pre-classical jurists treated *walā'* not as a replacement genealogy, but as a vestige of slavery.
20. Verse 33:37 makes it clear that the reason that genealogical language must reflect the biological truth is 'so that there would be no prohibition for the Muslims against [marrying] the wives of their adopted sons'.
21. Al-Qurṭubī, *Al-Jāmiʿ Li-Aḥkām Al-Qur'ān,* 17:59. See also al-Ṭabarī, *Jāmiʿ al-Bayān*, 19:13, where Abū Bakra only says, 'I am your brother in religion'; and Ibn ʿAsākir, *Tārīkh Madīnat Dimashq*, 62:213–214, where Abū Bakra says, 'I am your brother in religion and a *mawlā* of the messenger of God.' Apparently, some of Abū Bakra's companions had teased him for his unknown paternity,

for his mother was a prostitute. The meaning of Abū Bakra's so-called '*mawlā*' identity is the subject of the next chapter, but I suggest that here Abū Bakra is invoking this verse in its original, community-affirming sense.

22. The Quran uses a similar phrase when describing Abraham in verse 3:68: 'Indeed, the closest (*awlā*) of people to Abraham are surely those who followed him, and this prophet, and those who believe. For God is the *walī* of the believers.' Abraham, too, had valued belief over genealogy – he had broken the strongest tribal social bond, the bond between father and son, in the name of right belief.
23. For the idea that all followers are equal before the Imam, see Patricia Crone, '*Mawālī* and the Prophet's *Family:* An Early Shi'ite View', 185–187. According to Maria Massi Dakake, the Shii concept of walaya 'describes an all-encompassing bond of spiritual loyalty that describes, simultaneously, a Shiite believer's allegiance to God, the Prophet, the Imam, and the community of Shiite believers, collectively' (Maria Massi Dakake, *The Charismatic Community*, 7). The Shii concept of *walāya* also hinges on the term *mawlā,* not in the Quran, but in the Prophet Muḥammad's famous statement at Ghadīr Khumm: 'Whosoever I am his *mawlā,* Ali is also his *mawlā.*'
24. Al-Zamakhsharī precedes me in this reading. While most exegetes understand 'treat your *awilyā'* well' to mean that people should give their friends a *waṣiyya,* or voluntary bequeathal in their will, al-Zamakhsharī says: 'If you say, "the relative is closer than the stranger, except in *waṣiyya,*" what you mean is, he is more deserving of every help, inheritance, gift, present, charity and everything, except a *waṣiyya.*' That is, a person can remember his friend in his will, but every other form of social and legal help should go first and foremost to a person's relatives (Al-Zamakhsharī, *Al-Kashshāf,* 3:509).
25. In Arabic, masculine plural nouns, pronouns and verbs can refer either to a group of males, or to a mixed group of males and females. See Amina Wadud, *Qur'an and Woman,* 4–7 on the application of the Quran's masculine plural words to Muslim women as well as Muslim men.
26. See first and foremost Kecia Ali, *Sexual Ethics and Islam* and *Marriage and Slavery in Early Islam.* See also Harald Motzki, ed., 'Wal-Muhsanatu Mina N-Nisa'i'; Brockopp, *Early Mālikī Law*; and Mattson, 'A Believing Slave is Better than an Unbeliever'.
27. As expressed in Q 23:6: '[Believers should abstain from sex] except with their spouses and slaves, for they are blameless.' A nearly identical sentiment is expressed in Q 70:30.
28. It is a bit unclear whether the Quran exhorts or simply allows the marriage

of slaves. On the one hand, Q 24:32 appears to encourage Muslims to marry righteous slaves. However, Q 4:25 indicates that a man should only marry an enslaved woman if he cannot afford a free spouse, and does not trust himself to remain abstinent outside legal marriage.

29. That is, by getting married, the enslaved woman becomes a full *muḥṣina,* or chaste woman. See Motzki, 'Wal-Muhsinatu Mina N-Nisa'i', 200–201; Ali, *Marriage and Slavery in Early Islam,* 68–69; Brockopp, *Early Mālikī Law,* 202, n. 187.
30. On this point, see particularly J. Burton, 'The Meaning of "Ihsan"'. As Burton explains, classical Muslim jurists used the term *muḥṣana* to designate a free, married, Muslim woman who must remain chaste – and who is stoned to death if she commits adultery. These scholars almost universally did not consider slave women to be *muḥṣanāt,* and thus adulterous slave women were not stoned to death. This situation puzzled Burton, for Q 4:24 seems to include enslaved women in the category of *muḥṣana* when it says, 'And the *muḥṣanāt* among the women, except "those your right hands possess" [i.e. slaves]' (*wa-al-muḥṣanātu min al-nisā'i illā mā malakat aymānukum*). He argues that the non-stoning of enslaved women was already a well-established practice before the revelation of the Quran, and that jurists sought to justify this existing practice through selective interpretation of the Quran, rather than to use the Quran to reform existing practices. On the non-chastity of the enslaved woman, see also Motzki, 'Wal-Muhsinatu Mina N-Nisa'i'.
31. I am convinced by Motzki's argument that this term should usually be read in the active voice (*muḥṣināt*), and that it refers to anyone who abstains from illicit sex. However, I am less convinced by his reading of *taḥaṣṣun* in Q 4:25 as a state of voluntary, non-mandatory chastity for the unmarried slave woman. Motzki, 'Wal-Muhsinatu Mina N-Nisa'i', 199–200.
32. Motzki, 'Wal-Muhsinatu Mina N-Nisa'i', 199.
33. I can only attribute Motzki's oversight to the fact that he is focused on solving the puzzle of Q 4:24, not on explicating the meaning of Q 24:33. Moreover, like most scholars before him, he is not thinking about this issue from the perspective of the enslaved woman herself, or from the perspective of a community trying to figure out how to balance their need for both inclusivity and social order.
34. On the different forms, see W. Wright, *A Grammar of the Arabic Language,* 34–38. According to W. Lane, *Arabic-English Lexicon*, 1:586, classical Arabic dictionaries such as *Lisān al-ʿArab* and *Tāj al-ʿArūs* use the form IV verb to refer

to chastity and/or marriage, while they use the form V verb to mean to fortify oneself or hole oneself up in a fortress.

35. For example, the famous poet al-Mutanabbī's name is the form V participle of the word '*nabī*' (prophet), and it means 'to pretend to be a prophet'. Similarly, the word *ta'allama* is the form V verb of the word '*'ilm*' (knowledge), and it means 'to learn' – a reflexive word that denotes one's internal quest to gain knowledge.
36. This sense of intransitivity or incompletion is heightened by the phrasing in Q 24:33: 'if they *want* taḥaṣṣun'; emphasis added.
37. On this phrase, see Motzki, 'Wal-Muhsinatu Mina N-Nisa'i', 205–210; and Ali, *Sexual Ethics and Islam,* 39–55.
38. As previously mentioned, Motzki, 'Wal-Muhsinastu Mina N-Nisa'i', and Burton, 'The Meaning of "Ihsan"', have problematised this dichotomy. I suggest that there is not necessarily a contrast or contradiction here between *muḥṣināt* and *fatayāt,* so much as there is a difference. I read *muḥṣināt* as free, chaste women of any age or any marital status; while I read *fatayāt* here to mean young, unmarried slave women, and that it also implies that such young women are virginal or chaste.
39. Classical exegetes gloss the term *fatayāt* here as 'slave women' (*imā'*). They base their reading on a hadith in which Muhammad exhorts his followers to refer to their male and female slaves as 'my boy' (*fatāya*) or 'girl' (*fatātī*).
40. See also Q 16:90.
41. This reading corresponds with that of the exegetes; all classical exegetes from al-Ṭabarī to Fakhr al-Dīn to Ibn Kathīr gloss *bighā'* in Q 24:33 as *zinā,* or fornication.
42. Q 24:31 also provides a list of people before whom a Muslim woman may 'display her beauty', usually taken to mean to take off her veil.
43. Because this Quranic passage generally refers to marriage rather than manumission, Crone argues that the word *kitāba* here 'is a marriage document (cf. Hebrew *ketubah*), not a manumission agreement'. Crone, *Roman, Provincial and Islamic Law,* 145, n. 100. I find her reading entirely plausible; however, I think it is also plausible, given that the passage speaks about earning money, that it could refer to a writ of manumission.
44. See Motzki, 'Wal-Muhsinastu Mina N-Nisa'i', 199–201.
45. See also Q 4:24, and 33:50.
46. Jennifer A Glancy, *Slavery in Early Christianity,* 65. I thank Isabel Moreira for pointing me towards this connection.

47. *Ibid.*, 62.
48. *Ibid.*, 64.
49. I am not implying that such classical exegeses are wrong or meaningless, or that my interpretation is the only correct one. Rather, I am hoping to de-centre the classical exegetical view, and to highlight the ways that the classical exegetes view the Quran from an elite, male, slave-holding perspective.
50. For a recent re-interpretation of Zayd, see David Powers, *Muhammad is Not the Father of Any of Your Men*.
51. For a discussion of the 'brotherhood' agreement, see I. Lichtenstaedter, 'Fraternization (*Mu'ākhāt*) in Early Islamic society'. See also Jamal Juda, 'Die sozialen und wirtschaftlichen Aspekte der Mawālī in frühislamischer Zeit', 55–57.
52. These women are the subject of Chapter 4 of this monograph.
53. Muqātil ibn Sulaymān, *Tafsīr Muqātil ibn Sulaymān*, 3:473.
54. Most Sunni sources read this phrase as meaning that Muḥammad deserved the complete obedience and allegiance, while Shii authors read it as referring to the rightful political leadership of Muḥammad, ʿAlī, and the Imams after him. For the Shii view, see, for instance, ʿAlī ibn Ibrāhīm al-Qummī, *Tafsīr Al-Qummī*, 2:171–196.
55. For example, exegetes fail to adequately explain the problem with forcing unmarried slave women to prostitution if they 'desire chastity', given that they also view unmarried slave women as inherently unchaste – a non-existent state of chastity cannot be violated. Perhaps they take this verse to mean that married slaves cannot be forced into prostitution if they desire chastity, which would make sense according to the rules of marriage expressed in Q 4:25. However, the exegetes do not indicate that they only mean married slaves. J. Burton has already shown how exegetes and jurists miss out on the potential problems of slave women's chastity in the Quran, and he argues that they assume that enslaved women cannot be chaste not on the basis of the Quran, but on the basis of already existing juristic practice (Burton, 'The Meaning of "Ihsan"').
56. Al-Qurṭubī mentions that 'some' think this clause has been abrogated. Al-Qurṭubī, *Al-Jāmiʿ Li-Aḥkām Al-Qur'ān,* 15:252–254. The 'some' here seems to refer to the Shia, for, according to al-Qummī, Abū Jaʿfar (Imam al-Bāqir) said: 'This verse is abrogated by the phrase [from 4:25], "If they commit a sin they have half the punishment of free women."' Al-Qummī, *Tafsīr Al-Qummī,* 2:102. Al-Māturīdī interprets this verse as a prohibition of *mutʿa* marriage, *Tafsīr Al-Qur'ān Al-ʿAẓīm, Al-Musammá, Ta'wīlāt Ahl Al-Sunna*, 3:462.

57. For example, al-Ṭabarī treats each verse separately; al-Zamakhsharī treats 33:4–5 as a unit, and 33:6 separately; al-Ṭūsī treats 33:1–5 and then 33:6–10 as units; Fakhr al-Dīn al-Rāzī treats 33:1–4 as a unit, and then each of verses 5 and 6 separately.
58. See, for example, al-Ṭabarī, al-Zamakhsharī and Fakhr al-Dīn. A few exegetes, such as al-Māturīdī and al-Ṭūsī preserve the relationship of Q 24:33 to the surrounding verses, noting that they pertain to questions of marriage and slavery.
59. I will speak more in Chapter 4 about the way the exegeses of Q 24:33 can be read selectively to reconstruct first-/seventh-century history.
60. Al-Zamakhsharī, *al-Kashshāf*, 3:507–8.
61. After reading dozens of pre-modern and modern *tafsīrs*, I was surprised to find only a single exegete who explicates the community-building implications of the term *mawālī* in Q 33:5: the extremist ideologue Sayyid Qutb (d. 1966 CE). He explains of Q 33:5: 'Islam still provides a place for people of unknown paternity in Islamic society, based on brotherhood in religion and friendship. This is a cultural, emotional connection with no concomitant legal commitments . . . Rather, it is so that these people of unknown paternity will not be left without a connection to society.' Sayyid Qutb, *Fī Ẓilāl al-Qur'ān,* 5: 2,826. Unlike the medieval exegetes who appear to have taken the ascendancy of Islam for granted, Qutb apparently thinks that 'true' Muslims are a minority (even in ostensibly Muslim societies). Writing in a time of uncertainty, Qutb finds it important to demonstrate that outsiders can join Islam and find stability and community there. While Sayyid Qutb and I are diametrically opposed thinkers in many ways, we are clearly both denisens of a modern, globalised world concerned with questions of identity and belonging.
62. For more on the *qiyān*, see Chapter 6 of this monograph.
63. As Matthew Gordon says, there was 'evidence of a likely sex industry in . . . Abbasid society, into which, the assumption must be, a good number of enslaved women were forced' (Gordon, 'Introduction', 4).
64. Modern exegetes acknowledge a middle ground between the two extremes of women who 'want' to be prostitutes and women who are unequivocally 'forced' to be prostitutes. For instance, the nineteenth-century al-Shawkānī says: 'the slave woman might not want either right or wrong [*ḥalāl aw ḥarām*], or might not desire to get married; and minors might be described as "compelled" to fornication even if they do not desire chastity' (Al-Shawkānī, *Fatḥ Al-Qadīr*, 16:1,267–1,268). Likewise, the twentieth-century al-Shaʿrāwī says: 'Among these slave women were girls who had good, noble natures, but fate befell them

and they became captives during or after war, at a time when it was easy to be chaste when one was free and no one would expose them to harm.' Al-Shaʿrāwī, *Tafsīr Al-Shaʿrāwī*, 4:32–33.

65. Al-Zamakhsharī, *Al-Kashshāf*, 3:233–234.
66. Al-Bayḍāwī, *Tafsīr Qāḍī Bayḍāwī*, 2:141. Accessed on 28 July 2017 at Hathi Trust. https://babel.hathitrust.org/cgi/pt?id=mdp.39015053589746;view=1up;seq=149
67. Al-Zamakhsharī, *Al-Kashshāf*, 3:233.
68. On the haggadic (storytelling) and halakhic (legalistic) aspects of exegesis, see Wansbrough, *Quranic Studies*, 122–147, and 170–201.

3

Abū Bakra, Freedman of God

Building upon the foundation of the ambiguous term *mawālī* in the Quran, this chapter investigates an early Muslim freedman named Abū Bakra (d. 52/672) who appears in a few exegeses of Q 33:5, saying, 'I am one of those whose fathers is not known, so I am your brother in religion and your *mawlā*.' Abū Bakra is a relatively obscure figure who should not be confused with the famous second caliph, Abū Bakr; Abū Bakra is a bit player, a lowly curmudgeon on the sidelines of Islamic history. Yet, he is important as a window onto early Islamic history precisely because of his liminality. He provides a case study for how early Muslims navigated the tension between egalitarianism and social hierarchy inherent in the new *umma*, and he also allows us to see how later authors tried to make sense of his identity. I argue that during his lifetime in the first/seventh century, he was identified as a brother in religion, as a *mawlā* in its inclusive Quranic sense (without the overtones of later clientage), and as a 'freedman of God' (*ṭalīq allāh*). This latter anomalous phrase seems to indicate a radically inclusive, faith-based community that was not concerned with legal ownership, but instead focused on the mutual cooperation and support of all members. However, by the second/eighth and third/ninth centuries, these inclusive designations had become confusing or even meaningless to the authors of Islamic history, so they sought to place Abū Bakra into more familiar social categories. These sources alternatively describe him as an Arab and a *mawlā*, a moral authority and an unrepentant sinner, a powerless individual and a member of a powerful family. It is clear that none of these descriptions is simple or objective, but that different authors used Abū Bakra to represent their different worldviews. Thus, Abū Bakra's story helps us discern that seemingly straightforward identifiers such as *mawlā* and Arab are deeply intertwined in the wider narratives that authors hoped to tell about the trajectory of early Islamic history.

While the details of Abū Bakra's biography vary from source to source and will receive fuller analysis below, a brief overview will provide a sense of orientation.[1] His given name is Nufayʿ. He was born sometime in the early seventh century CE in the city of Taif, just east of Mecca. His mother was a slave-prostitute named Sumayya, who was also the mother of Nufayʿ's several half-brothers (including the infamous Umayyad governor, Ziyād ibn Abīhi).[2] The identity of Nufayʿ's father is uncertain. It could have been Sumayya's master, al-Ḥārith ibn Kalada, a well-to-do physician of the Arabian tribe of Thaqīf, or it could have been Masrūḥ, another one of al-Ḥārith's slaves. When Sumayya was pregnant, al-Ḥārith seems to have been fully prepared to accept her child as his own, as he had done for Nufayʿ's older brother Nāfiʿ. But when little Nufayʿ emerged with dark skin, al-Ḥārith declared that the father must have been the Abyssinian Masrūḥ, and Nufayʿ was raised as a slave.[3]

The sources next mention Nufayʿ in the year 8/630, when Muḥammad and his army of Muslims took control of Mecca and besieged nearby Taif. During the siege of Taif, the Muslims announced that any slave who fled his master and joined the cause of Islam would be freed. When they heard this promise, Nufayʿ and a handful of other slaves escaped to the Muslim camp. Nufayʿ reportedly rappelled down from Taif's high citadel wall on a rope and pulley, which is how he earned his moniker Abū Bakra, or 'father of the pulley'. Abū Bakra was manumitted and became the *mawlā* of the Prophet Muḥammad (according to some sources). While this particular siege of Taif proved abortive, the Muslims soon thereafter subdued the town and its main tribal contingent of Thaqīf. The town's leading tribesmen converted to Islam and asked to have their former slaves back, but Muḥammad denied their request – those slaves had been permanently freed by their prior acceptance of Islam.

The sources preserve little information about the relationship between Abū Bakra and the Prophet Muḥammad. The only clues about this relationship come from the hadiths that Abū Bakra transmitted, some of which depict him learning proper forms of religious observance directly from Muḥammad.[4] Instead, most historical sources skip ahead to Abū Bakra's career in the newly founded garrison town of Basra, Iraq, where he moved with his uterine brothers during the caliphate of ʿUmar ibn al-Khaṭṭāb (r. 13–23/634–644). Here transpired two events that would occupy the attention of later scholars, up to the present day. First, he became embroiled in a legal dispute that strained his relationship with his half-brother Ziyād (d. 53/673). In this dispute, which will be analysed in more detail below, Ziyād caused Abū Bakra to be found guilty of slander, or falsely accusing someone of adultery (*qadhf*). Second, Abū Bakra refused to take part in the Battle of the Camel, one of the battles of the First Civil War that took place near Basra. He excused himself from aiding one of the leaders of this battle – the Prophet's widow ʿĀ'isha, who encouraged the troops from atop her armour-clad camel – by quoting the hadith: 'Those who entrust their affairs to a woman will never know prosperity.'[5] While Abū Bakra unfortunately demurred in gender-specific terms that have had a lasting impact on gender ideologies in the Islamic world, it was not only ʿĀ'isha whom he refused to help in this conflict. He repeatedly expressed a politically detached attitude and a desire for reconciliation between the warring factions.[6] As a vocal advocate for political neutrality, he never held any political office in the Umayyad government.[7] After living a fruitful life, fathering many children, and amassing a great estate in Basra, Abū Bakra died in the year 52/672.

Transforming Arabian Society: Abū Bakra as 'Freedman of God'

A basic methodological approach to the early Islamic historical sources is to search for traces that do not fit neatly into the main historical narrative and therefore are not likely ideological back-projections. Far from destroying scholars' confidence in the historical narratives, such an against-the-grain reading confirms that our sources have not been altered beyond all recognition. Reading between the lines of the historical sources in this way, the sources provide circumstantial evidence that Abū Bakra was not a *mawlā* of the Prophet Muḥammad, or even a *mawlā* at all. For instance, several other slaves reportedly escaped from Taif and joined the Muslims along with Abū Bakra, yet none of these other slaves has been remembered as a *mawlā* of the Prophet.[8] Additionally, the historical narratives generally associate Abū Bakra more closely with his old master's tribe of Thaqīf than with Muḥammad's tribe of Quraysh – one report even says Abū Bakra was a *mawlā* of his master, al-Ḥārith ibn Kalada.[9] However, the most intriguing anomaly is that the phrase used to describe Abū Bakra's post-manumission status in several accounts is not *mawlā*, but *ṭalīq allāh* ('freedman of God').

According to two accounts presented in the *Al-Ṭabaqāt al-Kubrā* (Greatest Generations) of Ibn Saʿd (d. 230/845), after the city of Taif had surrendered and its leading tribe of Thaqīf had converted collectively to Islam, a delegation of Thaqīf tribesmen asked Muḥammad to return their former slave Abū Bakra to them. Muḥammad rebuffed the Thaqafis by saying, 'No, he is the one set loose by God and his apostle' (*ṭalīq allāh wa-ṭalīq rasūlihi*).[10] Al-Wāqidī (d. 207/823) and Ibn Hishām (d. 218/833) preserve similar accounts in which the Thaqafīs request all their slaves back, and the answer is: 'No, they are the ones freed by God' (*hum ʿutaqāʾ allāh*).[11] I take this unusual phrase, *ṭalīq* (or *ʿatīq*) *allāh*, to be Abū Bakra's original designation in the community of believers. The sources never explicitly describe what it meant to be a *ṭalīq allāh*, but they provide a few scant clues. Based on circumstantial evidence derived from a variety of sources, the *ṭalīq allāh* seems to be completely free from bondage, including the usual bonds of dependency inherent in *mawlā* status. The freedom of the *ṭalīq allāh* was justly ordained by God, and any attempts to re-enslave or reduce the *ṭalīq allāh* to a subordinate status were therefore unjust. The *ṭalīq allāh* fully belonged to the Muslim community and received care and support from the entire community, rather than from an individual kinsman or patron. As such, the term is a marker of the radical inclusiveness of the earliest Islamic community, bound together first and foremost by their monotheistic belief and their devotion to the Prophet Muḥammad.

The first clue for reconstructing the meaning of *ṭalīq allāh* comes from the many Arabic-Islamic historical sources that use the plural term *ṭulaqāʾ* to refer to the late, reluctant converts of the Quraysh tribe, who finally capitulated during the Muslim conquest of Mecca in 8/630. These conquered Qurashīs should legally have been the war captives of the Prophet, but he chose to release rather than to enslave them. On the one hand, Abū Bakra's case seems to be quite different from that of the Qurashi *ṭulaqāʾ*. Abū Bakra's designation as a *ṭalīq* is overwhelmingly positive, for it connotes his brave decision to adopt Islam before the rest of Taif, his freedom from bondage and possibly even his spiritual superiority over the freeborn members of Thaqīf.

On the other hand, both uses of the term *ṭalīq* share one salient feature: they both imply unconditional freedom, without any subordinate bonds of clientage. (Certainly, no source ever argues that the Qurashī *ṭulaqāʾ* became Muḥammad's *mawālī*.) Accordingly, I suggest that Abū Bakra's original designation as a *ṭalīq allāh* meant that he became no one's legal client or *mawlā*.

A few more glimmers of evidence come from two early Arabic poems. While these poems do not address Abū Bakra's case directly, they provide examples of how the phrase *ṭalīq allāh* was used and understood. The first poem was composed by a man named Imām ibn Aqram al-Numayrī, who was arrested by the notorious Umayyad governor al-Ḥajjāj ibn Yūsuf (d. 95/714). Imām managed to escape from prison using his own cunning, at which point he extemporised a poem declaring himself 'freedman of God' and ridiculing the ugly faces of the police who had incarcerated him:

> The freedman of God was shown no favours
> By Abū Dāwūd or Ibn Abī Kathīr
> Or Ḥajjāj, with eyes like a stork
> Who turns up her gaze, fearing vultures.[12]

Imam uses *ṭalīq allāh* to refer to his escape from jail rather than slavery, but it nevertheless expresses that his incarceration was unjust and that his escape was ordained by God. The second poem continues this theme of justice. It is a simple teaching tool used to explain the word *bahz* (a violent strike or blow) in early grammatical textbooks:

> I am the freedman of God, Ibn Hurmuz.
> He rescued me from a ruthless master,
> Vehement against the people, felling, striking.[13]

Here, the speaker appears to be a slave of Persian descent (Ibn Hurmuz), and to have escaped from an abusive master by the grace of God. The overarching message of both poems is that it is wrong to mistreat one's fellow Muslims, whether through political oppression or brutal violence. All Muslims deserve to be treated with dignity, and God will come to the rescue of those who are mistreated. This implication holds true for Abū Bakra as well, for his legal freedom was inextricable from his belief, and his former master's request to re-enslave him was unjust.

A third poem raises new conceptual issues about the *ṭalīq allāh*. In a panegyric poem in praise of the Abbasid caliph al-Mahdī (reigned 158–169/775–785), the court poet Marwān ibn Abī Ḥafṣa asks: 'The freedman of God, who is his manumitter? / The one killed by God, who is his killer?'[14] The answer to these rhetorical questions (in addition to the most obvious answer of 'God') is caliph al-Mahdī himself, as the lynchpin of the Islamic polity and upholder of God's statutes. While its phrasing here is poetic and underscores the ideological importance of the caliph, this question is also important from a social-historical standpoint: if God is the ultimate manumitter of the *ṭalīq allāh*, what human being bears the responsibility for his manumission and subsequent care? It is by no means conclusive, but some evidence exists that 'the freedman of God' became the joint responsibility of the entire Islamic community, rather than becoming the *mawlā* of any individual patron.

Al-Wāqidī, the only author who lists each of the freed slaves of Taif by name, says:

> The Messenger of God manumitted all of these [slaves], and gave each one of them to a Muslim to provide for him and look after him. Abū Bakra went to ʿAmr ibn Saʿīd ibn al-ʿĀṣ; al-Azraq went to Khālid ibn Saʿīd; Wardān went to Abān ibn Saʿīd; Yuḥannas al-Nabbāl went to ʿUthmān ibn ʿAffān; Yasār ibn Mālik went to Saʿd ibn ʿUbāda; and Ibrāhīm ibn Jābir went to Usayd ibn Ḥudayr. The messenger of God ordered them to read them the Quran and teach them the proper ways (*sunan*).[15]

From this account, it seems that Muḥammad divided up the responsibility for these patronless freedmen among individual members of the Islamic community as he saw fit. This responsibility had both a social aspect ('to provide for him and look after him') and a religious aspect ('to read them the Quran and teach them the *sunan*'.) It was not a tribal arrangement, as the patrons listed here are from the various tribes of Quraysh, Aws and Khazraj. Likewise, it does not seem to have been a permanent legal arrangement, for there is no mention of any *walā'* bonds forged between the freedmen and their new mentors, and no account indicates that Abū Bakra became the *mawlā* of ʿAmr ibn Saʿīd ibn al-ʿĀṣ. Rather, it seems to have been a temporary arrangement for the integration of these freedmen into the community, perhaps similar to the temporary 'brotherhood' (*mu'ākha*) arrangement that Muḥammad set up between the Meccan Emigrants and Medinan Helpers.

If al-Wāqidī's account is true, the 'freedman of God' seems akin to another category from early Islamic history: the *sā'iba*, or slave set completely free without becoming anyone's *mawlā*. (The term *sā'iba* literally refers to a camel left to wander alone in the desert without a caretaker, indicating that the absolute freedom of the *sā'iba* does not have the positive connotations that modern audiences might assume.) Early Muslim jurists debated the legality of manumitting someone as a *sā'iba*, until they ultimately disallowed the practice.[16] While the terms *ṭalīq allāh* and *sā'iba* are never explicitly connected in the sources and do not seem to be identical, both terms seem to connote manumission without subsequent *mawlā* status. Moreover, the one major scholar who did accept *sā'iba* manumission, the Medinan scholar Mālik ibn Anas, also gave legal responsibility for the *sā'iba* and other patronless freedmen to the community of Muslims at large.[17] Both terms seem to have worked best in the relatively small, homogenous environment of western Arabia, which could apparently accommodate a small number of foreigners, freedmen and other rootless people without relying on the specific institution of clientage.

Finally, a close examination of the accounts in Ibn Sa'd's *Ṭabaqāt* helps clarify the semantic difference between being a *ṭalīq allāh* and being a *mawlā* of the Prophet. Ibn Sa'd provides three alternative accounts of how the newly converted Thaqīf tribesmen asked to have Abū Bakra back and were rebuffed. In two of the accounts, the Thaqīf ask for Abū Bakra to be returned to them, presumably to be re-enslaved; in both of these accounts, the Prophet Muḥammad denies their request by declaring Abū Bakra to be a *ṭalīq allāh*. In the third account, however, the Thaqīf tribesmen instead ask to 'adopt' (*idda'ā*) Abū Bakra into their tribe.[18] Abū Bakra himself responds to the insolent request by saying, 'I am Masrūḥ (*sic*), the *mawlā* of the Messenger of God.' Thus, while *ṭalīq allāh* appears to entail freedom from slavery, *mawlā* here appears to entail genealogy and adoption. Additionally, the term used for 'adopt' in the above account is the same one used by Abū Bakra's infamous half-brother, Ziyād ibn Abīhi, when he 'adopts' a falsified Arabian lineage. As will become clear later in the chapter, Abū Bakra's refusal to adopt a fake Arabian lineage – in contrast to Ziyād – is a key element of his *mawlā* persona.

By tracing the oral transmissions of these three variations in Ibn Saʿd, it appears that the two *ṭalīq allāh* accounts are transmitted almost entirely by scholars from Kufa,[19] while the single *mawlā* account is transmitted exclusively by Basrans.[20] The death date of the earliest Basran transmitter, Khālid ibn Sumayr, is unknown, but it can be estimated to approximately 120/738. The identification of Abū Bakra as a *mawlā,* as well as the contrast between *mawlā* status and the adoption of a fake Arabian lineage, thus seems to have emerged in late-Umayyad Basra – a provenance that will be corroborated below in the hadith literature. On the one hand, it is perfectly understandable that Basran transmitters should celebrate Abū Bakra, for Abū Bakra lived there and was something of a hometown hero. Less expected is the fact that his identity has been changed from *ṭalīq allāh* to *mawlā* in the Basran tradition, or that his *mawlā*ness takes on specific connotations not just about manumission and conversion, but also about the proper use of genealogy.

The reasons for this development are speculative. The Arabian tribal migrations to Basra and Kufa followed different patterns, and Basra's original foundation was also much smaller than that of Kufa, which may have affected the meaning of the term *mawlā*. Moreover, the towns displayed divergent intellectual and sectarian trends: Kufa was a hotbed of pro-ʿAlī sentiment, whereas Basra was more known for its Kharijite and proto-Sufi tendencies.[21] Basra's particular association with early *mawlā*-ascetics, such as al-Ḥasan al-Baṣrī and Rābiʾa al-Baṣriyya, may have elevated *mawlā* identity into an emblem of spiritual pride. Perhaps it was even in Basra that *mawlā* came increasingly to mean 'non-Arab' and to be specifically contrasted with 'Arab'.[22] Whatever the case, Ibn Saʿd's alternative accounts highlight the crucial point that the meaning of the term *mawlā* is neither universal nor obvious, but rather reflects local traditions and specific contexts.

Based on this smattering of evidence, I suggest that the label 'freedman of God' reflects a time when Abū Bakra's primary identity was a believer whose freedom was ordained by God, rather than someone's *mawlā* with all the legal rights and responsibilities of classical Islamic clientage.[23] This finding seems to correspond with Crone's argument in *Roman, Provincial and Islamic Law*, that pre-Islamic Arabian ways of incorporating outsiders did not resemble classical Islamic *walāʾ*.[24] However, it seems that the term *ṭalīq allāh* disappeared as a salient designation relatively early in Islamic history.

It was probably lost because *ṭalīq* took on specific pejorative connotations about the late Meccan converts, and because the legal practice of clientage came to replace the more informal process of freeing slaves and caring for them communally. The far-flung garrison cities of Kufa, Basra, Fustat, Marw and Qayrawan were very different places from the Arabian towns of Mecca, Medina and Taif. As the Islamic empire expanded and became more diverse, its leaders developed more systematic ways of bringing freedmen into the fold.[25]

The *Mawlā* and the Arab: The Symbolism of a Brothers' Feud

Thanks to the scrupulous early scholars who preserved the anomalous phrase *ṭalīq allāh*, historians today are poised to interrogate Abū Bakra's more usual designations as a '*mawlā* of the Prophet' or an 'Arab of the Thaqīf tribe'. If Abū Bakra was known neither as the Prophet's *mawlā* nor as an Arab in his own day, later authors must have categorised him in these ways for a reason.[26] Close textual analysis shows that these categorisations involve more than simple legal definitions; they reflect deeper, more normative political and moral symbols that vary according to genre. Particularly, several biographers present Abū Bakra as a humble everyman, and '*mawlā*' is a quintessential marker of this pious identity. In these accounts, his *mawlā* status sets him apart from his powerful but wicked half-brother, Ziyād ibn Abīhi, who faked an Arabian lineage and ruined Abū Bakra's reputation by causing him unjustly to be convicted of slander. On the other hand, most hadith scholars identify Abū Bakra as an Arabian tribesman, and they view his slander conviction as a clear-cut legal verdict. They lose the communitarian meaning of Abū Bakra's *mawlā* identity, as well as the symbolic undertones of the slander affair.

Abū Bakra as 'Nufayʿ ibn Masrūḥ the Abyssinian, Mawlā of the Prophet'

Ziyād, Nāfiʿ, and Abū Bakra
Are very amusing to me.
Three men created in one woman's womb,
Yet with different genealogy:
One a Qurashi, or so he says; one a *mawlā*;
And one who claims an Arab to be.[27]

With this poem, the belles-lettrist and historian al-Masʿūdī (d. 345/956) reveals that Abū Bakra's social identity – as well as those of his half-brothers Ziyād and Nāfiʿ – was a source of interest in the narrative historical tradition. Several authors highlight the contrast between Abū Bakra's *mawlā* status and Ziyād's claim to belong to the Quraysh tribe. They pepper their accounts of Abū Bakra with accounts about Ziyād, treating the two half-brothers as inextricably linked and often diametrically opposed. Abū Bakra's *mawlā*-ness thus becomes a subtle marker of political ideology, used to contrast 'heroes' like Abū Bakra from 'villains' like Ziyād. I suggest that Abū Bakra's *mawlā* identity always alludes to the conflict between him and Ziyād, and more broadly to debates about morality and politics.

Like Abū Bakra, Ziyād was born to the enslaved prostitute Sumayya and raised as a slave in the household of al-Ḥārith ibn Kalada in Taif. Ziyād's actual father was likely a Byzantine slave named ʿUbayd, who belonged to al-Ḥārith and was married to Sumayya. However, in 44/664 the new Umayyad caliph Muʿāwiya suggested that his own father, Abū Sufyān – arguably the most powerful Arabian tribal chief of his day – had visited Sumayya's tent during one of his visits to Taif, and that the result of this visit was Ziyād.[28] It seems likely that neither Muʿāwiya nor Ziyād actually believed this tale. Rather, it was an olive branch extended from Muʿāwiya to Ziyād, meant to solidify their partnership. Ziyād had previously worked for Muʿāwiya's fallen arch-nemesis, ʿAlī ibn Abī Ṭālib. When ʿAlī was murdered, Ziyād withdrew to his Iranian citadel and refused to approach the new caliph in Damascus, likely fearing that Muʿāwiya would punish ʿAlī's former supporters. Indeed, Muʿāwiya initially tried to lure Ziyād out of his citadel by holding his children hostage (Abū Bakra negotiated their release). However, Muʿāwiya was known for his calm-headed political savvy, and he eventually declared Ziyād his half-brother to signal that he wanted to work with Ziyād rather than harm him. Overnight, Ziyād dropped his *mawlā* status and became an Arabian tribesman, member of the leading tribe of Quraysh and half-brother of the caliph. Because of his 'adoption', Ziyād is widely known by the derogatory name Ziyād ibn Abīhi, which means 'Ziyād, the son of his father (whoever *he* is)'.

Against this model of political manoeuvring and impious ambition, Abū Bakra reportedly revelled in his identity as *mawlā* of the Prophet, insisted that his children call him 'the son of Masrūḥ [the Abyssinian slave]' and flatly refused any attempt to claim him as an Arabian tribesman. He preferred to associate himself with the Prophet Muḥammad as his *mawlā* – even if *mawlā* status was disdained in the eyes of the Umayyad aristocracy – than to associate himself with secular power. He chose spiritual prestige over secular prestige in an age when people were scrambling to define the values of Islamic society and the structure of the Islamic state. Abū Bakra's self-designation as the *mawlā* of Muḥammad thus emerges as a marker of honesty and humility, as opposed to the crass opportunism of his brother.

Al-Balādhurī is the author who most explicitly draws out the ideological ramifications of Abū Bakra's *mawlā* status. In his *Ansāb al-Ashrāf*, he reports that the Prophet Muḥammad himself manumitted Nufayʿ after the siege of Taif, nicknamed him Abū Bakra and took him as his *mawlā*. As would be expected of the Prophet's humble *mawlā*, Abū Bakra emerges strongly as a foil to Ziyād ibn Abīhi throughout this account. For instance, al-Balādhurī transmits one vivid story in which two famous Basran figures – Anas ibn Mālik and al-Ḥasan al-Baṣrī – visit the elderly Abū Bakra at home when he is suffering from a bad case of haemorrhoids. During their conversation, Anas wonders whether Abū Bakra is angry with Ziyād for a matter concerning this world or the next world. Anas insists that Abū Bakra should not be angry with Ziyād for anything concerning this world, for Ziyād has bestowed high positions and wealth upon Abū Bakra's children. To this, Abū Bakra responds: 'What has he done for them, other than to ensure that they will enter Hell?'[29] Anas then insists that Abū Bakra should not be angry with Ziyād for anything concerning the next world, for Ziyād 'always strives to do what is right' (*innahu la-mujtahid*).[30] To this, Abū Bakra responds: 'The Kharijites of Harura claim that they strive to do what is right.'[31] With one flip comeback, Abū Bakra has reduced his half-brother to the same level as a band of dangerous Kharijite fanatics.[32]

While al-Balādhurī provides the most colourful anecdotes, the corpus in which Abū Bakra most clearly emerges as an ideological weapon against Ziyād is the hadith literature. Hadiths are accounts of the sayings and deeds of the Prophet Muḥammad, transmitted orally by the first generation of Muslims (the Companions of Muḥammad), and then by the second generation of Muslims (the Successors), and then by the third generation (Successors of the

Successors) and so on until they were finally written down in the hadith collections compiled in the third/ninth and fourth/tenth centuries. By analysing these chains of oral transmission, along with the accompanying variations of the hadith's text, scholars can get a better picture of the provenance of a particular hadith. At least, scholars can discover which transmitter likely introduced certain textual changes. The hadith that sheds light on Abū Bakra reads in its most basic form: 'Whoever claims a false father, knowing that he is not his father, will have Heaven forbidden to him.'[33] Of the twenty variants of this hadith, many present Abū Bakra as one of the Companion transmitters, and a few make it clear that his association with this hadith is meant to condemn Ziyād for 'adopting a false father'.

The hadith gains its initial sense of context through its Companion transmitter, the person who heard it directly from the Prophet. Almost all versions (nineteen out of twenty) are transmitted by the notable Companion and military hero Saʿd ibn Abī Waqqāṣ. Saʿd had asked for the Prophet's ruling in a paternity dispute involving his own brother, ʿUtba ibn Abī Waqqāṣ; the primary context of the hadith thus seems to have concerned this case of contested paternity.[34] While most versions of the hadith also contain Abū Bakra as a second Companion transmitter, it exists in two versions with Saʿd alone.[35] One of these 'Saʿd only' accounts is transmitted exclusively by scholars from Kufa, while all the versions that also include Abū Bakra come from the rival town of Basra. This shred of evidence is by no means conclusive, but it indicates that the ideological importance of Abū Bakra's *mawlā* status may have emerged in Basra, as was also indicated in Ibn Saʿd's *Ṭabaqāt*.

Although it is impossible to prove that the Kufan 'Saʿd only' account is the original version of the hadith, it at least hints that this hadith might not originally have been associated with Abū Bakra – scholars should be curious about Abū Bakra's appearance in most other versions. His incorporation into the hadith begins subtly. In two versions, Saʿd ibn Abī Waqqāṣ reports the hadith as usual, and Abū Bakra chimes in at the end: 'My two ears and my heart also heard [that] from Muḥammad.'[36] In twelve versions, Saʿd and Abū Bakra, 'both of them', are presented as the joint Companion transmitters, sometimes with extra information describing Saʿd (he was the first to shoot an arrow in Islam) and Abū Bakra (he climbed down from the citadel at Taif).[37] In all these cases, the text of the actual hadith remains essentially the same. It is only the Companion transmitter that changes, with the incorporation of Abū Bakra as the other Companion transmitter alongside Sa'd. Never is Ziyād ibn Abihi mentioned by name, although his contrast with Abū Bakra is quietly implied if one is already familiar with the brothers' biographies.

Almost all the hadiths that include Abū Bakra have a second-generation transmitter named Abū 'Uthmān al-Nahdī (d. *c.* 94/714).[38] Abū 'Uthmān was a friend of Abū Bakra's in Basra, and he reportedly transmitted the following account: 'Abū Bakra, the *mawlā* of the Messenger of God, said: "If the people insist on giving me a fatherly attribution, then let them call me Nufay' ibn Masrūḥ [the Abyssinian slave]."'[39] This saying of Abū 'Uthmān's indicates that the subtext of the above hadith is indeed Abū Bakra's *mawlā* status, which serves as an understated condemnation of Ziyād and also bolsters Abū Bakra's authority as a transmitter of the hadith by emphasising his closeness with the Prophet. Abū 'Uthmān himself may have been responsible for championing Abū Bakra's *mawlā* identity, or it may have been the third-generation transmitter of these hadiths, the Basran scholar 'Āṣim al-Aḥwal (d. *c.* 758).[40] In any case, taking 'Āṣim's death date of 141/758 as a guide, it seems that the presence of Abū Bakra in this hadith probably emerged sometime in mid-to-late Umayyad Basra.

While the previous hadith variations are subtle and their polemical overtones are veiled, several versions of the hadith make the connection with Ziyād more explicit. Three hadiths read:

> When Ziyād acknowledged [Abū Sufyān as his father], [Abū 'Uthmān al-Nahdī] met Abū Bakra and said: 'What is this that you have done? For I heard Sa'd ibn Abī Waqqāṣ saying: "My ear heard from the Messenger of God: whoever claims a father in Islam that is not his father, knowing that he is not his father, the Garden will be forbidden to him."' Abū Bakra said, 'I heard [that] from the Messenger of God.'[41]

The obvious new element in this version is the setup story of Ziyād's 'adoption', the purported reason for Abū Bakra's connection with this hadith. As for the chains of transmission, they all have the familiar second-generation transmitter, Abū 'Uthmān al-Nahdī, but a new third-generation transmitter, the Basran scholar Khālid al-Hadhdhā' (d. *c.* 142/759).[42] It thus seems to have been Khālid who was particularly interested in using Abū Bakra to condemn Ziyād, although it is difficult to pinpoint his motivation for doing so. Khālid was a student of al-Ḥasan al-Baṣrī, another early Basran *mawlā* and ascetic who is occasionally associated with Abū Bakra.[43] Moreover, H. P. Raddatz calls Khālid an early Mu'tazili,[44] and Abū Bakra does exhibit the political neutrality characteristic of the earliest Mu'tazila.[45] Perhaps it was an early ascetic, proto-Mu'tazili current within Basra that co-opted Abū Bakra for its own ideological needs.

A final version of the hadith can be easily dismissed as inauthentic,[46] but it illustrates Abū Bakra's ideological potential. It has a highly suspicious chain of transmitters[47] – although once again all Basran – and its text has been made into a transparent vehicle for polemic:

> Ziyād said to Abū Bakra: 'Don't you see that the Commander of Believers [Mu'āwiya] wants me for this and that [i.e. to adopt me]? I was born on the bed of 'Ubayd [the Byzantine slave] and so I attribute my paternity to him, for I know that the Messenger of God said: "Whoever claims a false father, let him occupy his seat in Hell."' Then the following year came, and he falsely adopted him.[48]

Not only are Ziyād and Abū Bakra shown having a face-to-face conversation that is presented in no other source, but Ziyād also incriminates himself by claiming to have heard the Prophetic hadith with his own ears. There is no mention of Sa'd ibn Abī Waqqāṣ at all. The entire context of the hadith has changed from Sa'd's paternity question into a condemnation of Ziyād and the Umayyad manipulation of genealogy. The silent presence of Abū Bakra, the pious *mawlā* of the Prophet, highlights Ziyād's hypocrisy and immorality.

Abū Bakra as the Arabian Tribesman, 'Nufay' ibn al-Ḥārith, of Thaqīf'

Whereas most early Islamic authors view Abū Bakra as a *mawlā*, those scholars who specialised in the collection and study of hadith categorise Abū Bakra differently.[49] Hadith compilers such as Ibn Abī Shayba (d. 234/848), Khalīfa ibn Khayyāṭ (d. 239/853), Aḥmad ibn Ḥanbal (d. 240/854), al-Bukhārī (d. 255/869) and Muslim (d. 260/874) consider Abū Bakra the son of his master al-Ḥārith ibn Kalada and therefore a member of the Arabian tribe of Thaqīf.[50] They never explain their reasoning in the biographical dictionaries they wrote to supplement their hadith compilations; their presentation of Abū Bakra is characteristically terse and aims only to identify him as a hadith transmitter. Reading between the lines, however, it seems that they back projected a particular hadith on to Abū Bakra, a hadith about paternity that was later systematised into law. This hadith, known as 'the child belongs to the master of the bed' dictum, states that in a case of disputed paternity, a child is automatically attributed to his mother's legal husband or master.

This maxim is most famously associated with ʿUtba ibn Abī Waqqāṣ – the brother of Saʿd ibn Abī Waqqāṣ introduced above. ʿUtba claimed to have fathered a son by an enslaved woman who did not belong to him, but belonged to a now-deceased man named Zamʿa (father of the Prophet's wife Sawda). The Prophet decided the boy's legal paternity in favour of Zamʿa rather than ʿUtba, even though the child resembled ʿUtba. This decision meant that the child could legally inherit from his late father Zamʿa, rather than becoming ʿUtba's heir.[51] The Prophet's reason for deciding the case in favour of Zamʿa was that 'the child belongs to the master of the bed', rather than whoever claims to be the child's father or even whoever most closely resembles the child. Zamʿa was the enslaved woman's legal owner, and thus he was her child's legal father. In an age before paternity testing, this dictum provided a way to determine a child's parentage and to confirm the child's legal rights. The 'child belongs' dictum seems to have been most commonly applied to the offspring of female slaves – such as Sumayya, mother of Abū Bakra and Ziyād – who were assumed to have many sexual partners.[52]

Uri Rubin has shown how this hadith also became associated with Ziyād ibn Abīhi and was used to condemn Ziyād's 'adoption' of Abū Sufyān.[53] According to this hadith, Ziyād should rightly be considered the son of ʿUbayd the Byzantine slave, who was the legal husband of Sumayya at the time of his birth. Given the close association between Abū Bakra and Ziyād, it thus seems probable that the hadith transmitters also applied this hadith to Abū Bakra. Because he was born 'on the bed of' his mother's master al-Ḥārith ibn Kalada (Sumayya appears to have been unmarried at the time of Abū Bakra's conception and birth), Abū Bakra should be reckoned 'Nufayʿ

ibn al-Ḥārith of Thaqīf'. The application of this hadith inverts the usual view of Abū Bakra as a *mawlā* and Ziyād as an 'Arab', although it still presents the two brothers as polar opposites.

Together, the two hadiths, 'Whoever claims a false father . . .' and 'The child belongs . . .' create a one–two punch against the practice of *diʿwa*, or claiming paternity without legal basis.[54] However, the difference between the two maxims is an important one: the 'whoever claims a false father' hadith merely condemns the practice of false adoption, while the 'child belongs' hadith provides a positive standard for determining identity. Many of the historical narratives about Abū Bakra focus on the first idea, the fact that Abū Bakra refused to claim a false father and instead revelled in his identity as a *mawlā* of the Prophet. The historians highlight Abū Bakra's integrity and personal agency, his choice to be socially lowly but spiritually lofty. However, the hadith compilers seem to have focused on the second idea, the application of a standard legal identity to all Muslims. They used the 'child belongs' dictum to determine Ziyād's and Abū Bakra's (and everyone else's) true identity. Despite the historical evidence that Abū Bakra did not know his father, always demurred when asked about it and refused to call himself an Arabian tribesman, these hadith scholars believed they knew better how to identify him.[55] The 'child belongs to the master of the bed' maxim may have led hadith scholars to feel they had found a systematic, legal and thoroughly Islamic notion of identity, but it also erases the moral significance that most historians found in Abū Bakra. By viewing this significant difference in the way narrative historians and hadith compilers categorise him, Abū Bakra provides insight into the development of particular genres of Islamic writing, with their unique symbols, identity markers and value systems.

Why Does Anybody Listen to Abū Bakra?

The foregoing illustration of Abū Bakra as a foil to Ziyād helps explain Abū Bakra's lasting authority as a hadith transmitter. The Moroccan feminist scholar Fatima Mernissi and the University of California, Los Angeles (UCLA) law professor Khaled Abou El Fadl have both wondered why Muslims have accepted Abū Bakra's transmission of the misogynistic hadith, 'Those who entrust their affairs to a woman will never know prosperity.'[56] Both scholars point out that Abū Bakra was found guilty of slander (*qadhf*) and refused to repent of his crime. As an unrepentant sinner (*fāsiq*), Abū Bakra should have no reliability as a hadith transmitter. And yet, this infamous hadith has remained in circulation for centuries.

I suggest that the answer to this puzzle lies in the way early Islamic historians treat Abū Bakra's slander case.[57] I will focus on two different accounts of the episode, one from al-Ṭabarī's *Tārīkh al-Rusul wa-al-Mulūk* (History of Apostles and Kings) and the other from al-Balādhurī's *Ansāb al-Ashrāf* (Genealogies of the Notables). While these two sources treat Abū Bakra quite differently,[58] both provide insight into his lasting religious authority. Al-Ṭabarī transmits one unusual account in which Abū Bakra is not found guilty of slander at all. This account raises questions about the historical accuracy of the other accounts, and it suggests that the slander episode should be read symbolically rather than literally. On the other hand, al-Balādhurī acknowledges the slander case, but he presents it from Abū Bakra's perspective. Abū Bakra appears as a speaker of truth and selfless defender of the faith. He submits his body to physical punishment and allows his reputation to suffer, not because he is wicked, but precisely because he is humble and righteous. In either case, recognising the complexities and subtexts of the slander affair helps explain why a lowly pietist convicted of a major crime retained so much authority as a hadith transmitter.

In order to appreciate what different authors do with this slander episode, one must know its basic parameters. In 16/637, Abū Bakra witnessed the governor of Basra, al-Mughīra ibn Shuʿba, having intercourse with a woman other than his wife. In the classical Islamic legal tradition, four witnesses are needed to prove an accusation of adultery, so Abū Bakra summoned three of his half-brothers (including Ziyād) to witness the scandal for themselves. After confirming that they had seen the dirty deed, the four witnesses sped to Medina and brought their case before the caliph, ʿUmar ibn al-Khaṭṭāb. At the last minute, Ziyād withdrew his testimony against al-Mughīra. Two other witnesses then rescinded their accusations and repented, but Abū Bakra stuck to his story. If someone makes an accusation of adultery but cannot produce the four necessary witnesses, he has committed the serious crime of slander, or false accusation of adultery (*qadhf*). The Quran lays down the punishment for this offence: eighty lashes, plus a permanent rejection of that person's veracity as a legal witness. By withdrawing his testimony against al-Mughīra,

Ziyād thus caused Abū Bakra to be found guilty of a grave crime and to be punished harshly for it.

It is worth noting that one feature of the slander affair, in its usual telling, already arouses a mild but nagging suspicion about the historical veracity of the episode. There is a striking intertextual resonance between Abū Bakra and the Prophet's wife, ʿĀ'isha. ʿĀ'isha is the original impetus behind contemporary scholars' interest in Abū Bakra's authority. It was to ʿĀ'isha's face that Abū Bakra quoted the hadith, 'Those who entrust their affairs to a woman will never know prosperity', as an excuse for refusing to join her side in the First Civil War. According to the Islamic tradition, ʿĀ'isha was also accused of adultery by three people and was vindicated by the Quranic verse making four witnesses necessary – she is widely understood to be the person for whom that verse was revealed in the first place. It seems convenient that Abū Bakra now finds himself on the wrong end of an adultery accusation that falls one witness short. The slander affair could be meant as an ironic inversion of ʿĀ'isha's and Abū Bakra's positions. Perhaps some political faction, such as the Zubayrids,[59] later disseminated this slander story to discredit those who refused to join their side, as Abū Bakra refused to join ʿĀ'isha's side. While these speculations are tentative and the evidence scanty, it is simply worth noting this dubious aspect of Abū Bakra's slander story.

More notably, al-Ṭabarī's account suggests that the slander affair may not have happened in quite this way. He presents two wildly divergent versions of the slander episode, one of which follows the outline provided above, and one of which indicates that there was no actual slander in the so-called slander affair. The former version, transmitted by Sayf ibn ʿUmar (d. late second/eighth century?), is full of dramatic conversations and colourful details – it makes a great story.[60] The other and more interesting version, which does not contain any slander, is transmitted by al-Wāqidī. In this account, Abū Bakra simply witnesses al-Mughīra's adultery and reports it to ʿUmar, who then sacks al-Mughīra. There is no mention of four witnesses, Ziyād's retraction of his testimony, Abū Bakra's refusal to repent or ʿUmar's application of the Quranic punishment. The only upshot is that Umar fires the 'horny old goat' al-Mughīra.[61]

Al-Ṭabarī dismisses al-Wāqidī's account as inaccurate, but historians should thank him for nevertheless preserving it. As with the *ṭalīq allāh* accounts above, al-Wāqidī's unusual report allows scholars to interrogate the usual version of events. Even if his narrative fails to provide conclusive answers, it raises the tantalising possibility that Abū Bakra never experienced any legal trouble. Perhaps his accusation against al-Mughīra had no legal ramifications at all, but only the rather mild political ramification of al-Mughīra's dismissal from office. Perhaps this affair even unfolded at a time before the four-witness criterion and *qadhf* punishment were regularly applied. After all, Islamic law did not spring out of the Quranic text fully formed, like Athena springing out of Zeus's thigh. It went through a period of development, which may have lasted more than a century.[62] But according to the traditional Islamic narrative, the caliph ʿUmar ibn al-Khaṭṭāb was largely responsible for formulating Islamic law in its classical form. For later authors living under classical Islamic law – which includes the four-witnesses criterion and *qadhf* punishment – it would have been unthinkable for the righteous ʿUmar to have ignored the law in this case. To suggest that he never demanded four witnesses or punished Abū Bakra for failing to produce them would have seemed blasphemous. Thus, the slander element may have been fabricated to highlight ʿUmar as a righteous caliph, and to back project Islamic law as already perfectly formed and implemented by his time.

Even if the slander affair never really happened, it remains that many historical accounts mention it. It was clearly in the minds of scholars in the second/eighth and third/ninth century, which means that Abū Bakra still potentially had an authority problem. I suggest, however, that some historians use the slander affair not to highlight Abū Bakra's iniquity, but rather his righteousness. If this slander affair is viewed as part of a wider saga of Abū Bakra versus Ziyād, it appears not as a clear-cut legal case, but a metaphor about piety and politics. This interpretation comes across most strongly in al-Balādhurī's *Ansāb al-Ashrāf*. As briefly mentioned above, al-Balādhurī often presents Abū Bakra as a lowly *mawlā* of the Prophet who clashes with the opportunistic 'Arab' Ziyād. This contrast also underlies the slander affair, which al-Balādhurī presents in a way that vindicates Abū Bakra of wrongdoing. Al-Balādhurī begins his account of this episode by declaring Abū Bakra to be one of 'those who walk upon the earth in humility' (*alladhīna yamshūna ʿalā al-arḍa hawnan*, Q 24:62).[63] Al-Balādhurī only quotes half of this Quranic verse, which in its entirety reads: 'The servants of the Merciful are those who walk upon the earth in humility, and when ignorant fools accost them, they say, "Peace".' The full verse reveals that the humility expressed here is not passive, but active; it is not solely an internal attitude or self-assessment strategy,[64] but a value that entails both *comportment* (walking upon the earth) and *speech* (saying 'peace'). By beginning with this verse, al-Balādhurī signals that the bold speech and action Abū Bakra is about to exhibit fits an authoritative Quranic definition of humility.

The next exceptional moment occurs after caliph ʿUmar has found Abū Bakra guilty and has dealt him one round of lashes. When ʿUmar moves to beat the unapologetic Abū Bakra a second time, Abū Bakra yells: 'I will not repent from the truth!' (*lā atūbu min al-ḥaqq*).[65] This outburst radically challenges the usual representative of the truth in early Islamic narratives, caliph ʿUmar himself. Elsewhere, al-Balādhurī states that 'God placed the truth in the mouth of ʿUmar', and Ibn Saʿd also reports the Prophetic hadith: 'The truth after me will be with ʿUmar, no matter what.'[66] Abū Bakra now turns this familiar association on its head: it is he who stands up for the truth and is willing to sacrifice his body and his reputation for it, and it is ʿUmar who is trying to suppress the truth. ʿUmar is not completely discredited here, but he comes across as more of a 'king' than a caliph, an elite who prefers practical politics to the inconvenient religious ideals espoused by ordinary Muslims.

Immediately after Abū Bakra declares that he will not repent from the truth, ʿAlī ibn Abī Ṭālib unexpectedly steps in and asks ʿUmar to stop beating Abū Bakra. The surprising – and historically unlikely – entrance of ʿAlī further indicates that something symbolic rather than strictly factual is happening in al-Balādhurī's account. As Tayeb El-Hibri has shown, ʿUmar often symbolically represents law, order, Arab mores and political pragmatism; ʿAlī represents non-Arabs, justice for the oppressed and a politically un-savvy sense of piety.[67] Whether these images of ʿUmar and ʿAlī are historically accurate is beside the point – it is their symbolic significance that resonates with Abū Bakra's image here, as a representative of non-elite folk oppressed by the powerful. The tragedy of Abū Bakra's beating, and ʿAlī's failure to prevent it, prefigures ʿAlī's failure to keep the Islamic government together by sheer force of piety during the First Civil War. Abū Bakra emerges here as a tragic hero who teaches his audience how to resist oppression and speak for justice, even if it entails tremendous personal sacrifice. Al-Balādhurī ends the episode with the pronouncement: 'Abū Bakra was a righteous man.'

For al-Balādhurī, the slander episode reveals Abū Bakra's integrity rather than his mendacity. It is Ziyād who is the antagonist in this account. In this way, the slander affair becomes a tale about how arrogant, power-hungry elites like Ziyād can destroy the standing of humble, honest everymen like Abū Bakra. From a moral standpoint, Abū Bakra retains his moral authority, even if from a legal standpoint he is now officially a sinner. This symbolic reading of Abū Bakra helps explain how he retained his authority as a hadith transmitter, even if he was actually found guilty of slander (which he may not have been). By exploring the slander affair from these many angles, it becomes clear that Islamic law and historiography have a complex relationship, sometimes harmonious, sometimes contradictory, each always informing the other. The legal view of Abū Bakra is not the only view, or even necessarily the most accurate view. The legal and historical must be viewed together if scholars are to uncover the range of meanings imbedded in the early Islamic past.

Conclusion

By unpacking the tangled strands of Abū Bakra's identity, we find this one obscure man can clarify both the first decades of Islamic history and the development of early Islamic historical writing. As a 'freedman of God' whose care fell collectively to the Islamic community, Abū Bakra provides insight into the organic way new members were incorporated into the *umma*. He appears to have been no one's *mawlā* but instead belonged to the nascent community merely as a brother in faith whose freedom was ordained by God. His identity as a *ṭalīq allāh* thus resonates with the more egalitarian reading of the word *mawālī* in the Quran, as expored in the previous chapter. As a *ṭalīq allāh,* Abū Bakra also better equips scholars to understand the values and underlying assumptions of authors who view him instead as a *mawlā* or an Arabian tribesman from Thaqīf. His *mawlā* identity signifies the values of piety, humility and political neutrality; these values are erased when Abū Bakra is viewed as an Arab tribesman according to literalistic legal standards. Similarly, Abū Bakra's lasting authority as a hadith transmitter is incomprehensible if the slander affair is viewed as a simple legal case. It is only by viewing Abū Bakra's legal case along with his *mawlā* morality tale that the complex relationship between law, historiography and social identity emerges.

Notes

1. For information on Abū Bakra in the early sources, see: ʿAbd al-Malik Ibn Hishām, *Al-Sīra,* 2:485; Muḥammad ibn ʿUmar al-Wāqidī, *Al-Maghāzī,* 3:931–932; Muḥammad Ibn Saʿd, *Al-Ṭabaqāt,* 7.1:8–9; Aḥmad ibn Yaḥyā al-Balādhurī, *Ansāb al-Ashrāf,* 1:579–84; Aḥmad ibn Yaḥyā al-Balādhurī, *Futūḥ al-Buldān,* 55–56, 344–346; Aḥmad ibn Abī Yaʿqūb al-Yaʿqūbī, *Tārīkh,* 167, 181, 273; ʿAlī ibn Ḥusayn al-Masʿūdī, *Murūj al-Dhahab,* 5:26; Khalīfa ibn Khayyāṭ al-ʿUṣfūrī, *Tārīkh,* 89, 135; ʿAbd al-Malik ibn Ḥabīb, *Kitāb al-Taʾrīj,* 105, 114; Muḥammad ibn Jarīr al-Ṭabarī, *Tārīkh,* I:1,782, 2,385, 2,529–2,533, II:11–14, and III:2,535. Many later sources from Ibn ʿAsākir to Ibn Ḥajar al-ʿAsqalānī also discuss Abū Bakra.
2. Sumayya will receive more attention in Chapter 4 of this monograph.
3. Al-Balādhurī, *Ansāb al-Ashrāf,* 1:580.
4. Such as how to do a prayer posture (*rakʿa*) correctly (Muḥammad ibn Ismāʿīl al-Bukhārī, *Ṣaḥīḥ*, 1:416–417); that one should do two *rakʿa*s during a solar or lunar eclipse (*ibid.*, 2:83, 88, 97; 7:455–456); and that the names of certain important days and months – such as Dhū al-Ḥijja – should retain their pre-Islamic names (*ibid.*, 1:58–60; 2:461–462; 9:155–156).
5. Fatima Mernissi, *The Veil and the Male Elite,* 49–60.
6. See, for instance, al-Bukhārī, *Ṣaḥīḥ*, 1:30: 'Al-Aḥnaf ibn Qays said: "While I was going to help [ʿAlī ibn Abī Ṭālib], Abū Bakra met me and asked, 'Where are you going?' I replied, 'I am going to help [ʿAlī].' He said, 'Turn back, for I have heard the Messenger of God saying, 'When two Muslims meet each other with their swords, both the killer and the killed will enter hell.' I said, 'O Messenger of God! That is fine for the killer, but what about the killed?' The Messenger of God said, 'He surely intended to kill his companion.'"' A similar account is found in Ibn Ḥabīb, *Kitāb al-Taʾrīj*, 114, where Abū Bakra's interlocutor is not al-Aḥnaf ibn Qays but rather Sulaymān al-Anṣārī. Abū Bakra also reportedly said: 'Once when the Prophet was making an address, al-Ḥasan [ibn ʿAlī] entered and the Prophet said: "This son of mine is a nobleman (*sayyid*), may God make peace between two groups of Muslims through him."' Al-Bukhārī, *Ṣaḥīḥ*, 9:174.
7. Although the caliph ʿUmar did apparently put him and his brother Nāfiʿ in

charge of the spoils from the battle of Ubulla, near Basra. (See ʿAbd al-Raḥmān Ibn ʿAbd al-Ḥakam, *The History of the Conquest of Egypt*, 147–148.) This position is probably where Abū Bakra gained his tremendous wealth. I thank Luke Yarborough for sharing this reference with me.

8. Most of these other slaves are anonymous or largely forgotten to history, but even those who do receive some treatment in the early sources are never considered *mawālī* of the Prophet. For example, al-Azraq, a Byzantine slave belonging either to al-Ḥārith ibn Kalada or his father Kalada – and married at one point to Abū Bakra's mother Sumayya – descended from the citadel along with Abū Bakra. Al-Azraq is not known as a *mawlā* of the Prophet in a single early historical or bibliographical source; indeed, he and his sons seem to have claimed an Arab heritage and intermarried with the Umayyads. See, for instance, Al-Wāqidī, *Al-Maghāzī*, 3:931–932; Ibn Saʿd, *Al-Ṭabaqāt*, 3.1:174; Balādhurī, *Ansāb al-Ashrāf*, 1:581; al-Balādhurī, *Futūḥ al-Buldān*, 55–56 (where he claims that the Azariqa Kharijite sect was named after al-Azraq!); and al-Ṭabarī, *Tārīkh*, III:2,315.
9. ʿAlī ibn al-Ḥasan Ibn ʿAsākir, *Tārīkh Madīnat Dimashq*, 62:208. Even if he were the *legal* client of Muḥammad, Abū Bakra would still have been allowed to maintain strong *social* ties with his kin in Thaqīf.
10. Ibn Saʿd, *Al-Ṭabaqāt*, 7.1:9. See also the much later Ibn ʿAsākir, *Tārīkh Madīnat Dimashq*, 62:212–213; and Ibn Qayyim al-Jawziyya, *Zād al-Maʿād*, 3:366. In some versions of this account, the Thaqafīs ask for three concessions from Muḥammad: to let them forego the ritual purifications during the winter because their land is a cold land; to let them eat the *dubba'* gourd; and to return Abū Bakra to them. Muḥammad refuses all requests.
11. Al-Wāqidī, *Al-Maghāzī*, 3:931–932; Ibn Hishām, *Al-Sīra*, 1:485. I prefer *ṭalīq allāh* as the original reading, based on the principle of *lectio difficilior potior* (the more difficult reading is the stronger). First, *ʿatīq* (pl. *ʿutaqā'*) is the more common word for freedman. Second, according to most sources, when the Quraysh tribe of Mecca surrendered to Muḥammad in 8/630, they became collectively known as *ṭulaqā'* (singular: *ṭalīq*)'. When the Thaqīf tribe of Taif surrendered several months later, they became collectively known as *ʿutaqā'* (singular: *ʿatīq*), 'those set free'. Abū Bakra belonged to the tribe of Thaqīf in Taif. Thus, it seems likely that an author or scribe might have changed the original word *ṭalīq* – an unusual term associated with Quraysh – to the more common and fitting *ʿatīq*.
12. Sibawayhī, *Al-Kitāb*, 2:158; Khalīl ibn Aḥmad, *Al-Jumal fi al-Naḥw*, 64; al-Jāḥiẓ,

Al-Bayān wa-al-Tabyīn, 1:386. Sibawayhī and Khalīl ibn Aḥmad indicate that this is an insulting description of 'apes' faces'. However, al-Jāḥiẓ makes the somewhat more convincing explanation that al-Ḥajjāj had small eyes with red, infected eyelids, and that all water birds (such as the stork in this description) also have small, ugly and infected eyes.

13. Al-Azharī, *Tahdhīb al-Lugha*, 4:402–403; Ibn Sīda, *Al-Muḥkam wa-al-Muḥīṭ*, 4:238–239. Ibn Sīda adds a fourth line to the poem: 'If he comes near me with the rod, it will not be held back.'
14. Marwān ibn Abī Ḥaf,a, *Shiʿr*, 95.
15. Al-Wāqidī, *Al-Maghāzī*, 3:932. Ibn Saʿd, who was Al-Wāqidī's student and scribe, summarises this account in his *Al-Ṭabaqāt*, 2.1:114: '[Muḥammad] gave each one of them to one of the Muslims, to take care of him.'
16. For a discussion of the legal issues involved in *sā'iba* manumission, or 'unconditional manumission', see Ulrike Mitter, 'Unconditional Manumission of Slaves in Early Islamic Law'. See also Crone, *Roman, Provincial and Islamic Law*, 68, 81.
17. For instance, Mālik says: 'Jews and Christians do not get custody [over Muslim slaves]; the custody of a Muslim slave [owned by a Jew or Christian] goes to the society of Muslims' (*jamāʿat al-muslimīn*). Mālik ibn Anas, *Al-Muwaṭṭaʾ*, 2:786 (book 38, section 13, hadith #25).
18. Ibn Saʿd, *Al-Ṭabaqāt*, 7.1:9; the same account is also found in the much later Ibn ʿAsākir, *Tārīkh Madīnat Dimashq*, 62:213–214.
19. The isnads for the *ṭalīq allāh* accounts are: 1) Al-Faḍl ibn Dukayn (d. 219/834, Kufan; Ibn Ḥajar al-ʿAsqalānī, Aḥmad ibn ʿAlī, *Tahdhīb al-Tahdhīb*, 5:250–555), from Abū al-Aḥwaṣ (d. 179/795, Kufan; *ibid.*, 3:112), from Mughīra ibn Miqsam (d. *c.* 133/750, Kufan; *ibid.*, 6:386–387), from Shibāk (n.d., Kufan; *ibid.*, 3:131), from an unnamed Thaqafī man; and 2) Yaḥyā ibn Ḥammād (d. 215/830, Basran; *ibid.*, 7:27–28), from Abū ʿAwāna (d. 175/791, Wāsiṭī; *ibid.*, 6:714–717), from Mughīra, from Shibāk, from ʿĀmir al-Shaʿbī (d. *c.* 107/725, Kufan; *ibid.*, 3:339–342).
20. They are Abū ʿĀmir al-ʿAqadī (d. *c.* 205/820; *ibid.*, 4:254–55), al-Aswad ibn Shaybān (d. 165/781; *ibid.*, 1:319.), and Khālid ibn Sumayr (n.d.; *ibid.*, 2:274–275).
21. For the most thorough discussion of early Islamic Basra, including its ethnic makeup, its intellectual currents and its political trends, see Pellat, *Le milieu basrien.*
22. Jamal Juda devotes much attention to the regional differences in clientage

between Kufa and Basra, 'Die sozialen und wirtschaftlichen Aspekte der Mawālī', vi–xi, 76–86, 163–171 and 189–193. For instance, he finds that *walā' al-tibāʿa* (conversion of free non-Muslims) was found predominantly in Syria and Basra, whereas *walā' ʿitāqa* (manumission of slaves) was found in Hijaz and Kufa. He argues that Kufan and Medinan legal schools did not put much value on genealogy, but rather advocated the idea that all believers were equal (contrast with Ziadeh's findings in 'Equality (*kafā'ah*) in the Muslim Law of Marriage'). On the other hand, in Basra, tribal pedigree was more highly valued and the *mawālī* and Persian ethnic minority more despised. He argues that Kufa had a greater tendency towards pro-*mawlā* and anti-Umayyad sentiment. However, his theories need more investigation, for my own study suggests that pro-*mawlā* and anti-Umayyad currents in Abū Bakra's biography seem to have emerged in Basra.

23. I do not wish to argue that Abū Bakra's identity as 'freedman of God' is the only way, or the only correct way, to view him, but simply a new way that sheds a different light on early Islamic history. It seems likely that he was always considered a *mawlā* in the inclusive 'all Muslims are *mawālī*' sense discussed in the previous chapter, and Abū Bakra certainly fits the phrase from Q 33:5, "If you do not know their fathers, they are your brothers in religion and your *mawālī*."' Rather, what this unique phrase *ṭalīq allāh* shows us is that Abū Bakra's life may not originally have carried overtones of legal clientage or non-Arab ethnicity.
24. Crone, *Roman, Provincial and Islamic Law.*
25. Crone suggests that Muʿāwiya may have been responsible for introducing the more systematic Roman law of patronage into Islamic law, *Roman, Provincial and Islamic Law,* 91.
26. The imposition of these new categories may even have begun during Abū Bakra's own long lifetime, as he survived into the early Umayyad period and experienced the systemisation that began under the Rightly Guided and Umayyad caliphs.
27. A poem by Khālid al-Najjārī, cited in al-Masʿūdī, *Murūj al-Dhahab*, 5:26.
28. This kind of genealogical manipulation is forbidden by the Quran, but in practice it persists even to this day. See, for instance, Szombathy, *The Roots of Arabic Genealogy*; and Conte, 'Agnatic Illusions'.
29. In a different account from al-Balādhurī, Abū Bakra responds, 'What in this world is graver than Ziyād's appointing [my son] ʿUbaydallāh over Sijistan and the matter of the [Zoroastrian] fires?' Al-Balādhurī, *Ansāb al-Ashrāf,* 0:585. Apparently Abū Bakra did not approve of 'fire temple demolishing' as a career for ʿUbaydallāh.

30. I have translated the Arabic word *mujtahid* in a slightly tortuous manner, hoping to convey both the idea of 'striving' and 'exercising independent judgment'.
31. Al-Balādhurī, *Ansāb al-Ashrāf,* 0:585. The Kharijites are the most notorious band of radicals in early Islamic history; they were responsible for many murders, including that of the pious caliph ʿAlī. Abū Bakra is essentially saying, 'The road to hell is paved with good intentions.'
32. Nowhere is Ziyād's 'adoption' or Abū Bakra's *mawlā* status mentioned in this account, but both are implied. First, the reference to Abū Bakra's children is based on the fact that they pretended to be 'Arabs' when they began working for the Umayyads. Second, the presence of Anas ibn Mālik and al-Ḥasan al-Basrī, two famous Basran *mawālī*, implies that Abū Bakra here stands as a representative of *mawlā* status.
33. For a discussion of this hadith in a different context, see Uri Rubin, '"Al-walad li-l-firāsh"'.
34. Or perhaps the context is meant to refer to Saʿd himself, who asked the Prophet whether he should be called Saʿd ibn Abī Waqqāṣ (as he is most commonly known), or Saʿd ibn Mālik (his actual name). The Prophet said: 'You are Saʿd ibn Mālik ibn Uhayb (or Wuhayb) ibn ʿAbd Manāf ibn Zuhra, and may God curse whoever says otherwise.' See G. R. Hawting, 'Saʿd b. Abī Waḳḳās', *EI*[1].
35. Abū Bakr Aḥmad ibn ʿAmr Al-Bazzār, *Al-Baḥr al-Zakhkhār,* 2:362; ʿAbd al-Razzāq ibn Ḥammām al-Ḥimyarī, *Al-Muṣannaf,* 8:50.
36. Aḥmad Ibn Ḥanbal, *Al-Musnad,* 2:55 and 2:76.
37. It is clear from the wording of these hadiths that that the fourth generation of transmitters added this extra information to help their audiences remember who Saʿd ibn Abī Waqqāṣ and Abū Bakra were. ʿAbd Allāh ibn Muḥammad Ibn Abī Shayba, *Al-Muṣannaf,* 7:515; ʿAbd al-Razzāq ibn Ḥammām al-Ḥimyarī, *Al-Muṣannaf,* 8:48–49; Ibn Ḥanbal, *Musnad,* 2:52; al-Bukhārī, *Ṣaḥīḥ*, 4:429; Muslim ibn Ḥajjāj al-Qushayrī, *Ṣaḥīḥ Muslim,* 3.1:45–46; I Muḥammad ibn Yazīd bn Māja, *Sunan,* 1:869; ʿAbd Allāh ibn ʿAbd al-Raḥmān al-Dārimī, *Musnad,* 2:1,644–1,645 and 3:1,888–1,889; Ibn ʿAsākir, *Tārīkh Madīnat Dimashq*, 61:209–210.
38. Ibn Ḥajar, *Tahdhīb al-Tahdhīb*, 3:134–135.
39. Ibn ʿAsākir, *Tārīkh Madīnat Dimashq*, 61:204.
40. In a formal hadith analysis, ʿĀṣim would be considered the 'common link', while Abū ʿUthmān is part of the more dubious 'single strand'. A good introduction to these terms and the scholarly debates surrounding them can be found in Harald Motzki, ed., *Hadith,* xxxviii–xli, and the sources cited therein. See also

the corpus of G. H. A. Juynboll, especially his articles: 'Some *Isnad*-Analytical Methods' and 'Nāfiʿ, the Mawlā of Ibn ʿUmar'.

41. Muslim, *Ṣaḥīḥ Muslim*, 3.1:45; Ibn Ḥanbal, *Musnad*, 2:31; Ibn ʿAsākir, *Tārīkh Madīnat Dimashq*, 18:175.
42. Ibn Ḥajar, *Tahdhīb al-Tahdhīb*, 1:294–296.
43. Khālid transmitted hadiths both from al-Ḥasan al-Baṣrī and his brother Saʿīd ibn Abī al-Ḥasan al-Baṣrī, see Ibn Ḥajar, *Tahdhīb al-Tahdhīb*, 1:295. Al-Ḥasan al-Baṣrī himself supposedly said: 'No one better ever lived in Basra than Abū Bakra and ʿImrān ibn al-Ḥusayn' (al-Dhahabī, *Siyar*, 3:4). Whether or not any of the reported interactions between Abū Bakra and al-Ḥasan al-Baṣrī actually took place, some kind of ideological connection exists between the two figures, and they both seem to represent an activist but not militant stance towards political oppression.
44. H. P. Raddatz, 'Sufyan al-Thawrī', *EI*[1]. Raddatz counts Khālid in the same group as Wāṣil ibn ʿAṭā' and ʿAmr ibn ʿUbayd. However, I have been unable to find any reference to Khālid's Muʿtazili leanings in any sources, including Muʿtazili biographical dictionaries and Josef van Ess's *Theologie und Gesellschaft*.
45. For the development of the term *iʿtizāl*, see Sarah Stroumsa, 'The Beginnings of the Muʿtazila Reconsidered'. Abū Bakra is not treated in works on Muʿtazilism, nor is he an ascetic (*zāhid/nāsik*) proper – he had legions of children, after all. But he withdrew from politics, as was characteristic of the early Muʿtazila.
46. This is not a controversial stance – this version of the hadith does not appear in any proper hadith collections, but rather in Ibn ʿAsākir, *Tārīkh Madīnat Dimashq*, 18:173.
47. This version replaces the usual Successor transmitter, Abū ʿUthmān al-Nahdī, with the famous Basran scholar Ibn Sīrīn. In my estimation, the chain of transmission is made up out of whole cloth.
48. Ibn ʿAsākir, *Tārīkh Madīnat Dimashq*, 18:173.
49. This seems somewhat ironic, given that the content of the 'whoever claims a false father' hadith hinges on Abū Bakra's identity as a *mawlā*.
50. Khalīfa ibn Khayyāṭ, *Al-Ṭabaqāt*, 124 and 429; Aḥmad Ibn Ḥanbal, *Kitāb al-Asāmī wa-al-Kunā*, 29; Muḥammad ibn Ismāʿīl al-Bukhārī, *Al-Tārīkh al-Kabīr*, 3.2: 111–112; and Muslim ibn Ḥajjāj al-Qushayrī, *Kitāb al-Kunā wa-al-Asmā'*, 15. For the opinion of Ibn Abī Shayba, as well as several other scholars, see Ibn ʿAsākir, *Tārīkh Madīnat Dimashq*, 61:201.
51. However, Muḥammad also told his wife Sawda to veil herself around the child,

indicating that he was not 'really' her brother (as women do not have to veil around their own brothers).

52. Rubin, 'Al-walad li-l-firāsh'. Rubin briefly mentions Abū Bakra in his discussion of Ziyād's false adoption, and he treats the 'whoever claims a false father' hadith as related to the 'child belongs to the bed' dictum. However, nowhere does he talk about Abū Bakra's own identity, or the idea that the hadith specialists may have applied this dictum to Abū Bakra and thus found him to be an Arabian tribesman, in contrast to Ziyād. For more on Sumayya, see Chapter 3.
53. Rubin, 'Al-walad li-l-firāsh'.
54. *Ibid.*, 5.
55. At the time of Abū Bakra's birth, the 'child belongs to the bed' dictum still seems to have been in its developmental stages; see Uri Rubin, ''Walad li-l-Firash'.' Also, if Abū Bakra is viewed as a freedman, there is a potential conflict between the 'child belongs to the bed' hadith and the '*walā'* belongs to the manumitter' hadith. According to the first hadith, Abū Bakra should be a Thaqafī tribesman; according to the second, he should be a *mawlā* of the Prohpet. There is no inherent conflict between the two, as in the pre-Islamic and earliest Islamic period Arabs could also be *mawālī*. (Good examples of 'Arab *mawālī*' from this period are the Prophet's adopted son-turned-*mawlā*, Zayd ibn Ḥāritha, and the founder of the Māliki school of law, Mālik ibn Anas.) However, the fact remains that the hadith scholars do not view Abū Bakra as a *mawlā* at all, and they avoid any potential conflict by focusing solely on Abū Bakra's Thaqīf lineage.
56. Khaled Abou El Fadl, *Speaking in God's Name,* 110–113; Fatima Mernissi, *The Veil and the Male Elite,* 48–59.
57. I would like to clarify here that I do not wish to condone the sentiment of the hadith that Abū Bakra transmitted, but rather to explore the issue of legal authority.
58. Generally, al-Ṭabarī presents Abū Bakra as an insignificant historical actor and rather a nuisance. Al-Ṭabarī does not emphasise his identity as a *mawlā*, nor does he seem to care much about his social identity. Perhaps this is because al-Ṭabarī views the *mawālī* as bearers of Persian values or as Turkish slave-soldiers, features that do not apply to Abū Bakra. Or perhaps it is simply because Abū Bakra was never very powerful, and al-Ṭabarī focuses on political events. Al-Balādhurī, as we shall see, cares much more about Abū Bakra as the humble *mawlā* par excellence. Abū Bakra also appears much more strongly as a foil to Ziyād in al-Balādhurī's account.
59. I suggest the Zubayrids because 'Ā'isha was allied with al-Zubayr in 'Awwām

in the First Civil War. Al-Zubayr's sons, ʿAbdallāh and Muṣʿab, were major participants in the Second Civil War that occurred about thirty years later.

60. Al-Ṭabarī, *Tārīkh,* I:2,529–2,532.
61. *Ibid.,* I:2,528-31.
62. The classic work exploring the slow development of Islamic law is Joseph Schacht, *Introduction to Islamic Law.*
63. Al-Balādhurī, *Ansāb al-Ashrāf,* 0:581.
64. In critical analyses of the concept, humility is often treated as an attitude about the self in comparison to others or to a higher standard. There is debate about whether humility entails an *accurate* self-assessment, or an *underestimating* self-assessment. See, for example, David Cooper, *The Measure of Things: Humanism, Humility, and Mystery,* 160–166; and Jamie Schillinger, 'Intellectual Humility and Interreligious Dialogue', 363. For more on Abū Bakra's humility, see Elizabeth Urban, 'Humble in Word and Body'.
65. Al-Balāhdurī, *Ansāb al-Ashrāf,* 0:582.
66. Al-Balādhurī, *Ansāb al-Ashrāf,* 0:357; Ibn Saʿd, *Ṭabaqāt,* 2:269. See also Tayeb El-Hibri, *Parable and Politics,* 78–80 for more reports of ʿUmar's righteousness and tremendous knowledge.
67. See El-Hibri, *Parable and Politics,* 83–90; Crone, '*Mawālī* and the Prophet's Family: An Early Shiite View'.

4

Enslaved Prostitutes in Early Islamic History

This chapter treats enslaved prostitutes, who are mostly marginal in the historical sources and have received little scholarly attention.[1] Upon closer analysis, enslaved prostitutes reveal many deep-seated thematic connections to the other people studied in this monograph. First, both Abū Bakra and early Islamic prostitutes reveal tensions about the more egalitarian/inclusive and the more hierarchical/exclusive interpretations of the Quran. Just as Abū Bakra reportedly invoked Q 33:5 to articulate his place in the early Islamic *umma*, so did two first-/seventh-century prostitutes apparently invoke Q 24:33 to seek inclusion in the earliest *umma*. The references to these women are as obscure and suggestive as Abū Bakra's identity as a *ṭaliq allāh*, and likewise they are only recoverable through a careful combing of the sources. By the third/ninth century, Arabic-Islamic authors had downplayed or even plain forgotten the stories of these two prostitutes and had replaced them with narratives that made more sense in their own contexts. Like the saga of the heroic Abū Bakra versus the villainous Ziyād, these authors created archetypes of the 'good' slave prostitute saved by Islam versus the 'bad' prostitute revelling in her debauchery. Thus, early Islamic slave prostitutes are illuminating case studies of liminal believers who navigated their belonging in the earliest *umma*, and whose identities were flattened by later authors who were not concerned with the inclusion of such outsiders.

Prostitutes are also connected to the coming chapters through their gender and status, that is, as enslaved women.[2] The coming chapters will analyse two prominent types of enslaved women from Umayyad and early Abbasid society – the concubine-mother (*umm walad*) and the courtesan (*qayna*). Both of these types of enslaved women play important roles in early Islamic history and literature, and, by contrast, they allow us to interrogate the near absence of the more mundane prostitute. On the one hand, most of our source authors are urban elites (often associated with or at least paid by a royal court), and they accordingly pay more attention to high-class literary soirées than to the local bar-and-brothel scene. On the other hand, I suggest that the sources can afford to ignore prostitutes because they are so easily dismissed as 'other' – as foreign non-Muslims at the fringes of Islamic society, or as vestiges of pre-Islamic sexual ethics. As we shall see in later chapters, because courtesans and concbubines were 'producing songs and sons'[3] their liminality could not be so easily resolved, and they continued to exercise the pens and the imaginations of scholars well into the Abbasid period.

Why and How to do Feminist History for Early Islam

The methodologies used in this chapter are similar to those of the previous chapter: I scour various narrative sources from multiple genres, searching for anomalous or surprising accounts that do not fit later ideological agendas. However, any scholar hoping to study women in early Islamic history is immediately faced with an additional problem: none of the early Arabic-Islamic narrative sources were written by women, and probably none of the early Islamic epigraphic, numismatic or archaeological sources were made by women.[4] Scholars of early Islam have no accounts to rival those of medieval European scholars, who have Hildegard of Bingen's *Scivias*, or those of Byzantininsts, who have Anna Komnena's *Alexiad.* Even those Arabic-Islamic sources that purport to centre on women, such as al-Iṣbahānī's (d. *c.* 360/971) *al-Imāʾ al-Shawāʿir* (Slave Poetesses) or Ibn al-Sāʿī's (d. 674/1276) *Nisāʾ al-Khulafāʾ* (Consorts of the Caliphs), are still filtered through the worldview of slave-holding, elite, urban male authors. A naive approach to these sources – that is, treating these texts as objective and descriptive, rather than subjective and normative – will inevitably fail to understand the ways that women experienced and navigated early Islamic history. A descriptive approach is bound to simply sprinkle a few women into existing, hegemonic, male-dominated narratives about the past.[5]

How can scholars proceed with such problematic source material? One possibility is to give up trying to recover female experiences at all, and to focus instead only on mnemohistory (the study of collective memory) or gender history (the study of gendered norms and expectations, for both men and women). However, mnemohistory and gender history often still reveal only what *male* authors remembered of famous women,[6] or how male authors expressed and upheld gender norms.[7] While such methods are incredibly valuable and shed new light on early Islamic historical sources, they ultimately provide insight into male perceptions of women. As medieval European historian Gisela Bock states more boldly, using male-authored texts to study women 'must in fact be viewed as men's history'.[8]

Feminist history provides another possibility. Feminist history challenges scholars not merely to fit women into already-existing historical categories, but to completely re-frame their understanding of the past to include female perspectives, experiences and interpretations. Feminist history insists that scholars must take seriously multiple perspectives if they are to uncover anything approximating the 'truth' of the historical past. It can be very difficult to challenge hegemonic male narratives about history, when the only sources we have are those very hegemonic narratives.[9] And yet, I suggest it can be done; even if the answers are tentative and suggestive, I find that the endeavour itself is valuable. Accordingly, I derive the following methodological suggestions from models in Islamic history, from studies of women in medieval Europe and from feminist history theory more broadly.

First, feminist historians can simply ask new questions of the sources – questions that did not motivate the original authors, but questions to which the sources nevertheless provide an answer. This is at heart what all historians do; as Aziz Al-Azmeh says, 'The main task of the historian [is] going beyond the limits of sources in an effort towards historical reconstruction.'[10] In order to avoid projecting anachronistic notions of feminism onto the texts, however, scholars should let feminist sensibilities guide their questions rather than dictate their answers. They should certainly not expect to find 'feminists' in the pages of medieval history, and they should avoid seeking evidence of loaded, modern concepts such as 'oppression'. Instead of lamenting oppressed victims or trumpeting feminist heroes, [11] scholars should interrogate the intersection of power structures, social norms and individual agency. They should consider what choices were available to women in any given historical context, and what were the costs and benefits of making certain choices.

Second, Judith Bennett, a prominent historian of Medieval European women's history, suggests that scholars should do micro-historical case studies of individual women. She further suggests that it might be particularly useful to focus on women who lived during 'times of crisis'; these moments of crisis help elucidate what forms of patriarchy certain women saw as intolerable, and which they saw as liveable or even desirable in certain contexts. In this chapter, I take Muḥammad's movement as just such a time of crisis.[12] Additionally, when analysing accounts about women, Ottoman historian Ehud Toledano has suggested that it is fruitful to analyse what women *do* (or fail to do) in these accounts, instead of accepting whatever motivation the authors ascribe to those actions.[13] The historian and theorist Gisela Bock similarly suggests that, in analysing female actions, scholars can seek to recover the possible underlying female interpretations of texts or reactions to patriarchal structures.[14] Finally, prosopography – the study of groups using large data sets – has the power to reveal trends that go beyond the level of individual authors' awareness. Arabic-Islamic genealogical material precisely lends itself to prosopographical analysis.[15] I offer examples of these methodologies in this chapter (as well as the following chapters), to suggest how feminist history can enhance our understanding of the experiences of enslaved women in the early Islamic period.

A model of such a methodology for early Islamic history is Asma Sayeed's study of the role of women in hadith transmission. Sayeed conducts a micro-historical analysis of several female hadith transmitters from the first to ninth/seventh to fifteenth centuries, as well as amassing data from thousands of *isnāds*. By doing so, she provides convincing explanations for the prominence of female transmitters of the Companion generation, the decline of female participation in hadith transmission in the second to fourth/eighth to tenth centuries, and the re-emergence of prominent female hadith scholars beginning in the late fourth/tenth century. Her explanations have little to do with people's misogyny on the one hand, or with individual women's heroic fight to join the ranks of the hadith scholars on the other. Rather, she attributes women's changing roles to wider social-historical developments, such as the canonisation of the major Sunni hadith collections and the acceptance of writing as a form of hadith transmission. She investigates a range of women's activities in specific historical contexts, and she avoids reducing these activities to over-simplified, over-politicised binaries. For example, Sayeed finds that, among the prophet Muḥammad's wives, ʿĀ'isha interpreted the idea of 'hijab' more loosely than did Sawda, allowing ʿĀ'isha to play a greater and more active role in the life of the early *umma*. Sayeed warns that we should not view Sawda as 'submitting to' and ʿĀ'isha as 'rebelling against' the idea of seclusion. 'On the contrary, this diversity of approaches highlights the right of interpretation that the wives exercised when confronted with what appears to us as a highly restrictive ruling.'[16] I take Sayeed's book as a model for how to do feminist history of the early Islamic period.

Transforming Arabian Society: Musayka and 'Abat' Seek Justice

Taking my inspiration from these feminist historical methodologies, I offer in this chapter a case study of two enslaved prostitutes from very early Islamic Arabia. One of these women was named Musayka, and she seems to have asked the community of Medina for help when her master was mistreating her. The second woman's name has been lost, but for the sake of simplicity, I will call her 'Abat' or 'she refused' – for she apparently stood up to her own people (*ahl*) and refused to continue working as a prostitute. During the time of crisis that Muḥammad's religious movement created for Arabian society, these women appear to have rejected the practice of prostitution (or perhaps even slave concubinage) as unjust and unacceptable. In rejecting prostitution, Musayka and Abat were not pushing for some twenty-first-century ideal of individual liberty or a free-love revolution. Rather, they seem to have been advocating for their ability to protect their chastity, likely in order to save their sexual activities for the more attractive patriarchal structure of marriage. Thus, I suggest that Musayka and Abat reveal brief flashes of the female interpretation of Islam's moral vision in general, and of Q 24:33 in particular.

It takes careful attention to genre, as well as careful literary analysis, to recover these women's histories. First, Musayka and 'Abat' are absent from the genres of prophetic biography (*sīra*), historical report (*tārīkh*/*akhbār*) and biographical dictionary (*ṭabaqāt*). Their stories are only found in exegeses of the Quranic verse 24:33, in accounts known as *asbāb al-nuzūl*. Classically, *asbāb al-nuzūl* are the 'occasions of revelation', or explanations of the events that caused God to reveal particular Quranic verses; this chapter uses the term to describe any account that purports to set the Quranic revelation in historical context.[17] Second, even within the genre of *asbāb al-nuzūl*, Musayka's and Abat's stories are hidden behind layers of literary polish. Most exegetes conflate or forget the women at the heart of the story, and many exegetes also include a character named Muʿādha, who is not to be understood as a historical figure, but as an ideological symbol of chastity and piety. I offer here an example of how feminist historical analysis helps scholars separate earlier, more historical *asbāb* material from later, more ideological material.

Exegetes associate Musayka and Abat with the clause in Q 24:33, 'Do not force your young slave women into whoredom if they want to try to be chaste.'[18] We have already seen this verse in Chapter 2, where I suggested that it reveals some of the questions enslaved women might have had about whether or not they could belong to the *umma*. I suggest that early exegeses – particularly those transmitted by the Arabian transmitters Jābir ibn ʿAbdallāh (d. 78/697) and Mujāhid ibn Jabr (d. 104/722) – provide more details about how such women participated in the creation of the earliest *umma*. Especially, they help us see that slave prostitution was not a monolithic practice, but that two different women faced slightly different situations and chose slightly different solutions to their problems. In the sections that follow, I will begin by closely analysing the two accounts that I find authentic, before turning to the accounts that I suggest have been embellished for ideological reasons.

Jābir's Tradition: Musayka's Plea for Help

The first account that I find authentic is transmitted by the Companion of Muḥammad, Jābir ibn ʿAbdallāh, on the authority of the hadith scholar Ibn Jurayj (d. 150/767).[19] There are three slight variants of this tradition, recorded in the early exegeses of al-Nasāʾī (d. 303/915) and al-Ṭabarī (d. 310/923), as well as in the canonical hadith compilation of Abū Dāʾūd (d. 275/889):

1) 'Musayka – the slave (*ama*) of one of the Anṣār – came and said: "My master forces me to whoredom (*bighāʾ*)." So God sent down this verse.'[20]
2) 'Musayka went to one of the Anṣār and said: "My master compels me to forncation (*zinā*)." So this verse came down regarding that.'[21]
3) 'A slave woman (*jāriya*) came to one of the Anṣār and said, "My master forces me to whoredom (*bighā*)." So this verse came down.'[22]

Several textual elements speak to these traditions' authenticity. First, the characters in these accounts are anonymous Anṣār – the Medinese 'Helpers' who accepted Islam and invited Muḥammad to build his community in Medina. Many later exegeses replace the Anṣār with the more symbolically significant Prophet Muḥammad.[23] Second, the story focuses on the woman and her actions, not on how the men treat her or how Islam saves her (which will become prominent themes in later traditions). The woman's name Musayka ('little musky') also seems like a typical slave name, unlike some of the other prostitute names analysed below.[24] Third, in none of these variations does Musayka's story operate as a true exegesis. The woman's story seems somewhat unconnected to the event of Quranic revelation, which descends at the end almost as an afterthought.[25]

If these accounts are indeed historically authentic, they indicate first that Musayka may have been seeking recourse from concubinage, rather than prostitution per se. There are no overt references to any markers of prostitution, such as multiple sexual partners, or the exchange of money. Thus, hearkening back to my analysis of Q 24:33 in Chapter 2, it seems possible here that the problem was that Musayka's master was forcing himself on her, when she wished to remain chaste. In any case, Musayka is presented as seeking help from the Anṣār. We can only infer why she turned to them, but perhaps it is because they had a reputation for righteousness, and she thought that she might find support among them. It is also possible that she had become a Believer by this point – perhaps attracted to a moral vision that frowned upon extra-marital sexual encounters – but the text makes no explicit statements about her religious status. The most we can say is that she, an *individual* suffering from perceived injustice, found recourse in a wider *group* or community that held a notion of sexual ethics that she found more agreeable. Finally, the picture it paints of early Islamic Medina is somewhat non-canonical; it seems more like a collaborative, ecumenical social experiment than a centralised, stratified society. The Anṣār apparently felt justified intervening in other people's extended households, in the name of helping the needy and reforming unethical practices.

Mujāhid's Tradition: Abat Refuses

The second tradition that rings historically true comes from the early Meccan exegete, Mujāhid ibn Jabr, as reported in al-Ṭabarī's exegesis.[26] Mujāhid's account has two basic variants that, when viewed in tandem, provide tantalising glimmers of information about early Islamic prostitution:

1) They used to compel their female household slaves (*walā'id*) to prostitution, so they (f.) did that, and they earned from it. ʿAbdallāh ibn Ubayy had a slave who did prostitution, but she did not like it, so she swore not to do it anymore. But her people (*ahluhā*) compelled her, so she went out and prostituted herself for a green garment, and she gave it to them. Then this verse came down.[27]
2) ʿAbdallāh ibn Ubayy ibn Salūl used to force his slave woman (*ama*) to fornication, and she brought him a dinar or a garment (Abu ʿĀṣim is unsure), and she gave it to him, and he said: 'Go back and keep doing *zinā* (fornication) with someone else.' She said: 'No I won't go back.' God forgives those who are forced to fornication.[28]

As with the Musayka story above, there are certain features that speak for this story's basic authenticity. Once again, these accounts are barely exegetical, as the woman's story exists as a coherent narrative without the revelation of the Quran. In fact, version 2 is not explicitly associated with the revelation of the verse at all, but is merely capped with a quote taken from the end of Q 24:33. Similarly, the woman is once again the protagonist of the account, and she is again not described as a Muslim – she simply 'does not like' working as a prostitute. Finally, like Musayka's story, these accounts depict a society undergoing a radical change. In this case, a slave woman is able to stand up to her master and/or her 'people' (*ahluhā*) in the name of justice; she is challenging the usual authority of the male over the female, the master over the slave.

Both Mujāhid traditions do contain the highly symbolic, historically suspicious character ʿAbdallāh ibn Ubayy. However, the second account hints that ʿAbdallāh ibn Ubayy was added later. While this second tradition names Ibn Ubayy at the top of the account, it drops him at the end. Instead, at the end of the account, it is her people (*ahl*) who forced her – meaning perhaps her natal family or tribe, but more likely her master's extended household. It also says she gave the cloak to 'them' (pl.) and not 'him', indicating that the original master in this tradition might not have been the individual Ibn Ubayy, but a collective household, family or tribe. This account also preserves the rather unusual term *al-walāʾid,* which describes females born into slavery in their master's household.[29] Later historical traditions are rife with stories about the slave trade and how masters would purchase slaves to use as concubines and prostitutes. Here, however, the context appears not to be the slave trade, but the slave's original birth household, which corresponds with the idea that it was her *ahl* who forced her. While the evidence is somewhat circumstantial, I suggest that there are enough threads of the original text showing through to detect Ibn Ubayy's presence as an emendation.

If the extraneous and suspicious details are cut away, the combined texts tell the story of a slave woman whose master forced her to prostitution, but she refused to continue working as a prostitute. Unlike the Musayka accounts above, the Abat accounts are clearly about actual prostitution, not merely concubinage; the unique detail of the woman earning a cloak is perhaps an accurate description of pre-Islamic prostitution practices. Also, unlike Musayka, who appears as an exploited individual who sought help from a righteous community, Abat is exploited precisely as a member of a group (slave household, *jāhiliyya* tribe) and she seeks salvation in her individual morality. One can only speculate as to what made Abat feel justified in standing up to her household, but the mere fact that she *did* register her complaint once again indicates a society in the midst of a radical upheaval. Given that the women in these two accounts *do* such different things – Musayka seeks communal help, while Abat individually refuses her master – I take these stories to refer to two different historical women.

The fact that there were two different women who employed two different strategies to escape prostitution (or concubinage) gives us insight into the changes taking place in Medina when Islam first took root there. Their diverse actions challenge a dichotomous male-authored model of how 'good' versus 'bad' slave prostitutes behaved. Instead, these women seem to have viewed prostitution unilaterally as a form of injustice, quite regardless of their own personal moral virtues or vices. They seem to have understood the 'crisis' of Muḥammad's reform movement as an opportunity to treat free men as their moral equals – the same class of people who had owned, used and dominated them – by either seeking their help or standing up to them. We do not know what became of either woman, but given that their stories are associated with a verse prohibiting forced fornication, I like to imagine that their situations improved.

Good Prostitute, Bad Prostitute: The Symbolic Undertones of Muʿādha and Sumayya

Just as the sources mostly obscure Abū Bakra's status as a 'brother in religion' and *ṭalīq allāh*, so the sources mostly obscure the radical actions of enslaved prostitutes such as Musayka and Abat. Instead, the Arabic-Islamic sources generally present one of two narratives about enslaved prostitutes, depending on genre. Quranic exegeses predominantly tell an uplifting tale about Muʿādha, a 'reformed harlot' character on the model of Mary Magdalene and familiar from Christian saints' lives.[30] Whether because she adopted Islam, or because Muḥammad intervened to protect her, this woman was saved from the plight of prostitution. On the other hand, biographies and narrative histories never mention Muʿādha or any other 'saved' prostitute, but instead focus on the wicked deeds of infamous prostitutes such as Abū Bakra's mother Sumayya. Neither genre begins to engage with the systematic problem of prostitution or tries to understand why women might remain prostitutes. Instead, both sources draw a black-and-white picture of female sexuality, and they use female sexuality as a symbol of Islamic values (or lack thereof). Somewhat surprisingly, both genres highlight the enslaved prostitute's agency and choice – either to choose chastity, or to revel in fornication. However, these sources put all the burden of agency on these individual women, not on the men who own them or use them, and certainly not on the wider system of prostitution and/or slavery that allows for their exploitation.

Moral Salvation and Male Intervention: The Case of the 'Good' Prostitute

While I argued above that Musayka and 'Abat' are historical women who inhabited early Islamic Medina, the exegetes mention a handful of other women whose historical existence is more questionable. Particularly, Iraqi transmitters such as al-Suddī (d. *c.* 127/745), Muqātil ibn Sulaymān (d. 150/767) and al-Maʿmar ibn Rāshid (d. 153/770) instead usually tell the tale of a 'reformed harlot' named Muʿādha. Instead of recounting a brave slave woman's resistance to injustice, these later narratives convey messages about Islam's moral triumph and Muḥammad's protection of the powerless. The woman in the story becomes merely a symbol, a representation of any woman who finds justice and righteousness in Islam. There is still enormous value in these accounts, but they should not be used to understand the practice of slave prostitution in first-/seventh-century Medina. Instead, they should be used to understand the elaboration of Sunni exegetical strategies in the second/eighth and third/ninth centuries, especially in Iraq.

Al-Zuhrī's Tradition: Muʿādha the Reformed Harlot

One of the most clearly ideological accounts about Muʿādha apparently originated with the Medinese scholar Ibn Shihāb al-Zuhrī (d. 124/742), and was transmitted by the Basran scholar Maʿmar ibn Rāshid:

> A man from Quraysh was taken captive on the day of Badr, and he was held in captivity at ʿAbdallāh ibn Ubayy's. ʿAbdallāh had a slave woman called Muʿādha, and the Qurashi captive wanted her for himself. But she was a Muslim, and she held back from him because of her Islam. Ibn Ubayy compelled her to do that, and he hit her, hoping that she would become pregnant by the Qurashi and he would pay the ransom money for his son. But God said [this verse].[31]

Many elements of this narrative indicate that it is symbolic rather than historical. First, ʿAbdallāh ibn Ubayy appears here as an arch-villain, the infamous 'head of the hypocrites' who hopes to cling to pre-Islamic practices despite claiming to be a Muslim. The Qurashi prisoner of war, dwelling at ʿAbdallāh ibn Ubayy's house, represents the other antagonistic group from Muḥammad's career, the Meccan Qurashi polytheists. By colluding to abuse a helpless, disenfranchised Muslim woman, Ibn Ubayy and the Qurashi represent the moral dissipation of both the idolaters of Mecca and the hypocrites of Medina. Their physical violence is both a sign of their depravity and proof that Muʿādha was truly 'compelled' to fornicate.[32] Second, the protagonist of this account is not Muʿādha, but rather God, who intervenes to protect an innocent Muslim from persecution. It is overtly Muʿādha's Islam that causes her to shrink away from the Qurashi's sexual desire. Even her name,

Muʿādha, 'she who seeks refuge in God', alludes to the final two Suras of the Quran and indicates that it is God and not she who is the hero. Muʿādha is not a slave prostitute from the early first/seventh century, but a classical Islamic symbol of piety and chastity, a recipient of God's grace.

Al-Suddī's Tradition: Sectarian Overtones

The second-/eighth-century Kufan storyteller al-Suddī presents an even more wildly unhistorical account. (I am not the first person to question al-Suddī's reliability; even his contemporaries apparently thought his stories were pure fantasy.) Although his account is far from accurate history, it is narratively vivid and hints at the political disputes of al-Suddī's own day. He says:

> This verse came down regarding [ʿAbdallāh ibn Ubayy] Ibn Salūl, the Head of the Hypocrites, who had a slave named Muʿādha. Whenever a guest came to stay with him, he would send her to have sex with him, hoping for payment, and also as a way of honouring him. So the woman came to Abū Bakr and complained to him, and he told the Prophet, who ordered him to take custody of her. Ibn Salūl yelled: 'Who will answer for Muḥammad? He has taken our slave!' So God revealed this verse.[33]

Al-Suddī's account is full of juicy details that make for an entertaining story. His description of the supposed pre-Islamic practice of providing a slave girl to pleasure a guest is found in no other exegeses of this verse. There are several potential explanations of this description – it could be a gloss on the Lot story, a satirical twist on traditional Arab hospitality, or an accurate description of slavery practices current in al-Suddī's day.[34] Moreover, in this account, the Quranic verse does not come down as a result of the woman's mistreatment per se. Rather, the verse comes as a response to ʿAbdallāh ibn Ubayy's shouted question, 'Who will answer for Muḥammad?' The verse comes as a dramatic, incontrovertible answer: God will justify Muḥammad!

Even more surprisingly, al-Suddī presents the complaint recipient not as Muḥammad, but as Abū Bakr, who then takes the complaint to Muḥammad. As al-Suddī preached in the highly charged sectarian environment of Umayyad-era Kufa, this mention of Abū Bakr would probably not have gone unnoticed. Abū Bakr seems to be an overtly political, proto-Sunni addition. The account presents Abū Bakr as Muḥammad's deputy, the one who follows the Prophet's *sunna* and upholds his decrees; the caliph is the intermediary between the Prophet and the *umma.* By extension, al-Suddī is perhaps indicating that the Umayyad caliphs of his own day are the ones who uphold and protect the *umma.* Perhaps al-Suddī's account was directed against the Shi'a, or it is also possible that it was directed against the proto-Sunni *ulamā'*, who were beginning to challenge the Umayyad caliphs for the authority to interpret doctrine and dictate law. In any case, the inclusion of Abū Bakr here is the most strikingly sectarian rendering of this verse. Later exegetes mostly ignore al-Suddī's melodrama and strip their traditions of any political overtones.

Muqātil's Tradition: Combined and Conflated

A third and final version of the Muʿādha account is transmitted by the Kufan exegete and storyteller, Muqātil ibn Sulaymān. His account is widely transmitted by later scholars, indicating that it served an enduring ideological purpose. Muqātil says:

> Do not compel your slave women (*walāʾid*) to fornication. This came down regarding ʿAbdallāh ibn Ubayy the Hyprocrite and his slave woman Umayma, and ʿAbdallāh ibn Nātil the Hypocrite and his slave woman Musayka, who was the daughter of Umayma. Among them also were Muʿādha, Arwā, ʿAmrā, and Qutayla. Umayma and her daughter Musayka came to the Messenger of God (s.a.w.), and she said: 'We are being compelled to fornicate.' So God Almighty revealed this verse.[35]

The most important new feature of Muqātil's account is the addition of Umayma, as well as the other women mentioned as an afterthought, 'also among them were Muʿādha, Arwā, ʿAmrā, and Qutayla'. Later exegetes often lump all six names into a simple list: 'This verse came down regarding six slave women belonging to ʿAbdallāh ibn Ubayy: Muʿādha, Musayka, Umayma, Qutayla, ʿAmrā, and Arwā.'[36] Muqātil seems to be responsible for introducing these extra names, as they appear in no other early sources. As for Umayma herself, her entire role in this story is as Musayka's mother (even her name, Umayma, means 'little mother'.) The mother–daughter story could serve one of several narrative purposes. Perhaps the audience is to understand that Umayma's daughter, Musayka, was under-age and needed her mother's protection against the depredations of immoral men. Perhaps the audience is supposed to wonder how Umayma and Musayka became separated, for in Islamic law a slave mother may often not be sold away from her child, who is automatically free-born.[37] In any case, Muqātil's story appears to add nothing historically reliable to the core tradition about a woman named Musayka who complained to the Anṣār. Instead, it appears to combine several different stories about several different women, conflating them all together. For Muqātil and those who transmit his account, it is the moral of the story, the symbolic upshot, that matters more than the individual identities of the women involved.

Bird's Eye View: From Women's Agency to Male Authority

If we turn away from close literary analysis and towards broad patterns of transmission, we can discern how different exegetes in different times and places conveyed different lessons in their accounts of the redeemed prostitute. For this analysis, I read twenty-one exegeses, in order to analyse which literary elements they highlight and which they downplay in their *asbāb al-nuzūl* for Q 24:33. In selecting these twenty-one exegeses, I was careful to include the earliest *tafsīrs*, such as those by ʿAbd al-Razzāq (d. 211/827), al-Qummī (fl. 3rd/9th c.), Hūd ibn Muḥakkam (fl. 3rd/9th c.), al-Nasāʾī and al-Ṭabarī. I was also careful to include classics in the genre, such as those by al-Wāḥidī (d. 468/1076), al-Zamakhsharī (d. 538/1144), al-Qurṭubī (567/1172), Fakhr al-Dīn al-Rāzī (d. 606/1209), Ibn Kathīr (d. 774/1373) and al-Jalālayn (al-Maḥallī, d. 864/1459; al-Suyūṭī, d. 911/1505). I then chose a sampling of other *tafsīrs* across time, place and sectarian affiliation, aiming for variety rather than comprehensiveness.[38] I provide here a brief survey of trends in the *tafsīrs* of Q 24:33, which can reveal how exegesis subtly morphed to meet new needs and speak to new audiences, even while preserving many of the same stories and building on older traditions. Particularly, I found that the earlier traditions tend to focus on the redeemed prostitute's individual agency, while later traditions tend to focus on how Muḥammad, male Muslims or Islam itself 'saves' fallen women.

The first and most common trend, which occurs in 22/55 (40 per cent) of the *asbāb al-nuzūl* traditions, focuses on the enslaved prostitute's personal agency. For instance, we saw in al-Zuhrī's account of Muʿādha above that

Muʿādha 'held back from him because of her Islam'. While sometimes the woman's refusal is presented in this rather passive way, in many accounts the woman directly and flatly says no to her master, sometimes in the highly unlikely (but satisfyingly pithy) phrase: 'If [prostitution] is good then I've done enough of it, and if it's bad then it's time for me to quit!'[39] Whenever the woman stands up for herself and refuses to continue serving as a prostitute, she is almost never depicted as asking Muḥammad or anyone else for help.[40] It is her decision to quit prostitution that matters and that is vindicated by the Quran. Perhaps more surprisingly, the woman in these accounts is only sometimes described as a Muslim. Her agency is not necessarily defined by her religion, as al-Māturīdī (d. 333/944) explains: 'This verse indicates that fornication is wrong in all religions.'[41] Instead, many sources imply that the reformed prostitute has an innately moral nature. For instance, Ibn Kathīr describes the woman as having 'no wrong in her' (*lā baʾsa bihā*), which is more about her moral character than her religious belief.[42] Al-Zamakhsharī likewise explains: 'No hint of unusual perversion can be found in Muʿādha and Musayka, so God will forgive them . . .'[43] This pronouncement is not about their Islam; it is about their sexual morality more broadly.

This highlighting of personal female agency is the most popular tactic overall, and it is especially the best-attested tactic among early, proto-Sunni transmitters of the second/eighth and third/ninth centuries (Mujāhid uses it in 1 out of 1 (1/1) of his traditions; ʿAbd al-Razzāq (3/3); and al-Ṭabarī (5/10).)[44] Perhaps these exegetes were addressing a society that was still majority non-Muslim, trying to convince non-Muslim women – especially enslaved women – to find both spiritual and bodily salvation through conversion. Perhaps these exegetes were subtly directing their words towards the elite courtesans of the Abbasid court, who were widely considered to be promiscuous. Or perhaps this version of Muʿādha is inspired by Christian stories of Mary Magdalene, proof that a fallen woman can be saved not just by Christianity but also by Islam. In any case, the woman in these accounts is anonymous and one-dimensional, and therefore flexible enough to stand in for any enslaved prostitute. If Muʿādha can choose chastity in her circumstances, then *anyone* can.

In the second most common trend, 17 out of 55 (31 per cent) of the accounts, the slave woman asks for help. We have already seen that in some early exegeses (such as those of al-Nasā'ī and al-Ṭabarī) the woman seeks help from an anonymous Anṣārī, but in the vast majority of accounts she instead asks for help from Muḥammad himself.[45] In these accounts, the woman does not speak up for herself or refuse her master's requests, and, once again, she is rarely identified as a Muslim. Perhaps she is simply assumed to be a Muslim, but ultimately it does not matter who she is – what matters is the position of Muḥammad as the protector of his community, the arbiter of justice and the recipient of divine revelation. This trend became especially prominent in the fifth–seventh/eleventh–thirteenth centuries: al-Ṭabarānī (2/2), al-Zamakhasharī (1/1), Fakhr al-Dīn (2/4), al-Qurṭubī (2/2) and al-Bayḍāwī (1/1) prefer this reading.[46] Perhaps these exegetes focused on Muḥammad's role because the field of hadith study – the study of Muḥammad's words – had become a canonical, authoritative field of scholarship by the fifth/eleventh century.[47] Similarly, perhaps exegetes were now more careful to ensure that their *asbāb al-nuzūl* traditions directly explained how the Quranic revelation worked, rather than simply providing details about pre- and early Islamic society.

Finally, the third most common trend (16 out of 55, 29 per cent) excises the woman's role almost entirely.[48] These texts retain the basic narrative of ʿAbdallāh ibn Ubayy's mistreating his slave, but they focus on the event of Quranic revelation instead of the woman's plight. For example, al-Wāḥidī says: 'ʿAbdallāh ibn Ubayy said to a slave of his, "Go and earn something for us by prostitution." So God revealed [this verse].' This erasure of the woman's story becomes common starting in the fourth–fifth/tenth–eleventh century. (Al-Ṭūsī (1/1), al-Wāḥidī (4/7), Ibn al-Jawzī (1/3), Ibn Kathīr (4/10), and *Tafsīr al-Jalalayn* (1/1) highlight this reading.) But the trend reaches its culmination in the eighth/fourteenth century with the *Tafsīr* of Ibn Kathīr, the most explicitly patriarchal of all the exegeses I surveyed. Ibn Kathīr glosses this verse in such a way as to give *male* Muslims the agency, as he explains: 'ʿAbdallāh ibn Ubayy had a slave woman (*jāriya*) called Muʿādha, and he forced her to fornication. When Islam came, God forbade the male believers (*al-mu'minūn*) from that.' Ibn Kathīr's focus is not on the woman's reaction to her unjust situation; it says nothing about what a slave woman should do *if* she was being prostituted against her will. Rather, it reminds male Muslims that they should not abuse their power over enslaved women. It seems that

Ibn Kathīr lived in a world where the patriarchal establishment regulated female sexual practices, such that he could not imagine that this verse should empower women instead of men.

Overall, it appears that the earlier exegetes focus more on the female characters in the story, while the later exegetes focus more on the male characters in the story, or strip the storytelling elements away to focus on the verse's legal core. These findings correspond with Asma Afsaruddin's study of biographical accounts of 'difficult' early Islamic women.[49] In her comparison of Ibn Saʿd's (d. 230/845) and Ibn Ḥajar's (d. 852/1449) biographies of Umm ʿUmara and Umm Waraqa, she finds that 'societal conceptions of women's agency and proper conduct in the public realm came to be progressively defined and restricted' by Ibn Ḥajar's time.[50] She shows that these biographers do not express these changing social expectations by inventing wildly new traditions about these women, but, rather, by subtly shifting the narrative focus, by selectively highlighting and omitting certain aspects of their biographies. Something similar seems to have happened in the realm of exegesis. What apparently began as a story about a mouthy woman refusing her master becomes a story about a woman seeking a more 'correct' form of recourse by seeking the Prophet Muḥammad's help, and eventually becomes about Islam's salvific power for women without acknowledging women's choices or actions at all.[51] No matter what lesson the exegetes highlight, however, they are never concerned to reconstruct first-/seventh-century history according to modern academic standards. Rather, they are concerned to present morality tales and edifying symbols of piety.

Moral Perversion and Victim Blaming: The Case of the 'Bad' Prostitute

On the one hand, it can be read as empowering that so many early exegetes highlight Muʿādha's agency. In this uplifting version of the tradition, God vindicates a lowly enslaved woman in her attempt to assert some control over her own body. These traditions recognise a remarkable level of individual, moral agency on the part of the enslaved woman, marking her as a full human and spiritual equal. However, the problem with this reading is that it treats agency simply as an internal, individual issue; it does not consider wider social pressures, power discrepancies or unjust systems that encourage sexual violence. Such traditions put the burden entirely on the slave woman herself to resist injustice, rather than exhorting free men to use their power to create more just systems.[52] Thus, the exegetes do not single out slave prostitution per se as being an unjust practice; it only becomes unjust when the slave woman in question 'desires chastity'. The implication is that any woman who continues as a prostitute must 'want' to be a prostitute and thus deserves whatever exploitation or injustice she experiences. Muʿādha might exhibit agency and morality, but she subtly condemns all other women who do not choose her path, no matter the injustice or violence of their social situations. And, indeed, we find precisely such a condemnation of 'bad' prostitutes in the historical and literary traditions, which completely ignore the figure of the reformed prostitute, and focus instead on the infamous, unredeemed, gleefully promiscuous reprobate.

These historical genres are not concerned with providing moral guidance for would-be Muslim women or explaining the ethical ramifications of the Quran. Rather, they are concerned with making sense of the early Islamic past by elaborating 'sites of memory' that give meaning to their own present identity as Muslims.[53] They use stock characters like the 'bad prostitute' to fill out these narratives. For example, authors such as Ibn ʿAbd Rabbih (d. 328/940) tell the story of Ẓulayma, a pre-Islamic Arabian prostitute who reportedly liked fornicating so much that even after she became too old to ply her trade, she made her pet goats copulate so that she could enjoy the sounds of their heavy breathing. Ẓulayma, which means 'the little unjust one', thereby becomes a caricature of pre-Islamic mores, and she draws a stark boundary between pre-Islamic and Islamic sexual ethics. Some modern scholars have unfortunately accepted the caricature of Ẓulayma as historically accurate, instead of reading her as a symbol with a specific narrative role to play.[54]

Similarly, several sources present Sumayya, the mother of Abū Bakra and Ziyād ibn Abīhi, as promiscuous and disgusting. In a graphic account, the Shii-leaning historian al-Masʿūdī (d. 345/956) explains: 'Abū Sufyān went to a wine-seller named Abū Maryam and asked for a prostitute. The wine seller said: "I have only Sumayya here." Abū Sufyān said: "I will take her, despite her drooping breasts, the stink of her armpits and her belly, and the stench of her breath."'[55] Later, this wine seller would testify that Abū Sufyān visited Sumayya despite her foulness, and that she emerged from the meeting dripping with semen. As a Shii-leaning author, al-Masʿūdī has a vested interest in denigrating Sumayya, as an oblique way of denigrating her son, Ziyād ibn Abīhi. Ziyād ibn Abīhi worked for the Umayyads, the house that had famously fought against the first Shii Imam, ʿAlī ibn Abī Ṭālib. Even more scandalously, Ziyād's son, ʿUbaydallāh, had orchestrated the slaughter of the third Shii Imam, al-Ḥusayn. Thus, Sumayya's sexual promiscuity does not merely represent her own moral failing, but also that of her son and grandson. Sumayya's real function in these sources is as a 'your mother' joke. She is not an individual in her own right, but a stand-in for the health of society, a barometer of injustice.

The sources barely speak about Sumayya as an individual, which makes it nigh impossible to reconstruct her history. However, when piecing together the tiny bits of her biography, it appears that the line between concubine and prostitute might have been quite thin for her. Al-Balūdhurī's *Ansāb al-Ashrāf* implies that Sumayya began her career as the concubine of her master, al-Ḥārith ibn Kalada. When al-Ḥārith wondered whether he was really the father of Sumayya's son Nufayʿ (Abū Bakra), an unnamed informant reportedly told him: 'Your slave woman is a source of doubt: she does not repel a groper's hand' (*inna jāriyataka dhāt rība: lā tadfaʿu kaff lāmis*).[56] It appears here that Sumayya was not yet a prostitute, for presumably neither al-Ḥārith nor this informant would *expect* a prostitute to refuse a 'groper's' proposition. After Nufayʿ's birth, it seems that al-Ḥārith made Sumayya work as a prostitute – whether as punishment for her transgression, or simply as a way of capitalising on her 'skills', one cannot know. However, it also seems that the difference between concubine and prostitute mattered very little to Sumayya, as an enslaved woman who had almost no sexual or bodily agency.[57] Certainly, we never get her side of the story.

This euphemism, 'She does not repel a groper's hand', is all too resonant in the twenty-first century; it is an underhanded, understated way to blame Sumayya for her own victimisation. And it shows the danger of speaking about slave prostitutes only in terms of individual agency. The 'groper' here is not blamed for groping. In fact, it almost seems assumed that the hand will grope, and that it is a woman's responsibility to repel the ever-present fondler. While the informant in this account apparently expects Sumayya to reject sexual advances, he does not even begin to interrogate how difficult it might have been for her to do so or to consider the costs she would have had to pay. Unlike Musayka and Abat, who experienced the radical transformations of early Islamic Medina, Sumayya lived in no such remarkable context. She lived in al-Taif, where she was owned by a master who reportedly impregnated her, married her off to another slave and pimped her out as a prostitute. The stakes for saying 'no' – especially to a powerful nobleman like Abū Sufyān – must have been high for a woman like Sumayya. There is a wider systematic injustice happening to Sumayya that the historians and exegetes ignore. Instead of praising good Muʿādhas and condemning bad Sumayyas, historians must unpack wider social contexts and seek examples of complex, dynamic women who navigated their situations to the best of their abilities.

Where are the Enslaved Prostitutes?

Scholars have previously noted that Arabic-Islamic sources discuss enslaved women more frequently than they do free women. These scholars have suggested that free women were private and taboo, to be kept behind closed doors and not even exposed to the public gaze on the pages of texts. While this interpretation is likely valid, it does not explain why the sources speak so much more about many other kinds of enslaved women – concubines, courtesans, chamberlains, even domestic servants – than they speak about prostitutes. Prostitutes are marginal and fairly difficult to find in the sources; even using searchable databases such as al-Jāmiʿ al-Kabīr, the results are meagre.[58] This silence may partly be due to the 'unseemly' nature of prostitutes. But I suggest that prostitutes are also mostly ignored because they are so easily excluded as 'other';[59] this is in contrast to other types of slaves, particularly concubines and courtesans, who forced Muslim scholars to grapple with what it meant to be Arab and Muslim. Prostitutes caused no such hand-wringing from the scholars. Instead, the sources associate prostitutes with pre-Islamic Arabia, and with travel and warfare in foreign lands – prostitutes represent memories of the distant past, or transitional moments that breach normal expectations.[60] Prostitutes were women to be decried, used or saved, but they did not challenge scholars' sense of where the Islamic community's boundary lay.

For instance, the geographer Yāqūt al-Ḥamawī (d. 626/1229) recounts the story of ʿUqayshir ('little scabby'), who was travelling to Syria to fight in the Second Civil War (60–73/680–92). On the way, ʿUqayshir stopped in an Iraqi village called Qubbīn and stayed with a Nabatean wine seller 'whose wife traded in sex' (*tabdhulu zawjatuhu al-fujūr*).[61] In Qubbīn, he sold his riding beast and spent the money, presumably enjoying the Nabatean's wife, until the army caught up with him. He later composed this poem:

> I went out from the garrison, a disciple of his people,
> without intention of gain or pay,
> to the army of the people of Syria. I was reluctantly
> equipped, foolishly without an iron sword or blade.
> But there is a hopeless contradiction in a sword which
> has no feud, or a spear with a weak tip.
> Al-Qubbāʿ's injustice dragged me along with it,
> and I had to follow his orders and set out.
> I set upon my course and became a warrior, and I gave
> the greeting of the warriors to my people.
> My steed was a bent-backed donkey, bearing the
> marks of water-skins and ropes.
> We visited Qubbīn day and night, like some prostitutes
> visiting a client.

ʿUqayshir, presumably reluctant to fight against his own *umma* during a time of devastating civil war, instead seeks refuge in a Nabatean village. The Nabatean barkeeper and his wife are almost certainly meant to be Christians. Thus, the prostitution of the Nabatean's wife is not a Muslim problem – it is rather a moral failing of the Iraqi Christians. A Muslim would only encounter such a figure during times of *fitna* or while travelling in the countryside. In short, prostitution was a transitional, temporary practice that merited no great social attention.

However, their marginality should not lead us to believe that enslaved prostitutes were unimportant to early Islamic history. They did change society in a way that apparently escaped the grasp of the exegetes, biographers and storytellers. They changed it obliquely through the act of motherhood. According to Uri Rubin, early Islamic lawyers adopted the 'child belongs to the owner of the bed' paternity dictum to accommodate the perceived promiscuity of enslaved women like Sumayya.[62] It may even have been in response to Ziyād ibn Abīhi's situation specifically that Islamic lawyers determined that a slave woman's child should be attributed to her husband (if she had one) or her master. Thus, women like Sumayya helped shape Islamic society by impelling legal protections for the children of enslaved mothers.

Conclusion

Scholars today are not doing their job if they uncritically accept the medieval sources' dichotomy between good and bad slave prostitutes, or if they uncritically accept the idea that such women make a simple, individual choice between morality and immorality. Such ideas reflect the worldviews of the free, male authors who wrote our sources. These authors tended not to interrogate the unjust systems of their own making, and they instead passed the responsibility on to the enslaved women who participated in those systems. However, it is important to note that the earliest Islamic sources, when read carefully, appear to grapple with such tensions and to acknowledge the difficulties that enslaved prostitutes faced. These early accounts reveal a brief irruption of enslaved prostitutes' voices in first-/seventh-century Medina; these voices do not present a dichotomy between 'good' versus 'bad' women, but rather offer different strategies for challenging unjust structures during a time of tremendous social upheaval. By interpreting Q 24:33 in ways that allowed them to escape prostitution and protect their own chastity, enslaved women helped negotiate the contours of the earliest *umma*.

Notes

1. A few works of secondary scholarship mention prostitutes from early Islamic history, but none of them focus on the topic. See particularly Abdelwahab Bouhdiba, *Sexuality in Islam*, 187–195; Nadia M. El Cheikh, 'Describing the Other to Get at the Self', 239–250; Camilo Álvarez de Morales, 'Transgresiones sexuales en el Islam medieval'; and most recently Gary Leiser, *Prostitution in the Eastern Mediterranean World*, especially chapter 2. I was excited to read a recent Arabic article on the topic, Salameh al-Naimat and Aysha al-Sweidat, 'Al-Bighā' 'inda al-ʿArab qabla al-Islām'. However, this article is disappointingly descriptive rather than analytical. It mines several Arabic primary sources, such as Ibn

ʿAbd Rabbih's *Al-Iqd al-Farīd*, for references to prostitution, but it applies no critical apparatus to these sources.

2. Baber Johansen has shown that Hanafi theorists treat female slaves as a separate genus of humanity, different from both free women and male slaves. The female slave's raison d'être is 'concubinage, and bearing children for their masters'. Johansen, 'The Valorization of the Human Body', 83–84.
3. I take this felicitous turn of phrase from Matthew Gordon, 'Introduction', 1.
4. Scholars of early Islam have access to a few papyri and other documents that mention women, but we do not have anything like the Cairo Geniza or the archives of Ottoman history.
5. On the differences between women's history and feminist history, see Jill Matthews, 'Feminist History'. Unfortunately, some Arabic scholarship produced in the Middle East falls into the former category. See, for instance, Al-Naimat and al-Sweidat, 'Al-Bighā'', and the sources cited therein; see also Buthayna Bin Husayn, *Nisā' al-Khulafā' al-Umawīyīn*. Such sources tend more towards thorough description than critical analysis. While such works are still immensely valuable, their contribution would be even greater if they interrogated the narrative strategies of their primary sources.
6. See, for example, Denise A. Spellberg, *Politics, Gender, and the Islamic Past*, which suggests that scholars cannot hope to reconstruct an accurate, objective biography of the Prophet Muḥammad's wife ʿĀ'isha. Instead, Spellberg studies the shaping of ʿĀ'isha's 'legacy' in later Sunni and Shii sources, who present ʿĀ'isha as a hero and a villain, respectively.
7. For a foundational example of scholarship on early Islamic gender roles, see Julia Bray, 'Men, Women and Slaves in Abbasid Society'. Bray has shown that the romantic trope of the enslaved courtesan who 'enslaves' her own master with infatuation is caught up in male authors' changing notions of masculinity. In the Abbasid period, free Arab men felt both subordinated and feminised by working mundane government jobs for an autocratic caliph. To regain some sense of masculine individuality, Abbasid men fantasised about romantic love with slave poetesses. They also highlighted the trope of the slave woman enslaving her master to enact their own fantasy of turning the tables on the autocratic power structures that rendered them subservient. Bray thus reminds her readers that historical texts are not transparent or innocent; they must be read with careful attention to authorship and audience.
8. Gisela Bock, 'Women's History and Gender History', 17–18.
9. Narrative shaping and hegemonic narratives are always problems for the

historian. However, scholars of early Islamic history can interrogate and compare sources that have, say, a Sunni bias versus a Shii bias, because we have representatives of both schools. Because we *only* have representatives of a 'male' school of historical thought, we cannot easily cross-reference our sources to discover other perspectives.

10. Aziz Al-Azmeh, *Arabic Sources*, 5.
11. As Judith Bennett says, 'Women have always been both victims and agents' (Judith Bennett, 'Feminism and History', 262). Bennett also reminds us that 'agency' does not always mean to choose equality, freedom, or resistance – women often *choose* to participate in and support unequal power structures. (Saba Mahmood also reminds us of this fact in *Politics of Piety*, 5–10.)
12. Bennett, 'Feminism and History', 251–272.
13. Ehud R. Toledano, 'Understanding Enslavement as a Human Bond', Chapter 1 in *As if Silent and Absent: Bonds of Enslavement in the Islamic Middle East*, 35–36. As Toledano says, '"Actions speak louder than words" will be an essential concept and motto in our working space' (*ibid.*, 36).
14. Bock, 'Women's History and Gender History'.
15. I employ this methodology in the next chapter of this monograph.
16. Asma Sayeed, *Women and the Transmission of Religious Knowledge in Islam*, 43.
17. On the meaning and development of *asbāb al-nuzūl*, see Andrew Rippin, 'The Exegetical Genre *Asbāb Al-Nuzūl*' and 'The Function of *Asbāb Al-Nuzūl* in Qurʾānic Exegesis'; and Hans-Thomas Tillschneider, 'Les *Asbāb an-Nuzūl*: Une Branche de La Tradition Prophétique'. This last article is a digest of Tillschneider's German doctoral thesis.
18. See Chapter 2 of this monograph for a detailed analysis of this verse, and for an explanation of this translation.
19. I argue in more detail for the authenticity of this Ibn Jurayj transmission, as opposed to a more embellished tradition transmitted by al-Aʿmash, in Urban, 'A Tale of Two Prostitutes', *Arabica* (forthcoming).
20. Al-Nasāʾī, *Tafsīr al-Nasāʾī,* 2:123–124; al-Ṭabarī, *Jāmiʿ al-Bayān,* 17:291; Sulaymān ibn al-Ashʿath al-Sijistānī Abū Dāʾūd, *Sunan*, 2:294.
21. Al-Ṭabarī, *Jāmiʿ al-Bayān,* 17:290.
22. *Ibid.*, 17:291.
23. There are many versions of this Musayka tradition where ʿAbdallāh ibn Ubayy and Muḥammad have been added. But the fact that it exists in three separate traditions without these suspicious names speaks for the authenticity of this pared-down version. It is worth mentioning that all three of these more authen-

tic-seeming accounts are transmitted from Ibn Jurayj, from Abū al-Zubayr, from Jābir ibn ʿAbdallāh. Many of the more suspicious traditions have different chains of transmission, supposedly coming from people like ʿIkrima. For more details on the analyses of the different traditions with their different chains, see Urban, 'A Tale of Two Prostitutes'.

24. Musayka's name seems particularly authentic when compared to Muʿādha, whose name is Islamic and probably symbolic. See S. D. Goitein, 'Slaves and Slavegirls in the Cairo Geniza Records', for slave names in medieval Islamic history. Slave names are often either objects or physical descriptors – things like 'dinar', 'goldy', 'arsenic', 'happy' and 'bamboo'.
25. Tillschneider has suggested that when the *asbāb al-nuzūl* material stands alone with little narrative connection to the Quranic verse – that is, when the Quranic verse is tacked on at the end, essentially as an excuse for introducing the historical reference – the material is more likely to preserve early historical information. Tillschneider, 'Les *Asbāb al-Nuzūl*', 177–178.
26. Mujāhid's '*tafsīr*' has been reconstructed based on the transmission of Mujāhid's accounts in al-Ṭabarī's *Jāmiʿ al-Bayān*. For a detailed analysis of Mujāhid's exegetical style and the transmission of his ideas, see Claude Gilliot, 'Mujāhid's Exegesis'.
27. Al-Ṭabarī, *Jāmiʿ al-Bayān*, 17:294.
28. *Ibid.*, 17:293. ʿAbd al-Razzāq provides a similar account on the authority of the Kufan transmitter al-Shaʿbī, rather than Mujāhid: 'ʿAbdallāh ibn Ubayy had Muʿādha and Musayka, and he sent one of them to prostitute herself. She earned a cloak, and he wanted her to do it again, but she refused. Forgiveness came down for them despite him.' ʿAbd al-Razzāq, *Tafsīr Al-Qurʾān*, 22:59–60. I suggest elsewhere that ʿAbd al-Razzāq's transmission from al-Shaʿbī is less likely to be authentic than al-Ṭabarī's transmission from Mujāhid. See Urban, 'A Tale of Two Prostitutes'.
29. The gloss of '*fatayāt*' as '*walāʾid*' is characteristic of Mujāhid's paraphrastic style. See Claude Gilliot, 'The Beginnings of Qur'anic Exegesis', 13–14. While Gilliot argues that 'pseudo-historical' material was later added to this earliest paraphrastic core of exegesis (20–21), I find it telling that the historical material attached to Mujāhid's account is substantially different from the narratives attached to later accounts (such as those of al-Zuhrī and Muqātil). That is, perhaps the material attached to this early, paraphrastic exegesis is not so 'pseudo' after all. Perhaps it is the later, more narrativizing exegetes, whose accounts are more historically suspect.

30. See Leiser, *Prostitution*, Chapter 1. Leiser later states, 'It is striking that there is nothing in early Arabic Muslim literature that is remotely comparable to the edifying Christian stories of holy harlots – or even tales of women who had committed "fornication," seen the error of their ways and then had become virtuous examples to others' (Leiser, *Prostitution,* 85). While this statement may hold true for most genres of Arabic-Islamic historical literature, it fails to take into account the *asbāb al-nuzūl* genre, which presents precisely such tales of reformed 'holy harlots'. Moreover, Rkia Cornell has argued that Rabiʿah al-ʿAdawiyyah functions precisely as such a 'reformed harlot' in many Sufi narratives of her life (Rkia Cornell, 'Rabiʿah al-ʿAdawiyyah', 292–298.)
31. ʿAbd al-Razzāq, *Tafsīr al-Qurʾān,* 2:59; al-Ṭabarī, *Jāmiʿ al-Bayān,* 17:292. A shorter variation of this account is also given in the *tafsīr* of the Ibadi exegete Hūd ibn Muḥakkam al-Hawwārī: 'This came down regarding the slave woman of ʿAbdallāh ibn Ubayy ibn Salūl whom he compelled to [have sex with] a man from Quraysh, hoping that she would bear his child and he would ransom his child' (Hūd ibn Muḥakkam Al-Hawwārī, *Tafsīr Kitāb Allāh al-ʿAzīz,* 3:179).
32. In my forthcoming 'A Tale of Two Prostitutes', I suggest that the original narrative contains no element of violence. The reading 'he hit her' seems to stem from a mis-reading of the Arabic term *ḍaraba,* which can mean 'to hit', but more likely in this context meant 'to charge a fee'.
33. Al-Suddī, *Tafsīr Al-Suddī Al-Kabīr,* 361.
34. On the practice of providing slave women for guests to enjoy in Safavid Iran, see Rudi Matthee, 'Prostitutes, Courtesans, and Dancing Girls: Women Entertainers in Safavid Iran'.
35. Muqātil ibn Sulaymān, *Tafsīr Muqātil ibn Sulaymān,* 3:198.
36. Abū al-Faraj ʿAbd al-Raḥmān ibn ʿAlī Ibn al-Jawzī, *Zād Al-Masīr,* 5:381. See also al-Rāzī, *Al-Tafsīr al-Kabīr,* 23:220; al-Zamakhsharī, *Al-Kashshāf,* 3:233; and al-Ṭabarānī, *Al-Tafsīr al-Kabīr,* 4:432.
37. Islamic law has a special category for the slave woman who bears a child for her master. She becomes a 'mother of a child' (*umm walad*), with the following general rights: 1) She cannot be sold away. 2) She is automatically freed upon the death of her master. 3) Her child is considered freeborn and legitimate. For more on this category, see Chapter 5.
38. In alphabetical order by author's last name, the exegeses I consulted are: ʿAbd al-Razzāq's *Tafsīr*; al-Bayḍāwī's *Tafsīr*; Fakhr al-Dīn al-Rāzī's *Al-Tafsīr al-Kabīr*; Hawwārī's *Tafsīr*; Ibn al-Jawzī's *Zād Al-Masīr*; Ibn Kathīr's *Tafsīr*; al-Maḥallī and al-Suyūṭī's *Tafsīr al-Jalālayn*; Makkī ibn Abī Ṭālib's *Tafsīr*; al-Māturīdī's

Tafsīr; Mujāhid ibn Jabr's *Tafsīr*; Muqātil ibn Sulaymān's *Tafsīr Muqātil ibn Sulaymān*; al-Nasā'is *Tafsīr*; al-Qummī's *Tafsīr Al-Qummī*; al-Qurṭubī's *Al-Jāmiʿ Li-Aḥkām Al-Qur'ān*; al-Shawkānī's *Fatḥ al-Qadīr*; al-Suddī's *Tafsīr Al-Suddī Al-Kabīr*; al-Ṭabarānī's *Al-Tafsīr Al-Kabīr*; al-Ṭabarī's *Jāmiʿ al-Bayān*; al-Ṭūsī's *al-Tibyān*; al-Wāḥidī's *Asbāb al-Nuzūl*; and al-Zamakhsharī's *al-Kashshāf*. I also consulted several other exegeses that did not contain any further information on this passage of Q 24:33, which I have left off this list.

39. ʿAbd al-Razzāq, *Tafsīr*, 22:59–60; al-Ṭabarī, *Jāmiʿ al-Bayān*, 17:291; al-Ṭabarānī, *Al-Tafsīr Al-Kabīr*, 4:432; al-Wāḥidī, *Asbāb Al-Nuzūl*, 220; Ibn al-Jawzī, *Zād Al-Masīr*, 5:381.
40. There is only one exception to this rule, a wildly composite account found in al-Wāḥidī's *Asbāb al-Nuzūl* (and erroneously attributed to Muqātil ibn Sulaymān) that compiles as many names and themes as possible into one account: 'This verse came down regarding six slaves of ʿAbdallāh ibn Ubayy's, whom he used to force to fornicate and took their wages. They were Muʿādha, Musayka, Umayma, ʿAmrā, ʿArwā and Qutayla. One of them came that day with a dinar and another came with a cloak. He said to them, go back and fornicate some more. They said, "By God, we won't do it. God has brought us Islam and made fornication unlawful." So they came to the Messenger of God (s.a.w.) and complained to him, and God revealed this verse.' Al-Wāḥidī, *Asbāb Al-Nuzūl*, 220.
41. Al-Māturīdī, *Tafsīr Al-Qur'ān Al-ʿAẓīm, Al-Musammá, Ta'wīlāt Ahl Al-Sunna*, 3:461–462.
42. Ibn Kathīr, *Tafsīr Al-Qur'ān Al-ʿAẓīm*, 10:232.
43. Al-Zamakhsharī, al-*Kashshāf*, 3:233.
44. The trend continues into the fourth/tenth and fifth/eleventh centuries with al-Ṭabarānī 1/2; Makkī ibn Abī Ṭālib 1/1; Ibn al-Jawzī 1/3; Fakhr al-Dīn 1/3; Ibn Kathīr 4/10.
45. The only exegete after al-Ṭabarī who presents an account where the woman complains to 'someone' instead of Muḥammad is Fakhr al-Dīn al-Rāzī, *Al-Tafsīr al-Kabīr*, 23:220.
46. Although this reading was always popular: al-Suddī 1/1; Muqātil 1/1; al-Nasā'ī 1/1; al-Ṭabarī 3/10; Fakhr al-Dīn 1/3.
47. On the canonisation of al-Bukhārī's and Muslim's *Ṣaḥīḥayn* in the fourth/tenth century, see Jonathan Brown, *The Canonization of Al-Bukhari and Muslim*.
48. Anyone keeping track of the numbers will realise that there are three texts left unaccounted for. The remaining three texts are vague descriptions of the

jāhiliyya period, found usually in non-Sunni texts. For instance, the Ibadi Hūd ibn al-Muḥakkam writes: 'Men used to force their slave woman (*mamlūka*) to prostitution in order to increase her children.' Likewise, the Shii al-Qummī writes, 'In the *jāhiliyya* they used to force their slave women to fornication, and they took their wages, so God revealed [this verse].' These accounts do not contain stories about individual enslaved prostitutes at all.

49. Asma Afsaruddin, 'Literature, Scholarship, and Piety'.
50. *Ibid.*, 117.
51. It is important to note here that Asma Sayeed has found an opposite trend in hadith transmission – women are cut out in the third/ninth century, but play huge role by the eighth/fourteenth (Sayeed, *Women and the Transmission of Religious Knowledge*). These exegeses do not tell us the entire story about women's participation or women's roles in Islamic society on a grand scale. The restriction of women's stories happening in my exegetical accounts particularly concerns women as arbiters of their own sexual ethics, and their ability to boldly stand up to their own oppressors – they tell us nothing about whether women can be hadith transmitters or contribute to society in other ways.
52. Ibn Kathīr's reading seems to exhort men to uphold justice; however, the flip side is that he does not seem to recognise female agency.
53. On the concept of 'sites of memory', see Pierre Nora, *Les Lieux De Mémoire.* This concept has been adopted with great effect into the study of early Islamic historical narratives. See Antoine Borrut, *Entre mémoire et pouvoir;* and Sarah Bowen Savant, *The New Muslims of Post-Conquest Iran.*
54. Ibn ʿAbd Rabbih, *Al-ʿIqd al-Farīd,* 3:71–72. The uncritical portrayal of Ẓulayma is one of the many problems with Al-Naimat and Al-Sweidat's 'Al-Bighā''.
55. Al-Masʿūdi, *Murūj al-Dhahab,* ed. Charles Pellat, 3:193. The seventh-/thirteeth--century Shii author Ibn Ṭiqṭaqā repeats this story (Muḥammad ibn ʿAlī Ibn Ṭiqṭaqā, *Al-Fakhrī fī al-Ādāb al-Sulṭāniyya wa-l-Duwal al-Islāmiyya*, 109–110).
56. Al-Balādhurī, *Ansāb al-Ashrāf,* 1:580. According to a hadith found in the *Sunans* of al-Nasā'ī and Abū Dā'ūd (but denounced by Aḥmad ibn Ḥanbal as weak), a man reportedly came to Muḥammad to complain that his wife 'does not repel a groper's hand'. Muḥammad first advised him to divorce her, but upon the man's protestation that he would miss her, the prophet then reportedly told him that he could continue to enjoy his wife, despite her promiscuity. (Abū Dāʾūd, *Sunan*, 2:220 (hadith #2,049); al-Nasā'ī, *Sunan,* 4:257 (hadith #3,494).)
57. The difference may also have mattered little to the *qiyān.*
58. For example, the search term '*baghāya*' (prostitutes) results in twenty-one hits

in History works, and fourteen hits in Biography. By way of comparison, the term '*jawārī*' (slave girls) results in 234 hits in History and 316 in Biography; the term '*qiyān*' (courtesans) results in thirty-two hits in History and eighty-four in Biography (and the singular *qayna* produces a few hundred more hits). The algorithm is not able to do a multi-term search for '*umm walad*', but my own human brain calculates that the results are in the several hundreds, if not thousands.

59. El-Cheikh, 'Describing the Other to Get at the Self' likewise finds that Arab-Muslim sources treat prostitution as a Christian problem.
60. Gary Leiser, *Prostitution*, also argues that prostitution was associated with travelling merchants and soldiers garrisoned away from home.
61. Yāqūt ibn ʿAbdallāh al-Ḥamawī, *Muʿjam al-Buldān*, 4:309.
62. Rubin, 'Al-walad li-l-firāsh'.

5

Concubines and their Sons: The Changing Political Notion of Arabness

Unlike prostitutes, who are mostly marginalised in the source material, concubine-mothers (*umm walads*) are ubiquitous; they lurk behind the scenes as nameless mothers and take centre stage as queens. The sources had to acknowledge concubines because they were contributing so much to Islamic society – in this case, they were contributing children, and particularly sons.[1] Concubine-mothers and their sons must be viewed together, for questions regarding the son's position in society are tied to the mother's identity, and the mother herself gains a special status by bearing children. Mothers and sons are also connected in terms of changing political ideologies: the rise of the concubine-born caliph in the mid-second/eighth century is soon accompanied by the rise of the powerful concubine-queen. Thus, in this chapter, I analyse enslaved mothers and their sons together in order to elucidate how social identities and political ideologies were changing in the Umayyad period. First, I trace changing rates of concubinage and concubines' birth-rates across a large data set, in order to reveal the underlying demographic trends that were impelling social and political change. Second, I closely read historical narratives that first highlight the liminality or questionable status of 'mixed-breed' children born to enslaved mothers, and then resolve this tension by championing such children as true Muslims and full Arabs.

Based on these two forms of analysis, I argue that questions about the identity of concubine-born men only arose in the Marwanid period (64–132/684–749), not earlier. Muslim men had used concubines from the first decades of Islam and showed no concern to keep their bloodlines 'pure'. It was not until the Marwanid period that large numbers of these children began to attain adulthood and to make a marked impact on early Islamic society. Scholars have long noted that the Marwanid caliph ʿAbd al-Malik (r. 65–86/685–705) instituted many centralising, empire-building reforms that strongly defined the caliphate as Arab and Muslim. Scholars have viewed these reforms as ʿAbd al-Malik's attempt to gain control after the Great Fitna (60–72/680–692), to bolster the religious legitimacy of the Umayyad caliphs, and to distinguish the conqueror-elites from the conquered populations (especially Christians). However, it is also during this time of contraction, of more strictly defining and controlling the boundaries of the Islamic polity, that some people seemed to have questioned the place of concubines' children. These questions about the status of concubines' children should not be viewed as prejudice against non-Arabs or Arab chauvinism, but simply as grappling with the grey areas and fuzzy boundaries of a community that was seeking to define itself more clearly. In order to be embraced as full insiders, concubines' children first had to demonstrate that they were true Muslims, loyal to the Islamic empire and knowledgeable in religious lore. Next, in order to gain political power as caliphs, concubines' children had to re-define themselves as full 'Arabs'. To do so, they dismissed their mothers as essentially inconsequential, and they justified this dismissal by invoking paradigmatic examples of enslaved mothers from the Islamic religious tradition. Their language captures a pivotal moment in Islamic history, when concubine-mothers became intimately entwined in rhetoric about political legitimacy and Arab lineage. By viewing how powerful men spoke about their enslaved mothers, we discover that women not only shaped early Islamic political institutions, but also affected the very ideologies that underlay those institutions.

Part One: Prosopography of Early Islamic Concubinage

As discussed in the previous chapter, one way to overcome the difficulties of the early Islamic source material is to engage in prosopography – to trace trends in groups by amassing large data sets, rather than focusing on individual narrative accounts.[2] Prosopography is valuable because it can reveal historical trends that run deeper than the level of an individual text, author or school of thought. It provides a big-picture, trans-historical overview of the 'slow simmer' of social change, against which to contextualise narrative accounts about specific people or events of early Islamic history.[3]

Two recent works of prosopography have particularly inspired this chapter. Asad Q. Ahmed's analysis of five elite families of the early Islamic Hijaz reveals how important cognate (maternal) tribal ties were to early Islamic politics.[4] Ahmed also shows that these cognate ties not only linked people with their own mothers' clans, but also with the clans of their maternal grandmothers, as well as with their uterine brothers (half-siblings through the mother) and *their* mother's clans. That is, cognate ties did not form a single, straight branch of a family tree, but a dense shrubbery of connections. Additionally, Majied Robinson has analysed al-Zubayrī's (d. ca. 235/850) *Nasab Quraysh* (The Genealogy of Quraysh) to reveal trends in early Islamic concubinage.[5] He shows that Muslims – including the Umayyads – practised concubinage from the very beginning of the Islamic conquests, and that there was no apparent prejudice against bearing children from enslaved women. He likewise finds that the 'late emergence of the concubine-born caliph was not a result of discrimination, but a consequence of structural changes to the network of relationships which constituted the Muslim polity'.[6]

In this section, I complement Ahmed's and Robinson's prosopographical analyses by exploring concubinage practices in Ibn Saʿd's (d. 230/845) *Al-Ṭabaqāt al-Kubrā*. I find that the height of concubinage occurs in the fourth generation of Muslims, or roughly the late Marwanid period. I also find that concubinage is a more dynamic practice than marriage – more liable to fluctuate depending on historical circumstances. Finally, I find that the Hāshim clan of Quraysh relied the most heavily on concubinage, and it appears to have embraced the practice of concubinage earlier than other clans. The following analysis draws out the ramifications of these findings for early Islamic society, politics and law.

The Source: Ibn Saʿd's Ṭabaqāt

Several criteria recommend Ibn Saʿd's *al-Ṭabaqāt al-Kubrā* for prosopographical research.[7] First, it was penned sometime in the early third/ninth century, making it a relatively early source. Second, its roughly chronological organisation into *ṭabaqat*, or generations, makes it convenient for historical analysis. It is easier to trace change over time in Ibn Saʿd's *Ṭabaqāt* than, for instance, al-Balādhurī's (d. 278/892) massive, mostly tribally organised *Ansāb al-Ashrāf*. Third, it provides fairly extensive genealogical information for many of its entries. Unlike Ibn al-Kalbī's (d. 204/819) *Jamharat al-Nasab* (Compendium of Genealogy), for instance, which often only lists people's prominent male offspring, Ibn Saʿd lists all known offspring. Finally, unlike works that only trace the genealogies of Quraysh, such as al-Zubayrī's *Nasab Quraysh*, Ibn Saʿd also traces the lineages of the Anṣār, and a few tribes allied with Quraysh or the Anṣār. As such, his work allows for at least some comparison of tribal practice.

However, Ibn Saʿd's *Ṭabaqāt* is not a perfect source. Despite its wide geographical coverage, it unfortunately only provides complete genealogical information for people who lived in Medina.[8] Additionally, it only mentions genealogical information for Quraysh and the Anṣār, making it impossible to extend the analysis to other Arabian tribes. Finally, Ibn Saʿd focuses almost entirely on hadith transmitters and legal scholars, excluding the genealogies of more secular warriors, aristocrats and politicians.[9] His work does not paint a sharp image of all Muslims in the early Islamic empire, but an incomplete and impressionistic image of the religio-tribal elites of Medina. Nevertheless, these impressionistic insights help scholars better understand the deep currents of social change that underlie early Islamic history.

Structuring the Data

Ibn Saʿd organises his work around 'generations', which are technically levels of hadith transmission. Generation one comprises the Ṣaḥābīs (Companions) who knew Muḥammad. Generation two includes people who transmitted from one of Muḥammad's oldest Companions, and generation three includes people who transmitted from a younger Companion or child of a Companion.[10] Generations four, five and six include people who transmitted from the previous generations. However, the exact chronology of these generations is unclear. For instance, someone from the first generation of Companions might have been ten years old, or seventy years old, when Muḥammad began his career. Likewise, Ibn Saʿd does not provide death dates for many of his entries, making it impossible to provide clear parameters for the beginning and end of each generation. In order to make the chronological analysis possible, I have delineated each generation using a representative range of death dates (see Table 5.1).[11] These generations have porous boundaries and overlap to some degree, and this scheme should be taken as a general guideline rather than a perfectly accurate chronometer.

Table 5.1 Generational scheme derived from Ibn Saʿd's Ṭabaqāt

Generation **Approx. dates**	**One** **630–680** CE	**Two** **680–700** CE	**Three** **700–720** CE	**Four** **720–740** CE	**Five** **740–760** CE	**Six** **760–790** CE
Examples of entries from this Generation	Muḥammad ibn ʿAbdallāh, d. 632; ʿUthmān ibn ʿAffān, d. 656	Saʿīd ibn al-ʿĀṣ, d. 679; Muḥammad Ibn al-Hanafiyya, d. 700	ʿUrwa ibn al-Zubayr, d. 713; al-Qāsim ibn Muḥammad, d. 727	Muḥammad ibn ʿAlī al-Bāqir, d. 733; Muḥammad ibn Ibrāhīm, d. 738	al-Ḥārith ibn ʿAbd al-Raḥmān, d. 745; Hishām ibn ʿUrwa, d. 763	Muḥammad ibn ʿAbdallāh, d. 762; ʿUbaydallāh ibn ʿUmar, d. 789
Major events of this Generation	Muḥammad; Rāshidūn caliphs; First Fitna	Sufyanids; Second Fitna	Marwanids I: ʿAbd al-Malik	Marwanids II: Hishām ibn ʿAbd al-Malik	Third Fitna; Abbasid Revolution	Early Abbasids: al-Manṣūr and al-Mahdī

Table 5.2 Database categories

Entry #	**Generation**	**Name** including father's name	**Mother's name**	**Tribe** (and mother's tribe)	**Total # of children**	**# Children from free wives** (FWs)	**# Children from *umm walads*** (UWs)	**# of FWs**	**# of UWs**

Table 5.3 Sample database entry

#	**Generation**	**Name**	**Mother's name**	**Tribe** (mother's tribe)	**Total # children**	**# Children from FWs**	**# Children from UWs**	**# FWs**	**# UWs**
662	2	Saʿīd ibn Saʿd ibn ʿUbāda	Ghuzayya bint Saʿd ibn Khalīfa	Khazraj (Khazraj)	15	9	6	2	4.5

For each of Ibn Saʿd's entries on the people of Medina, I entered the following information into a database (see Table 5.2).[12] To help illustrate this method, I provide here a typical example of an Ibn Saʿd entry, translated into a database entry (see Table 5.3). I have added bold font to guide the reader.

> **#662:** **<u>Saʿīd ibn Saʿd ibn ʿUbāda</u>** ibn Dulaym ibn Ḥāritha ibn Abī Ḥazīma ibn Thaʿlaba ibn Ṭarīf ibn al-Khazraj ibn Sāʿida ibn Kaʿb ibn **Khazraj. His mother is Ghuzayya bint Saʿd** ibn Khalīfa ibn al-Ashraf ibn Abī Ḥazīma ibn Thaʿlaba ibn Ṭarīf ibn al-Khazraj ibn Sāʿida ibn Kaʿb ibn **Khazraj. Saʿīd ibn Saʿd bore Shuraḥbīl, Khālid, Ismāʿīl, Zakariyyā', Muḥammad, ʿAbd al-Raḥmān, Ḥafṣa, and ʿĀ'isha – their mother is Buthayna bint Abī al-Dardā'** ʿUwaymir ibn Zayd ibn Qays ibn ʿĀ'isha ibn Umayya ibn Mālik ibn ʿĀmir ibn ʿAdī ibn Kaʿb ibn al-Khazraj ibn al-Ḥārith ibn al-Khazraj. **[Saʿīd ibn Saʿd also bore] Yūsuf – his mother is Umm Yūsuf Bint Hammām** from the Banī Naṣr ibn Muʿāwiya of Hawzān. **[Saʿīd ibn Saʿd also bore] Yaḥyā, ʿUthmān, Ghuzayya, ʿAbd al-ʿAzīz, Umm Abān, and Umm al-Banīn, to various *umm walads*.**[13]

Many entries (including this one) indicate that a man's children were born to 'various *umm walads*'. In such a case, I always take the fewest number of *umm walads* to be three, since the Arabic plural indicates at least this number. I take the greatest number of *umm walads* to be the total number of children born to these 'various *umm walads*', as each of these children might have been born to a different *umm walad*. In Saʿīd ibn Saʿd's case, that number is six. Averaging these minimum (3) and maximum (6) numbers gives the result of 4.5.

The Chronological View: Change over Time

After compiling this database, perhaps the simplest snapshot of a changing early Islamic society comes from the percentage of children born to *umm walads* in each generation (see Figure 5.1). As Majied Robinson has also shown, the first generation of Muslims used *umm walads* to bear children (I find 16 per cent total, while Robinson finds 12 per cent). This finding challenges those scholars who have claimed that procreation with concubines was abhorrent to the early generations of Muslims.[14] The percentage

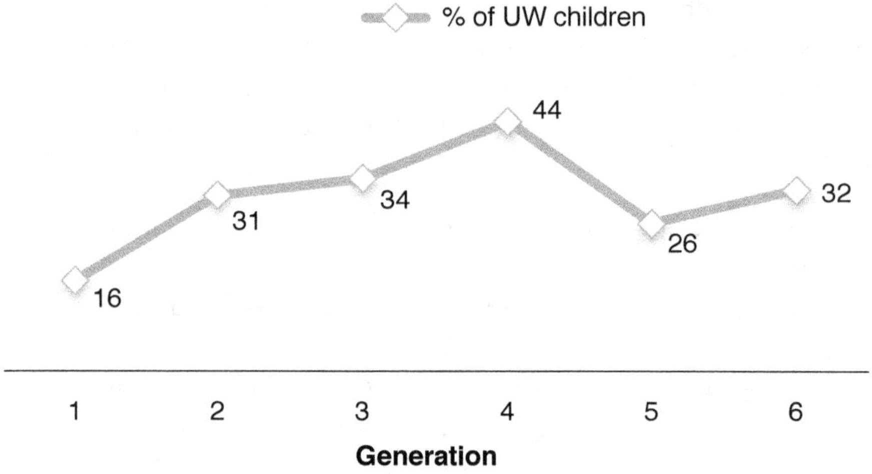

Figure 5.1 Percentage of children born of *umm walads* (UWs)

then doubles between the first and second generations, and it continues to grow until it reaches its height of 44 per cent in generation four (which corresponds roughly to the late Marwanid period, 720–740 CE).[15] The explanation for this growing percentage is fairly straightforward: the Islamic conquests brought in huge numbers of concubines who bore children for their conqueror-masters.

More intriguing is the precipitous drop in generation five, which roughly corresponds to the period of the Abbasid revolution. Perhaps the late-Umayyad tribal breakdown, the turmoil of the Third Fitna and the Abbasid revolution simply caused widespread social disruption – for there is also a drop in the number of wives and children at this time. However, the fact that the percentage of concubines' children remains relatively low in generation six perhaps hints at a more lasting social change rather than a revolutionary disruption. It seems likely that, as the major conquests of the Umayyad 'jihad state' ended with Hishām's reign around generation four, men simply had access to fewer *umm walads* in the early Abbasid polity.[16] There was probably a shift away from taking huge numbers of prisoners of war as concubines, and towards the more routinised slave trade of the Abbasid period.[17] *Umm walads* still existed as a prominent part of elite society, but they were not as prevalent as they had been during the heyday of the Umayyad period.

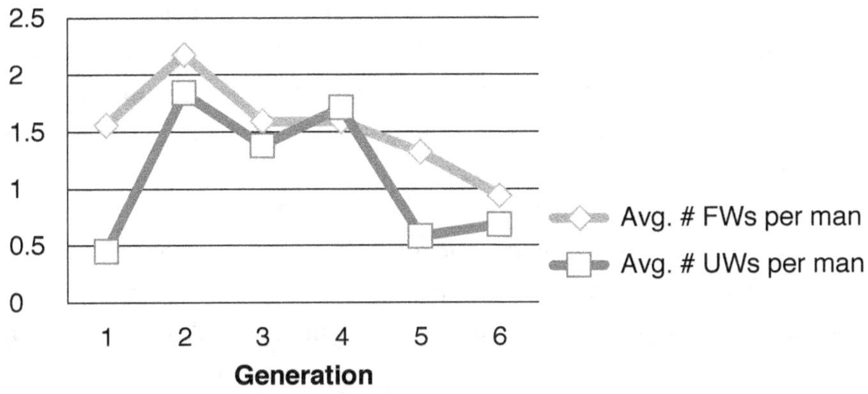

Figure 5.2 Average number of free wives (FWs) and *umm walads* (UWs) per man

In addition to tracing overall rates of concubinage, one of the goals of this research was to determine whether marriage and concubinage were complementary or competing practices. To answer this question, I calculated the overall numbers of free wives and concubines in every generation, and I then adjusted these total numbers to account for sample size.[18] What these adjusted numbers show in a practical sense is how many children, wives and concubines any individual man had, on average (see Figure 5.2):

According to this data, marriage and concubinage were independent reproductive strategies; they did not compete with each other. There is no indication that as the number of wives goes up, the number of concubines goes down, or vice versa. In fact, with the exception of generation two, marital practice generally holds quite steady. If one removes generation two as an anomalous data point (analysed further below), the wife data appears as a simple, slightly downward curve. It is the concubinage rate, not the marriage rate, which fluctuates wildly, leaping from small to large, large to small. It thus seems that marriage was a fairly stable practice – people always married fairly frequently and had children with those wives. On the other hand, concubinage was a more dynamic practice; it seems to have depended on a wider range of factors, such as availability of prisoners of war, or general political stability.

Additionally, the data indicate that marriage was usually the primary strategy for reproduction, with concubinage only secondary. The average man almost always had more wives than concubines – the notable exception is again generation four, when the number of concubines remarkably exceeds the number of wives. (This finding falls in line with the previous discussion of the high concubinage rates in generation four.) The primacy of marriage over concubinage is particularly conspicuous in generation five, when the average number of concubines plummets compared to the number of wives. It is possible that this drastic drop in concubinage in generation five represents a reaction to the high rate of concubinage in generation four. That is, perhaps widespread concubinage proved disruptive to marriage alliances and tribal ties in generation four, and, as a corrective measure, men in generation five made comparatively more marriages to try to repair weakened tribal alliances. Or, perhaps, this plummet merely indicates the end of the expansive conquest state and an end to the flood of prisoners of war, as previously discussed.

It is also worth noting that the data indicate a general reproductive boom in generation two (approximately 680–700 CE): the number of concubines leaps up, but so does the number of wives and children.[19] (In generation one, the average man has 4.13 children; in generation two, the number more than doubles to 8.93 children per man.) The increasing number of wives perhaps points to the new prestige of the Muslim conquerors, who likely made widespread, exogamous marriages with local elites in order to solidify their tribal networks and their political authority. Perhaps the Muslims were also trying to be fruitful and multiply, in order to gain some demographic ground on the vast conquered population. In any case, marriage and concubinage were complementary, not competing, strategies in this period of rampant reproduction.

The data also illuminate childbirth rates from the perspective of the wives and concubines themselves (see Figure 5.3). Throughout the generations, the average number of children per free wife is always higher than that of concubines. The trend holds true even when men use large numbers of concubines and have many children from concubines, as in generation four.[20]

This finding indicates that during the first few generations of Islamic history, reproduction was one of the main goals of marriage, but reproduction was not one of the main goals of concubinage. Put more bluntly, concubines were used first and foremost for sexual pleasure, not reproduction. Men were likely practising *coitus interruptus* with their concubines, but not with their

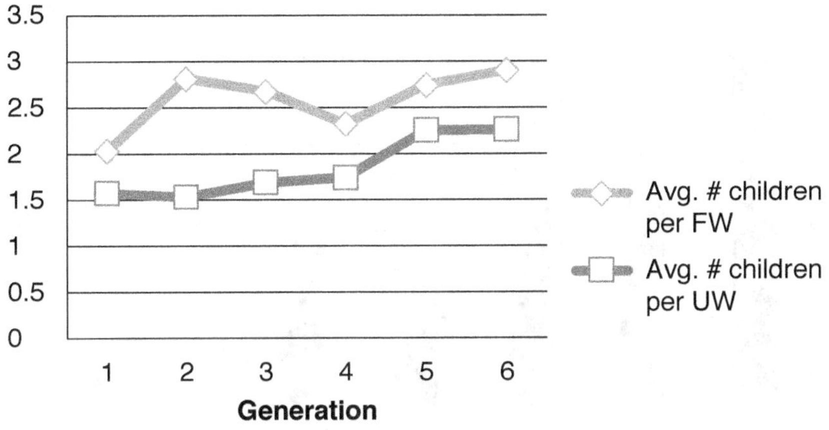

Figure 5.3 Birth rates of free wives (FWs) vs *umm walads* (UWs)

free wives.[21] This finding also hints that men had many more concubines than the data allow us to see – a concubine only appears in the data when she bears a child, which was probably often accidental. The other concubines who did not become accidentally pregnant by their masters are simply invisible, and we can only guess at their numbers.

Finally, it is worth noting that concubine birth rates rise above two children per concubine only in generations five and six (although they never overtake the free wives' rates). We have already seen that a man's average number of concubines also drops quite a bit in these generations (see Figure 5.2). Put in narrative terms, in generations five and six, men have fewer concubines on the whole, but each individual concubine is producing slightly more children. It is possible that this indicates a slight shift in concubinage practice in early Abbasid history, a shift towards using slave concubines for child-bearing purposes – as something like a replacement for a wife, or a supplement to a wife – and not merely for sexual enjoyment purposes. Such a change in reproductive practice would make sense in a post-conquest world where concubines were not pouring in as war booty, but where each man only had one or two concubines throughout their entire lives who were more fully integrated into their households, or were treated as more scarce (and thus more precious) commodities.

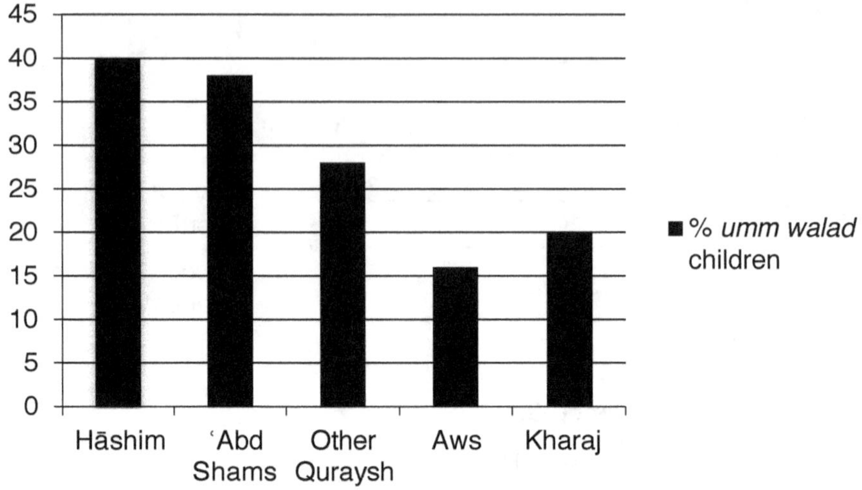

Figure 5.4 Percentage of children born to *umm walads* according to tribe

Tribal Practice

In addition to tracing change over time, I analysed tribal practice by breaking Ibn Saʿd's data into the following categories: Hāshim of Quraysh, ʿAbd Shams of Quraysh, Other Quraysh (including prominent clans such as Zuhra, Asad and Makhzūm), Aws of the Anṣār and Khazraj of the Anṣār. In terms of both percentage of children born to concubines (see Figure 5.4) and sheer numbers of concubines (see Figure 5.5), the Hāshim clan stands out.

Overall, Hāshim has the highest percentage of concubines' children, and it is the only clan to have more concubines than free wives on average. Perhaps more remarkably, Hāshim has a high concubine rate from the very beginning of Islamic history. Already in generation one, 27 per cent of Hāshim's children come from concubines. (The next highest rate is the other clans of Quraysh at 14 per cent, and recall from Figure 5.1 above that the average rate overall from this generation is 16 per cent.) Similarly, in generation one, Hāshim has almost as many concubines as wives (1.31 wives per one concubine), while the other tribes in this generation have from four to ten times as many wives as concubines.

Hāshim's early adoption of concubinage raises questions about the relationship between concubinage practice and early Islamic law. As other

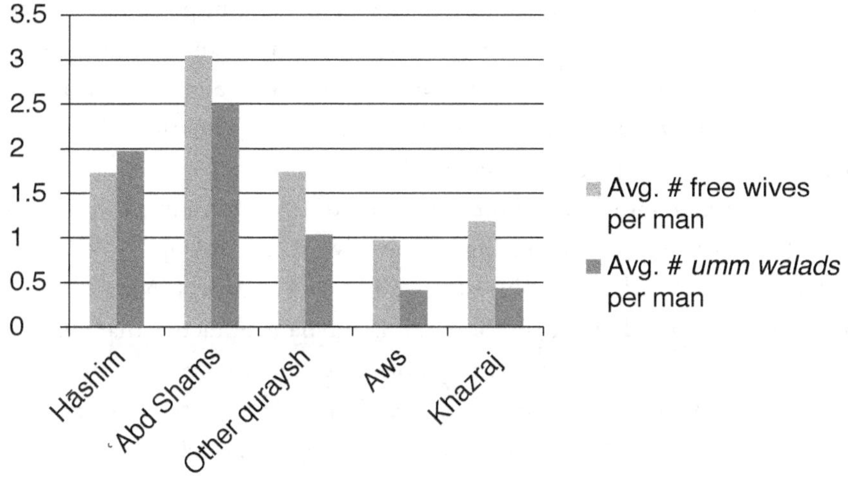

Figure 5.5 Adjusted numbers of free wives and *umm walads* according to tribe

scholars have shown, Shii law treats the *umm walad* essentially as a slave – she may be sold, she is not automatically freed upon her master's death, she may be inherited as part of her master's estate. On the other hand, Sunni law treats the *umm walad* as inhabiting a more special and protected status – she may not be sold, she is automatically freed upon her master's death and in some law schools she has more comforts and less menial labour.[22] Did the Hāshim clan take many concubines during this first generation because they considered them to be essentially slaves? Or, conversely, did Shii law treat concubines essentially as slaves because this clan was making such heavy use of concubines? The latter seems more likely to me, working from the assumption that law derives from practice. In either case, it seems to have been in the Hāshimīs' vested interest to limit the concubine's status and to maintain the master's full rights over his concubinal property.

Finally, the data indicates that Quraysh had many more concubines overall, and many more children from concubines, than did the Anṣār. In the absence of other data, this finding suggests that concubinage was an elite political practice, with the day's political contenders also having access to the most concubines. This makes sense in terms of sheer power and resources – the political contenders are the ones who have the most wealth and the greatest access to war spoils. However, this trend also makes sense in terms of political marital alliances. Compared to the main Qurashi political families, who could consolidate their power by using concubines (thus excluding rival clans from marrying into their family and sharing their power), the relatively disenfranchised Aws and Kharaj needed to make strategic marital alliances in order to retain a modicum of political clout. Even if they could monetarily afford to purchase more concubines, they could not politically afford to dissipate their local alliances by relying too heavily on concubinage.[23]

Ultimately, the demographic data indicate that concubinage is not a static, 'one-size-fits-all' practice. Rather, it is a dynamic practice that changes over time and across different demographics; as such, it requires dynamic, complex explanations, not simplistic ones. Certainly, the assertion that the Umayyads were Arab chauvinists who despised the children of concubines is overly simplistic – the Umayyad clan of ʿAbd Shams used concubines heavily, along with the rest of Quraysh. While the demographic data do not tell us much about the concubines themselves or the children they bore, they do provide a backdrop against which to better understand the changes happening in early Islamic society. Indeed, the narrative sources make it clear that the widespread practice of concubinage had an impact on the ideologies and institutions of the early Islamic period. Particularly, the narrative sources indicate that the children of slave mothers inhabited the liminal position of *hajīn* or 'mixed breed' for much of the early Islamic period; however, by the late Marwanid period, these children of concubines had articulated their belonging to the conquering elite as good Muslims and full-blooded Arabs.

Part Two: Close Narrative Analysis

While I suggest that Arab chauvinism is an overly simplistic explanation for the position of slave-born children in the Umayyad period, it is clear that some people in early Islamic society had questions about the identity and belonging of the children of concubines. I find that these questions (and their eventual resolutions) fall into three categories. First, there are legal questions about what practices were allowed and who could become an *umm walad*. I find evidence that early Islamic men sometimes took their wives' slaves as *umm walad*s, which would violate the later, classical Islamic definition of the *umm walad*. Second, there are community-defining questions about whether concubines' children truly belonged to the Islamic polity, or whether they instead belonged to the communities of their foreign mothers. I find that people first started questioning the place of *umm walads*' children in the mid-Umayyad period, and they eventually resolved these questions by vindicating concubines' children as devoted, knowledgeable and loyal Muslims. Finally, there are political questions about whether concubines' children could become caliphs. Scholars have sometimes argued that, from the beginning of the Umayyad period, the Umayyads deliberately and consistently barred concubines' children from attaining the caliphate. However, I find that the eligibility of the concubine-born caliph is a novel question that arises for the first time in the Marwanid period. Moreover, the controversy does not divide neatly into chauvinist Umayyads versus their cosmopolitan opponents; the Ḥusaynids, Ḥasanids, Abbasids and Umayyads all tried out a variety of answers to this novel question. Eventually, late-Umayyad and early Abbasid actors resolved this controversy by articulating a notion of purely patrilineal descent, which redefined concubines' children as full 'Arabs' and thus fully deserving of the caliphate.

Legal Theory and Historical Practice

Previous studies of *umm walads* have almost always focused on Islamic law.[24] Legal works are incredibly useful, but it is often difficult to know whether they are normative or descriptive. Thus, it is useful to find historical examples of practices that do not quite fit the legal mould, in order to judge how closely legal theory and historical practice coincide. For instance, legal sources on the *umm walad* always start from the premise that the *umm walad* is a female slave who becomes impregnated by her own master.[25] However, I have found some historical evidence suggesting that early Islamic men sometimes took their wives' slaves as their own *umm walads*. For example, according to Ibn al-Kalbī's *Jamharat al-Nasab*, ʿAnbasa ibn Saʿīd ibn al-ʿĀṣ (d. early second/eighth century?) was born to an *umm walad* called ʿAṣmāʾ. ʿAṣmāʾ belonged to Bint Jarīr ibn ʿAbdallāh, Saʿīd ibn al-ʿĀṣ's wife. And yet, ʿAṣmāʾ became Saʿīd ibn al-ʿĀṣ's *umm walad* and ʿAnbasa became the legitimate, freeborn son of Saʿīd ibn al-ʿĀṣ (and not a slave belonging to the estate of Bint Jarīr ibn ʿAbdallāh).[26]

Al-Balādhurī's *Ansāb al-Ashrāf* presents another, more controversial case involving the nobleman ʿAbdallāh ibn Khālid ibn Usayd ibn Abī al-ʿĀṣ in the early Umayyad period. ʿAbdallāh ibn Khālid was married to a wealthy woman, Umm Ḥujr, who lent him a black Qazāniyya slave woman to accompany him on a long journey to visit Muʿāwiya in Syria.[27] When ʿAbdallāh and the enslaved woman returned from their journey, the woman revealed that she was pregnant and told Umm Ḥujr that the baby was ʿAbdallāh's. Confronted with the accusation, ʿAbdallāh said, 'By God, I did not sleep with her at all. Does someone like me sleep with someone like her?'[28] The child, named Rashīd, was raised as Umm Ḥujr's slave. The exact reason for ʿAbdallāh's protestation is unclear, for he had seven other children from *umm walads*. The source hints that he was dismissive of the woman's colour or place of origin, or perhaps of her menial status as a domestic labourer.[29] But more importantly for the purposes of this chapter, the drama of the account revolves around the question of whether ʿAbdallāh fathered this woman's child, not the fact that she belonged to Umm Ḥujr in the first place. The implication seems to be that, if he had acknowledged the child as his own, the slave woman would have become his *umm walad* and the child would have been known as his son (as Rashīd himself always claimed to be). While this practice of taking one's wife's slave as an *umm walad* does not correspond to classical Islamic law, it does correspond to the paradigmatic religious figure of Hagar, who did not actually belong to Abraham, but to Abraham's wife Sarah. Hagar will appear below as a paradigmatic example of slave motherhood in the Islamic tradition.

Concubines' Children as Good Muslims: Warriors and Scholars

The more pressing questions raised in the historical narratives are not about legal rules, but about identity and belonging. There originally seems to have been some confusion about how concubines' children fit into Islamic society and how they contributed to its success.[30] For example, al-Ṭabarī transmits an apocalyptic tradition that associates the children of slave mothers with the dissolution of the Umayyad caliphate. In this historically suspect account, the third caliph ʿUthmān ibn ʿAffān sends a letter to the people, warning them: 'This community will fall into innovation when three things happen: complete material prosperity, the attainment of adulthood by the children of concubines, and the recitation of the Quran by both Arabs and non-Arabs.'[31] As ʿUthmān is the ancestor of the Umayyad house and should perhaps be considered the first Umayyad caliph, this account likely alludes to the downfall of the Umayyads. ʿUthmān presents concubines' children and non-Arabs as two direct causes of this downfall – as two liminal groups that represent the same fear of social change or religious 'innovation' brought about by the successful conquests.[32] However, non-Arabs and the children of concubines present slightly different problems in this account. The problem with the non-Arabs is that they try to read the Quran, which they apparently mangle with their bad pronunciations or translate into their native languages. The problem with the sons of concubines is not that they read the Quran – presumably their Arabic is good and they can recite the words correctly – but simply that they 'attain adulthood'.[33] Perhaps these adult concubines' children cause problems by rebelling, claiming the caliphate or taking other political actions; but perhaps they simply cause a problem by existing, and thereby blurring the edges of the Islamic community.

This late-Umayyad-era worry about what would happen when the children of concubines attained adulthood seems to reflect demographic trends in Ibn Saʿd's *Ṭabaqāt.* Ibn Saʿd provides no biographical entries in generations one or two for men who were unequivocally born of concubines.[34] We have already seen that some men were bearing children with concubines from the earliest decades of Islamic history, and therefore we might expect at least some children of concubines to attain prominence in the first generations of Ibn Saʿd's text. However, Ibn Saʿd also makes it clear that many of the children born during any generation died young, before they could either transmit hadiths or produce children of their own. The number of times Ibn Saʿd uses the phrases 'died young' (*daraja*) and 'has no progeny' (*laysa lahu ʿaqb*) throughout his work makes it clear that many children did not reach maturity. Thus, if only a minority of children in generation one were born of *umm walads*, and a high percentage of children were not living into adulthood, it makes sense that few or no concubine-born children would survive to make their marks on generation two. As the percentage of concubine-born children begins to skyrocket in generations two, three and especially four, it becomes more likely that these children would live into adulthood and contribute to Islamic society (and thus get their own individual entries in Ibn Saʿd's *Ṭabaqāt*). I thus find it telling that ʿUthmān's dire pronouncement singles out the children of concubines not as political rivals or religious heretics, but simply as 'adults'. Demographic change lies at the heart of this fear.

While ʿUthmān's account identifies concubines' children as a problem for Islamic society, other accounts suggest solutions to this problem. For instance, a previously under-appreciated apocalyptic account raises the possibility that concubines' children were suspicious outsiders with possible ties to the Byzantine enemy; however, this account ultimately vindicates these 'half-bloods' (*hujanāʾ*) as valuable contributors to Islamic society. This account comes from the *Kitāb al-Fitan* (Book of Tribulations) by Nuʿaym ibn Ḥammād (d. 228/843), which contains valuable apocalyptic material from early Islamic Syria. Nuʿaym's account describes a mythical, ultimate showdown between the Byzantines and the Muslims. The two sides reach a stalemate, at which point the Byzantines and Muslims exchange the following words:

> The Byzantines will say: 'Leave our land to us, and return to us every "red" (*ḥamrāʾ*) and half-blood (*hajīn*) among you, as well as the children of concubines (*banū sarārī).*' The Muslims will say: 'Whoever wants to will join you and whoever wants to will defend his religion and himself.' The half-bloods and concubines' children and 'reds' will become angry, and they will give the banner [of leadership] to one of the 'reds' – he is the authority which Abraham and Isaac promised would be brought at the end of time. They will pledge allegiance to him, then they will fight the Byzantines alone, and they will defeat the Byzantines. The settled Arabs and their hypocrites will fly away to the Byzantines when they see the victory of the *mawālī* over the Byzantines . . .[35]

While apocalyptic material should not be taken as strictly historical, it nevertheless reveals the attitudes of its transmitters and its intended audience. This account uses shifting vocabulary to describe the groups involved in the battle: 'reds',[36] half-bloods and children of concubines at the beginning of the account, and *mawālī* at the end of the account. In other versions of this account, the Byzantines instead ask the Muslims to return their non-Arabs (*ʿajam*),[37] 'those other than you' (*ghayrakum*)[38] and 'those whose origins are among us [Byzantines] (*alladhīna aṣluhum minnā*)'.[39] This semantic slippage indicates that the status of the concubines' children was initially just as unclear and liminal as the status of foreigners and *mawālī*.

The 'Muslims' in this account (presumably meaning Syrian/Arabian tribesmen) seem perfectly willing to let their liminal brethren return to the Byzantine side. In one variant account, the Muslims even explicitly command the liminal members to 'join the Byzantines'.[40] The question at the heart of this apocalyptic drama is not whether the children of concubines are good, noble or capable. Rather, the question is whether the 'half-bloods' and concubines' children are truly loyal to the Islamic empire. The accusation seems to be that half-bloods might actually belong to the Byzantines – that their mothers are Byzantine Christians, and that the half-bloods may be unduly influenced by Greek and/or Christian ideas. Moreover, as Asad Q. Ahmed has shown that motherhood ties were important and that 'cognate pull' was strong among the early Muslim elite, it makes sense that Arabian tribesmen would assume a concubine's son might want to move to his motherland or might find a natural set of allies among his maternal kin.

In Nuʿaym's account, the liminal Muslims themselves insist that their religion trumps their ethnic origins, mother's identities or previous cultural traditions. In fact, the half-bloods turn the tide of battle in the Muslims' favour; the concubines' children are the saviours of Islam. The moral of the story is that the children of concubines truly belong to the Islamic world, as committed Muslims and loyal soldiers of the Islamic empire. Perhaps the 'leader of the reds' in this account is even meant to be Maslama ibn ʿAbd al-Malik, the famously brilliant concubine-born general who waged successful military campaigns against the Byzantines in 88–95/707–714 and even laid siege to Constantinople in 98–99/717–718.[41] In any case, this account appears to be a late-Umayyad tale, and it makes sense that such questions were arising during this period, when the children of concubines were attaining maturity.

In addition to proving themselves in battle, the Umayyad-era *hujanāʾ* could apparently prove themselves through scholarship. The Syrian historian Ibn ʿAsākir transmits the following account on the authority of Abū al-Zinād (d. 130/747–748):

> The people of Medina used to be reluctant to take *umm walads*, until there grew up among them the Quran-reciting gentlemen: ʿAlī ibn al-Ḥusayn ibn ʿAlī ibn Abī Ṭālib [d. 95/713], al-Qāsim ibn Muḥammad ibn Abī

> Bakr al-Ṣiddīq [d. ca. 102/720], and Sālim ibn ʿAbdallāh ibn ʿUmar ibn al-Khaṭṭāb [d. ca. 106/725], the jurisprudents. They surpassed the people of Medina in knowledge, godliness, worship, and piety. Thereafter, the people wanted concubines (*al-sarārī*).[42]

The three men named in this account are grandchildren of three so-called 'Rightly Guided' caliphs of the Sunni tradition (ʿAlī, Abū Bakr and ʿUmar, respectively), who had been some of the Prophet Muḥammad's closest companions and supporters. Moreover, these grandchildren all lived in Medina in the late first/seventh and early second/eighth century (that is, the early Marwanid period), which is presented here as the historical turning point in people's attitudes towards slave mothers.[43] Finally, all three of these men are most famous in the Sunni tradition for their great Islamic knowledge, their transmission of hadiths and their mastery of jurisprudence. This account therefore highlights the egalitarian teachings of Islam as the great social equaliser that changed the status of slave mothers and their children in the Umayyad period.

Nuʿaym and Ibn ʿAsākir both present something like a 'Great Man' model of social change. According to this model, early Islamic society was widely prejudiced against the 'mixed-breed' children of enslaved concubines, until great warriors and scholars emerged to challenge those beliefs. Until the mid-twentieth century, researchers often accepted such a 'great man' model of social change at face value, rather than as a particular narrative strategy. However, the authors of our Arabic-Islamic source material had a vested interest in presenting great individuals as the source of historical change. These authors were the 'great men' of their own societies, and they had little incentive to consider seriously the indirect influence of women and slaves. Talented men may indeed have been important in changing Umayyad-era attitudes, but great men do not emerge from nowhere, and they only become 'great' if wider social and political systems allow them to be considered as such. I suggest that a more compelling explanation for the changing status of the *hujanāʾ* emerges from Ibn Saʿd's prosopographical data, which indicates that the appearance of concubine-born men such as Maslama ibn ʿAbd al-Malik and these 'Quran-reciting gentlemen' is an *effect* of already-rising concubine rates, not a *cause* of rising concubine rates. Ultimately, these questions about the role of concubines' children only come into sharp focus in the Marwanid period because it is only then that enough concubine-born children are actually surviving into adulthood to have an impact on Islamic society and politics.

Concubine-born Caliphs

Scholars have long noted that the political fortunes of slave-born men increased between the Umayyad and Abbasid periods. All the so-called 'Rightly Guided' caliphs and almost all the Umayyad caliphs were born of free Arabian mothers; conversely, the last three Umayyad caliphs and the vast majority of the Abbasid caliphs were born of slave concubines. For many decades, scholars explained this change by claiming that the Umayyads were Arab chauvinists who despised ignoble 'half-bloods', while the Abbasids were cosmopolitan thinkers who embraced the egalitarian teachings of Islam.[44] However, more recently, scholars such as Majied Robinson have convincingly challenged this view. It is clear that members of the Umayyad family used concubines widely from the first decades of Islamic history; moreover, Umayyad concubines' children could become famous scholars, generals and governors, and they could also make marriages with freeborn noblewomen.[45] It is not as though concubine-born children were being kept in ashamed seclusion. Rather, it is only the caliphate itself that the children of enslaved mothers did not achieve until the 120s/740s. Finally, even when concubine-born men did begin claiming the caliphate, it was not only certain Umayyads who protested their claims, but also certain Ḥasanids. Thus, it is clear that a more comprehensive and satisfactory explanation is needed for the rise of the concubine-born caliph at the end of the Umayyad period than Umayyad chauvinism.

I suggest there are two possible, related, explanations for the late appearance of the concubine-born caliph. One explanation, championed by Majied Robinson, involves the changing system of tribal politics in the late-Umayyad empire.[46] The sources indicate that, as long as Umayyad politics was based on complex tribal networks, the children of slave mothers were never considered suitable caliphal candidates. This was not necessarily because they were considered genetically inferior to their 'pure blood' siblings,[47] but because they lacked the maternal kinship ties needed in a tribal system.[48] For example, the sources highlight this aspect of tribal politics during the reign of the second Umayyad caliph, Yazīd I ibn Muʿāwiya (r. 60–64/680–683). His own mother was from the powerful tribe of Kalb, granting him important maternal kinship ties that might explain why he was nominated for the caliphate over his older half-brother, whose mother was from Quraysh. When Yazīd died and the Umayyad family fought over who should become the next caliph, a powerful leader of the Kinda tribe urged his kinsmen to support Yazīd's young son Khālid: 'Come, let us pledge allegiance to this young man whose father we begat, for he is descended from one of our women . . . Accept the authority of Khālid, the descendent of a woman of your own tribe.'[49]

However, as the Arabian tribesmen gradually migrated to the garrison towns and frontiers – away from their wives, mothers, other kin groups – these tribal ties ceased to operate and were replaced by other types of political networks, most notably military factionalism.[50] This factionalism was not based on tribal kinship ties, but on the ideology of shared descent through the paternal line from one of two distant ancestors: Qaḥṭān for the Southern faction, ʿAdnān for the Northern faction. The sources imply that it was a great political detriment to have a father from one faction and a mother from the other faction, for one's allegiance would become hopelessly split. For instance, when the slave-born revolutionary Yazīd III ibn al-Walīd (r. 126/744) seised the caliphate, he imprisoned two of his young cousins and political rivals. One of these cousins, al-Ḥakam ibn al-Walīd II (d. 126/744), whose mother was a free Arabian tribeswoman, composed these bitter lines in prison:

> Did you renounce your pledge of allegiance to me because of my mother?
> You have sooner pledged allegiance to a half-blood.
> Would that my maternal uncles were not from Kalb
> And had been born to some other tribe.[51]

Most of Yazīd III's supporters came from the Southern factions of Kalb and Yaman, while the supporters of the deposed caliph al-Walīd II (and his son al-Ḥakam here) were predominantly from the Northern factions of Qays and Muḍar.[52] It seems that these Northerners were reluctant to throw their full support behind a young man whose mother was from the rival faction of Kalb. They would rather pledge allegiance to a concubine's son than to a man with ties to the wrong faction. In this new factional context, the sources indicate that being the child of a slave mother could prove a political boon rather than a burden.

This factional explanation for the increasing political prospects of slave-born men raises the 'chicken and the egg' question: did the increasing power of slave mothers' children give rise to factionalism, or did factionalism lead to the increasing power of slave mothers' children? I suggest that both processes worked together as a kind of political feedback loop. Demographic changes (including the influx of female slaves into the Islamic polity) were likely the root cause of tribal breakdown and the rise of factionalism. But, in turn, the system of political factionalism created new opportunities for the children of slave mothers, who no longer relied on tribal ties for their power. This feedback loop skewed the political system ever more in favour of the children of slave mothers, creating a system in which they could not only reign as caliphs, but were eventually preferred as caliphal candidates.[53]

Another explanation for the rise of the slave-born caliph involves changing imperial marriage practices. Scholars who study other pre-modern contexts have shown that, as leading families amass political power, they change their marital practices. When they begin as petty regional kings, these families marry widely in order to cement their alliances and gain political support. For instance, the Spanish Umayyads married with local Christians, the early Ottomans married with local tribes and the Sufyanids married widely with Kalb.[54] However, as such leading families gain more power relative to other noble families, they begin to practise more endogamy – marrying their own relatives, especially cousins. This practice prevents competing clans from hijacking the leading family's power through claims of marriage and/or motherhood ties. For instance, Ahmed has shown that in the later Umayyad and early Abbasid period, elite families of Medina (particularly the Ḥasanids) increasingly practised endogamy.[55] Likewise, Robinson has shown that the Umayyads followed this pattern of increasingly endogamous reproductive politics.[56] Finally, as leading families transition into a truly centralised, absolutist imperial dynasty, they sometimes transition away even from endogamy and instead rely heavily on concubinage for their reproductive politics. Concubinage solidifies political power not only within one clan or extended family, but even more tightly within one line of patrilineal descent. Such a reliance on concubinage is familiar from Abbasid, Spanish Umayyad and

Ottoman history.[57] This changing reproductive practice also helps explain the rise of the concubine-queen herself, who gains power in the context of a centralised, bureucratic harem based on proximity to the autocratic monarch.[58]

No matter how this change happened, it remains that concubines' children rose to political prominence in the mid-second/eighth century. The political ascendancy of the children of slave mothers to the caliphate was accompanied by rhetoric about the nature of motherhood and the nature of lineage. For example, the first slave-born caliph, Yazīd III, exalted the lineage of his own enslaved mother, claiming that she was a foreign princess descended from great kings.[59] He boasted of his doubly royal ancestry: 'I am the son of Kisrā [Khusraw]; my father is Marwān. One grandfather is a Caesar, the other a Khāqān.'[60] But I focus here on a more novel, and more lasting, strategy that uses two paradigmatic slave mothers from the Islamic religious tradition to justify the political ambitions of slave-born caliphs. These slave mothers are Hagar and Māriya, the enslaved concubines of the prophets Abraham and Muḥammad, respectively.

The first man to call upon this religious model of slave motherhood is the revolutionary Zayd ibn ʿAlī (d. 122/740), the eponymous founder of the Zaydiyya sect of Shiism. Zayd might have invoked the model of Hagar against his own Ḥasanid cousin, al-Ḥasan ibn al-Ḥasan, in order to claim his right to the custody of ʿAlī's estate.[61] More commonly, however, Zayd is presented as using this rhetoric when he revolted against the Umayyad state in 122/740. The Umayyad caliph Hishām reportedly scoffed, 'You claim the imamate [that is the caliphate] when your mother is a slave? The imamate is not suitable for the children of slave women.'[62] The sources record several variations of Zayd's reply to Hishām, but he always reminds Hishām that Ishmael was born of a slave woman (Hagar), and that God chose Ishmael as both a Prophet and the ancestor of Muḥammad. For instance, in al-Yaʿqūbī's (d. ca. 292/905) *Tārīkh* (History), Zayd says:

> Woe to you! The status of my mother puts me in [a good] position. By God, Isaac was the son of a free woman while Ishmael was the son of a slave woman, and God Almighty singled out the descendants of Ishmael and made the Arabs come from them, and that continued until the Messenger of God came from them. Fear God, O Hishām![63]

On its most basic level, Zayd simply invokes Ishmael and Hagar in order to justify his own claim to the caliphate – if God chose the slave-born Ishmael as a prophet, why should God not choose the slave-born Zayd as a caliph? But by claiming Ishmael as the ancestor of both Muḥammad and 'the Arabs', Zayd is also asserting that his own slave ancestress does not dilute his Arab lineage – Zayd is just as much of an 'Arab' as Hishām. Thus, this invocation of Hagar does not merely elaborate the concept of prophethood, but it also subtly advocates a new definition of lineage that only accounts for the father, discounting the mother.

Some versions of Zayd's reply to Hishām make it clear that, while this invocation of Hagar may have begun as a political strategy, it had broader ramifications for society. For instance, in al-Balādhurī's account, Zayd bluntly adds: 'Mothers serve no purpose for men other than to reach the goal [of bearing children].'[64] Ibn ʿAsākir's Syrian source, ʿAbd al-Aʿlā ibn ʿAbdallāh al-Shāmī, likewise concludes, 'If there were some deficiency in *umm walad*s, then God would not have sent Ishmael as a prophet while his mother was Hagar.'[65] Here, mothers appear as nothing more than a means to an end, namely the passing along of the paternal lineage. Hagar was simply an instrument that God gave Abraham to provide him with a son. By implication, mothers do not affect caliphal lineage, Arab lineage or *any* kind of lineage whatsoever. Thus, Hagar becomes a figure that any concubine-born man could use to defend his lineage and define himself as a 'pure' Arab. Ibn Qutayba (d. 276/889) indicates as much when he defends Hagar – as the mother of the Arabs – from the insults of Persian 'bigots' and 'apostates'.[66] Ibn Qutayba's defence of Hagar is divorced from its original political context of debates about the caliphate, and it has been extended into the notion that 'Arabs' can be born of concubines and still be noble and pure.

Although Zayd's revolt of 122/740 failed, the question of whether a slave-born man could legitimately hold the caliphate remained open. Twenty years later, the second Abbasid caliph Abū Jaʿfar al-Manṣūr (r. 136–158/754–775) also defended his right to rule as the son of a slave woman. In this case, the Ḥasanid revolutionary Muḥammad al-Nafs al-Zakiyya ('The Pure Soul', d. 145/762) challenged al-Manṣūr's right to rule and claimed his own political authority. Al-Nafs al-Zakiyya bragged that he was 'the centre of the Hāshimites in terms of genealogy', and he added, 'I am the purest of both mother and father – the non-Arabs have put down no roots in me.'[67] Al-Manṣūr, whose own mother was an *umm walad*, responded by calling upon the family of the Prophet Muḥammad:

> You are proud that the non-Arabs never bore you, meaning that you have no blood from *umm walads*. But you have boasted over someone who is better than you in genealogy from beginning to end: Ibrāhīm [Abraham], the son of the Messenger of God (peace be upon him), whose mother was Māriya the Copt.[68]

Al-Manṣūr goes on to claim that the concubine-born ʿAlī Zayn al-ʿĀbidīn (d. ca. 95/713) was the best of all the Alids, and he finishes by refuting the Shiite doctrine of descent through Fāṭima. By invoking Māriya and her son Ibrāhīm, al-Manṣūr condemns al-Nafs al-Zakiyya's concern about 'non-Arab blood' and his pride in his 'purest' Arabic lineage as insults to the Prophet Muḥammad's family. Once again, it is Ibrāhīm's identity as Muḥammad's son, not as Māriya's son, which matters – only patrilineage counts. Al-Manṣūr's invocation of Māriya likewise expands the notion of Arab to include anyone who was descended through the male line from an Arab ancestor, and this patrilineal notion of Arabness is given an Islamic justification – it was the Prophet's *sunna*.

These invocations of Hagar and Māriya create a complex identity for the slave mother herself. On the one hand, Hagar and Māriya are positive models of slave motherhood, for they are remembered as pious and beloved women; perhaps such exalted models even encouraged some slave mothers to convert to Islam. However, the deeper effect of these invocations is to reduce mothers to the role of mere vessels of the male seed. Zayd and al-Manṣūr highlight paradigmatic slave mothers precisely so that they can demonstrate that 'mothers serve no purpose other than to reach the goal'. Thus, what some scholars have regarded as the Abbasids' 'egalitarian' acceptance of concubines' children only occurs alongside a highly un-egalitarian dismissal of women's identities as inconsequential. Moreover, far from celebrating their foreign mothers as evidence of their cosmopolitanism, the Ḥusaynid contender Zayd ibn ʿAlī and the Abbasid caliph Abū Jaʿfar al-Manṣūr took great pains to re-define themselves as true Arabs. From my perspective, this novel rhetorical strategy does not look like egalitarianism, but rather a rearticulation of patriarchal and hierarchical structures to fit a new historical setting.

Conclusion

Enslaved women are often overlooked as agents of historical change. Especially given that the Arabic-Islamic source material often mutes or silences slave women's voices, it can be easy to dismiss their contributions to early Islamic history. However, this chapter has suggested the many ways that enslaved women influenced early Islamic history through the act of motherhood. Most directly, these women changed the demographic make-up of the Islamic polity. According to Ibn Saʿd's account, by the mid-Umayyad period, more than one-third of all children born to Arabian noblemen were born to enslaved concubines. These children apparently began as liminal members of the Islamic community, disconnected from maternal tribal networks and potentially harbouring ties to the non-Muslim world through their mothers. They had one foot in the land of the conquerors, and one foot in the land of the conquered. Such liminal Muslims could demonstrate their true belonging to the *umma* either by fighting for it, or by producing Arabic-Islamic scholarship. By the late second/eighth century, the sons of enslaved concubines no longer had to prove that they belonged to the *umma* or the empire, for they had attained the caliphate itself. In doing so, they articulated a new notion of Arab identity that was based entirely on patrilineage. They invoked paradigmatic mothers from the Islamic religious tradition – Hagar and Māriya – in order to demonstrate that enslaved mothers were no barrier to prophethood or power. While the models of Hagar and Māriya tell us little about the lives, experiences, hopes or fears of Umayyad-era concubines, they do demonstrate the enormous (if indirect) impact that enslaved women had on early Islamic institutions and ideologies.

Notes

1. The genealogical sources do mention the female children born to concubine mothers, but, unfortunately, the narrative histories do not tell us very much about them. More research is needed to investigate the biographies (if they exist) of the daughters of concubines in narratives of Umayyad history. For the Abbasid period, Matthew Gordon has found that fathers sometimes deliberately

refused to acknowledge the daughters they had with concubines, or sometimes even revoked their acknowledgment of paternity after initially giving it (personal communication with Matthew Gordon). They did this because there was a lucrative trade in elite, educated, enslaved women – the courtesans or *qiyān* – and these fathers thought they would do better to raise their daughters as enslaved *qiyān* than as free women.

2. Previous scholars have fruitfully used prosopgraphy to study a number of groups from early Islamic history. See, for instance, Richard Bulliet, *Conversion to Islam in the Medieval Period*; Patricia Crone, *Slaves on Horses*; Fred Donner, 'Tribal Settlement in Basra during the First Century A.H'; and Monique Bernards and John Nawas, 'A Preliminary Report of the Netherlands Ulama Project (NUP)'.
3. I take this felicitous turn of phrase from Asad Q. Ahmed, who writes: '[Early Islamic historiography] paid undue attention to even the most mundane details of certain events of mythological proportions . . . at the cost of our knowledge of the slow simmer of local histories that were the impetus behind them.' Asad Q. Ahmed, *The Religious Elite of the Early Islamic Ḥijāz*, 3.
4. Ahmed finds that 'cognate links were at least as important as agnatic relations for sociopolitics on the ground'. Ahmed, *Religious Elite*, 13. Ḥayāt Qaṭṭāṭ has also shown how crucial matrilineal ties were in early Islamic society and politics, even if the Abbasid-era genealogies obscure the importance of such ties (*al-'Arab fi al-Jāhiliyya al-Akhīra wa-al-Islām al-Mubakkir*).
5. Majied Robinson, 'Statistical Approaches'.
6. Majied Robinson, 'Statistical Approaches', 14.
7. The best edition of this work remains the Sachau edition*: Ibn Saad: Biographien Muhammeds, seiner Gefährten und der späteren Träger des Islams bis zum Jahre 230 der Flucht* (Leiden: Brill, 1904–1940). However, for ease of use (particularly, the numbered entries), I relied on the Muḥammad ʿAbd al-Qadīr ʿAṭā' edition: Ibn Saʿd, *Al-Ṭabaqāt al-Kubrā*, ed. Muḥammad ʿAbd al-Qadīr ʿAṭā (Beirut: Dār al-Kutub al-'Ilmiyya, 1990). When faced with a textual question or problem, I cross-checked with the Sachau edition, but all page numbers refer to the ʿAṭā' edition.
8. I was initially excited to compare the generations from Medina, Basra, Kufa, Syria and Egypt. However, Ibn Saʿd rarely provides even the identity of people's mothers for these entries, much less their marriages and children.
9. For instance, Ibn Saʿd lists no progeny in the entry of the famous (and famously procreative) Makhzumi warrior, Khālid ibn al-Walīd. There is no entry at all for the Umayyad caliph Hishām ibn ʿAbd al-Malik.

10. For example, people from generation two transmitted from the likes of Abū Bakr, ʿUmar, ʿUthmān, ʿAlī, al-Zubayr and Talḥa. People from generation three transmitted from people such as ʿĀʾisha, ʿAbdallāh ibn ʿUmar and Usāma ibn Zayd.
11. Robinson uses a different method for defining generations, based on levels of descent from a common ancestor within Quraysh (see Robinson, 'Statistical Approaches', 14.) Our generations nevertheless appear to correspond nicely, with my generation one matching up with his generation five, my generation two with his generation six and so forth.
12. I also included children's names, wives' names and tribes, and *umm walads*' names and/or descriptors (when given). However, I include here only the pertinent information used in the data analysis.
13. Ibn Saʿd, *Ṭabaqāt,* 5:59–60.
14. For example, take Athamina's unequivocal and largely unsupportable statements that 'the Arab aristocracy was appalled at the idea of their daughters' marrying princes born to mothers who were *umm walad*', and '[the sons of concubines] were not accepted by the Arab society'. Khalil Athamina, 'How did Islam Contribute', 195–196. Robinson provides an admirable review and critique of the previous literature expounding Umayyad prejudice against *umm walads* and their children, 'Statistical Approaches', 12–14.
15. Similarly, Robinson finds a peak of 42.41 per cent concubines' children in this generation (which is his generation eight). Robinson, 'Statistical Approaches', 18.
16. I take this phrase from Khalid Yahya Blankinship, *The End of the Jihād State.*
17. On slavery and the slave trade in the Abbasid period, see Matthew Gordon, 'Introduction', 4–6 and 'Preliminary Remarks on Slaves and Slave Labor'; Fuad Matthew Caswell, *The Slave Girls of Baghdad*; and Julia Bray, 'Men, Women and Slaves in Abbasid Society'.
18. The sample sizes for each generation are as follows: generation one (171), generation two (71), generation three (100), generation four (51), generation five (84) and generation six (35). When presented in absolute terms, these numbers can be misleading; for instance, it might appear that there was a massive drop in concubinage in generation two, when in fact there was merely a drop in the total number of entries.
19. This reproductive boom does not necessarily indicate overall population growth, as the sample size for generation two is much smaller than generation one.
20. There are of course individual exceptions to this rule, such as ʿUmar ibn ʿAbd

al-ʿAzīz, who reportedly had nine children from a single concubine. However, the data bears out the general rule that an individual wife had more children, on average, than an individual *umm walad.*

21. Free wives had a legal right to procreative sex; their husbands could only perform *coitus interruptus* or use other forms of birth control with their wives' permission. Men needed no such permission from their concubines, who had no legal right to procreative sex. See Kecia Ali, *Marriage and Slavery in Early Islam*, 166; and Basim Musallam, *Sex and Society in Islam*, especially Chapter 2, 'Contraception and the Rights of Women'.
22. On the law of the *umm walad*, see most recently Younus Mirza, 'Remembering the *Umm al-Walad*', 297–323; and Marion Katz, 'Concubinage, in Islamic Law', *Encyclopedia of Islam THREE*, accessed online 18 April 2019. See also J. Schacht, *The Origins of Muhammadan Jurisprudence*, 264–266 and 'Umm al-Walad', *EI2;* Shaun Marmon, 'Concubinage, Islamic', *Dictionary of the Middle Ages*, 3:527–29; Baber Johansen, 'The Valorization of the Human Body', 71–112; Brockopp, *Early Mālikī Law*; and Ali, *Marriage and Slavery in Early Islam*.

    It is worth noting that there is no clear legal precedent on the *umm walad* in the Quranic text or Prophetic practice. Legal views on the *umm walad* probably developed relatively late, in response to the Islamic conquests and their influx of concubines (see Brockopp, *Early Mālikī Law*, 155). Even after the law schools began to crystallise, there was never a clear consensus about the *umm walad*'s legal status, and jurists practised their *ijtihād* or independent reasoning on the matter (see Mirza, 'Remembering the *Umm al-Walad*').
23. The role of marriage and concubinage in reproductive politics will be discussed further below.
24. See the references listed above in Note 22 of this chapter.
25. An enslaved woman could not be married to her own master; if the master wished to marry her, he had to manumit her first. An enslaved woman could be married to another man (most likely another slave), but if she bore that husband a child, the child was legally the slave of her master. Only a child born of the master's own unmarried concubine, and acknowledged by the master as his child, was considered freeborn. On the case of the married enslaved woman, see particularly Ali, *Marriage and Slavery in Early Islam*, Chapter 2.
26. Muḥammad Ibn al-Kalbī, *Jamharat Al-Nasab*, 128. ʿAnbasa also appears in generation three of Ibn Saʿd's *Ṭabaqāt*, but Ibn Saʿd merely describes ʿAnbasa's mother as an *umm walad.* Ibn Saʿd, *Ṭabaqāt*, 5:185.

27. Qazān is a place in Iran. The identity of this slave woman is quite unclear, for this account describes her alternately as black, Abyssinian, Qazaniyya, a *jāriya* (slave girl) and a *qayna* (a more elite form of singing slave).
28. Al-Balādhurī, *Ansāb al-Ashrāf*, 5:55.
29. As Ibn Qutayba says, 'menial servants who look after camels, gather firewood, draw water, do the milking, and perform similar chores' are considered unclean. Ibn Qutayba, *The Excellence of the Arabs*, 20 (Arabic), 21 (English translation).
30. The children of concubines also appear to have had a liminal status in pre-Islamic Arabia. There is a healthy corpus of Arabic poetry lambasting and lampooning the 'half-blood' (*hajīn*) offspring of slave women, who were considered inferior to their 'pure-blood' siblings. See B. Lewis, *Race and Slavery*, 39–40. (Lewis's discussion of the 'half-breeds' is provocative but not always thoroughly convincing.)
31. Al-Ṭabarī, *Tārīkh*, I:2,803–2,804.
32. Goldziher long ago noticed the similarity between *mawālī* and *hujāna'* as subalterns or disenfranchised groups (*Muslim Studies*, 121 ff.) Following him, scholars such as Bernard Lewis, Jamal Juda and Patricia Crone have also noted this similarity between the two groups, although they have not deeply interrogated it. For instance, Crone mentions that pre-Islamic Arabian tribesmen distinguished between full or noble (*ṣamīm/ṣarīḥ*) members of a tribe, and 'resident protegés' or dependent members of the tribe (often termed *mawālī*). Pre- and early-Islamic poetry suggests that anyone with servile origins, including the *hajīn,* was considered a mere 'follower' to an Arabian tribe, rather than a full tribesman (Crone, *Roman, Provincial and Islamic Law,* 59–60).
33. Another account does mention specifically the Umayyads' supposed attitude towards the caliphate. Ibn ʿAsākir transmits: 'The Umayyads thought that they would be divested of the caliphate when the son of an *umm walad* ruled over them, so they would not give the pledge of allegiance to anyone but the son of a pure Arab woman (*ibn ṣarīḥa*), until Marwān ibn Muḥammad took the caliphate by force (*ʿanwatan*) – he was the son of an *umm walad.* Then the Abbasids killed him and took the caliphate from him.' Ibn ʿAsākir, *Tārīkh Madīnat Dimashq*, 57:330. This account seems concerned only with the issue of imperial rule, while the ʿUthmān account cited above cites concubines' children as a source of widespread 'innovation'.
34. In my database, I only counted someone as born from an *umm walad* when Ibn Saʿd uses that specific phrase to describe their mothers. There are many

people whose mothers are not mentioned, or whose mothers receive unclear descriptions, such as 'a woman from the Banū Taghlib' or 'a Roman (Rūmiyya) woman'. In these cases, I did not count the mother as an *umm walad* or as a free wife, but as unknown. Thus, the total number of children in my database is sometimes greater than the sum of free wives' children and *umm walads*' children. A famous example of such a case is Muḥammad ibn al-Hanafiyya, whose mother seems to have been a prisoner of war from the Banū Hanīfa. Further investigation is required to figure out whether such tribal women, taken as prisoners of war during the first waves of conquest in Arabia, provided their children with cognate links into their original tribes, or whether on the other hand they were natally alienated from their original through enslavement.

35. Nuʿaym ibn Ḥammād al-Marwazī, *Kitāb al-Fitan*, 274–275.
36. On 'reds' (*ḥamrāʾ*) see Lewis, *Race and Slavery*, 63, where he says this term was 'commonly applied by the Arabs to the Iranians and later extended to their Central Asian neighbors'. There was also an early Islamic military corps known as the Ḥamrāʾ, which should not be confused with the term as it is used here (see, for instance, Crone, *Roman Provincial and Islamic Law,* 54 and 89). In Nuʿaym's account, *aḥmar/ḥamrāʾ* seems to be used as a synonym for concubine's child and half-blood – it seems to be a physical descriptor, perhaps referring to a child with red hair or ruddy cheeks.
37. Nuʿaym ibn Ḥammād al-Marwazī, *Kitāb al-Fitan*, 262–263.
38. *Ibid.*, 299.
39. *Ibid.*, 281, 290.
40. *Ibid.*, 290.
41. On Maslama's legacy in the Arabic-Islamic sources, see Borrut, *Entre mémoire et pouvoir,* especially Chapter 5.
42. Ibn ʿAsākir, *Tārīkh Madīnat Dimashq*, 20:57. A similar account in *ibid.*, 41:375, reads: 'Quraysh began to prefer *umm walads* and to make use of them, after having been abstinent from them, when ʿAlī ibn al-Ḥusayn was born, and al-Qāsim ibn Muḥammad ibn Abī Bakr, and Sālim ibn ʿAbdallāh ibn ʿUmar.'
43. Khalil Athamina also notes this point in his article, 'How did Islam Contribute', 396.
44. The fact that authors such as Goldziher saw the widespread use of concubinage as more 'egalitarian' than relying on free marriages for procreation indicates that people have different definitions of 'egalitarian'.
45. For example, Muḥammad ibn Marwān married two noblewomen (one from ʿAbd Shams, one from ʿAdī ibn Kaʿb); ʿUbaydallāh ibn ʿAbdallāh ibn ʿUmar

married two Taymi noblewomen; ʿAnbasa ibn Saʿīd ibn al-ʿĀṣ married widely and exogamously. These examples all contravene Athamina's claim that the aristocracy would have recoiled in horror at such unions; see Note 14 of this chapter.

46. As noted above, see Note 6 of this chapter.
47. Although, this viewpoint was certainly advanced in certain Arabic poetry of the pre-Islamic and early Islamic period.
48. Natal alienation, or an absence of family ties, is one of the hallmarks of slavery across societies; see Orlando Patterson, *Slavery and Social Death,* 7–8. Even though William Robertson Smith views marriage in Arabia as tantamount to slavery, he nevertheless admits that the difference between true slavery and marriage is that a wife 'continued to have a claim on the help and protection of her own people'. Robertson Smith, *Kinship and Marriage,* 122, 129. For a discussion of the importance of maternal kinship ties in tribal systems, see Ahmed, *Religious Elite*; Conte, 'Agnatic Illusions'; Juda, 'Die sozialen und wirtschaftlichen Aspekte der Mawālī', 175.
49. Al-Ṭabarī, *Tārīkh,* II:475.
50. Robertson Smith, *Kinship and Marriage,* 130, points out that if a free woman's kinship networks are important for the proper functioning of the tribal system, then moving her out away from the main area of her kinsmen – out to Khurasan, for instance – would effectively nullify the political and social benefits of her kinship groups for her and her husband alike.
51. Al-Ṭabarī, *Tārīkh,* II:1,892.
52. See G. R. Hawting, *First Dynasty,* 93.
53. For example, in the Abbasid system, almost all the caliphs were the sons of concubines. Leslie Peirce has also investigated the transition in Ottoman dynastic politics from free wives to slave concubines (Peirce, *Imperial Harem,* 28–56).
54. Moreover, all five families that Ahmed studied in his *Religious Elite* married exogamously in their first generation and moved gradually towards endogamy over time.
55. On Ḥasanid endogamy, see Ahmed, *Religious Elite,* Chapter 5 (particularly pages 148–166).
56. Robinson, 'Statistical Approaches', 19–20.
57. On the Spanish Umayyads' transition from exogamy to endogamy to concubinage, see Simon Barton, *Conquerors, Brides, and Concubines,* Chapter 1; on the same pattern in the Ottoman world, see Peirce, *Imperial Harem,* Chapter 2.
58. For more on the harem system, particularly Peirce, *Imperial Harem.* See also

Chapter 6 of this book; and Urban, 'Gender and Slavery in Islamic Political Thought', and the sources cited therein.

59. This rhetorical technique was also applied, probably some time later, to the fourth Shii imam, 'Alī ibn al-Ḥusayn Zayn al-'Ābidīn. On this phenomenon, see Amir-Moezzi, 'Šahrbanu', *Encyclopaedia Iranica,* an excellent article that focuses on the Persian legend of Zayn al-'Ābidīn's mother. Because of the unknown provenance of most captive women and slaves, some concubines in history have been recast as 'secret princesses'. A famous example of this phenomenon is Nakhshidil (d. 1817 CE), the concubine queen mother of the Ottoman Sultan Mahmud II; according to legend, Nakshidil was actually Aimée du Buc, a French heiress and cousin of Empress Josephine who had been captured as a young girl by Barbary Pirates. See Isom-Verhaaren, 'Royal French Women in the Ottoman Sultans' Harem'.

60. Al-Ṭabarī, *Tārīkh* II:1,874. Moreover, when the man who bought her asked whether any child of hers would be half-blooded, the surrounding people answered him: 'Yes, he will be half-blooded through his father.' Al-Ṭabarī, *Tārīkh*, II:1,247.

61. Al-Ṭabarī, *Tārīkh*, II:1,672. It is worth remembering that it was not only the Umayyads who seem to have excluded concubine-born men from the highest echelons of power. The Ḥasanids seem to have believed that, in order to be considered 'noble', a man's mother and the father had to be highborn; it is unclear whether this was because they were a tribal aristocracy, or because their own claim to religio-political authority rested on the identity of a mother (Fāṭima). In any case, al-Ḥasan ibn al-Ḥasan's son, Muḥammad al-Nafs al-Zakiyya, would soon make a bit for power in his own right.

62. Ibn 'Asākir, *Tārīkh Madīnat Dimashq*, 19:368. 'Imamate' refers to the office combining religious and political authority over the Muslim community; in this context, it is synonymous with caliphate.

63. Al-Ya'qūbī, *Tārīkh*, 2:390. Al-Ṭabarī's account is quite similar, although it emphasises a bit more strongly that God preferred the slave-born Ishmael to the free-born Isaac – and, by implication, that God preferred Zayd to Hishām (al-Ṭabarī, *Tārīkh*, II:1,676.) Al-Ṭabarī's account does not have a proper *isnād*, but is introduced by the vague phrase, 'it is said'.

64. The rest of his account says, 'The mother of Ismā'īl was a slave, and that did not prevent God from sending him as a prophet, or from making him the father of the Arabs, or from sending out Muḥammad from his loins.' Al-Balādhurī, *Ansāb al-Ashrāf*, 7:363–364.

65. Ibn ʿAsākir, *Tārīkh Madinat Dimashq*, 19:471.
66. Ibn Qutayba, *The Excellence of the Arabs,* 20 (Arabic), 21 (English translation).
67. Al-Balādhurī, *Ansāb al-Ashrāf*, 2:419–421; Al-Ṭabarī, *Tārīkh*, III:211–213.
68. Al-Balādhurī, *Ansāb al-Ashrāf*, 2:422; Al-Ṭabarī, *Tārīkh*, III:212–213.

6

Singers and Scribes: The Limits of Language and Power

While the previous chapter discussed demographic changes and the impact of enslaved concubines on early Islamic ideologies, this chapter traces how enslaved and unfree persons accessed political power in the Umayyad empire. Particularly, it interrogates the ways that two unfree groups – courtesans and scribes – used their education, training and linguistic expertise to participate in Umayyad politics. When viewed together, these two groups indicate that the increasing centralisation of the Umayyad ruling household during the Marwanid period (64–132/684–749) provided increased opportunities for educated slaves and freedmen to exercise political power. However, these subaltern groups were always in a precarious position, for they had to use their linguistic mastery in ways that pleased their imperial masters. If they did something to upset the balance of power, they could be dismissed or even killed without a second thought.

This chapter also analyses the complex, contested development of the term 'Arab' as it was slowly crystallising during the late Umayyad period.[1] Like the 'mixed-breeds' studied in the previous chapter, these courtesans and scribes seem to have inhabited a liminal position. But unlike the 'mixed breeds', the tensions that the courtesans and scribes raised were not so much about lineage – the question was not necessarily whether they had 'non-Arab blood'. Rather, courtesans and scribes seem to have raised questions about the meaning of linguistic and cultural attributes, about the 'cultural stuff' that people use to express ethnic identity.[2] These subaltern groups' entire job was to master Arabic language and learning and to produce Arabic culture. As such, concubines and scribes represent a somewhat open, cosmopolitan definition of 'Arabness', based on language mastery and accessible to anyone steeped in Arabic lore. I suggest that many Arabic-Islamic authors spill much ink trying to resolve the question of whether such linguistic and cultural masters are truly 'Arabs', although they are never able to fully resolve the issue.

Courtesans and Scribes: Two Sides of the Same Coin

Many previous scholars have separately studied either the courtesans (*qiyān*) or the secretaries (*kuttāb*), but I suggest that both groups can fruitfully be viewed together in order to illuminate these questions of language, power and cultural definitions of 'Arabness'. The *qiyān* were enslaved women, raised in Arabian cultural centres such as Mecca and Medina, and trained from an early age to master the arts of music, dance, witty banter and Arabic poetry. The *qiyān* may have been beautiful and sexually alluring, but their real power lay in their language expertise. Even a physically blemished *qayna* could gain attention and win a patron through her poetic and musical skill.[3] The heyday of the *qiyān* was in third–fourth/ninth–tenth century Baghdad, where they would perform at literary soirées attended by the notables of the day. At these soirées, *qiyān* could earn money for their performances, and they could also gain the favour and patronage of the powerful men (including caliphs) in attendance. The most talented Abbasid-era *qiyān* could become great celebrities, such as Inān, Faḍl and ʿArīb, the divas of their day. As for the *kuttāb*, they were bureaucrats in charge of many of the daily functions of the early Islamic empire, including collecting taxes and writing official correspondence. *Kuttāb* worked on all levels of politics; they can be found serving local notables, regional governors and caliphs.[4] By the mid-second/eighth century, freedmen and the descendants of freedmen (*mawālī*) had come to dominate the bureaucracy, and two of these *mawlā*-secretaries – ʿAbd al-Ḥamīd al-Kātib (d. 132/750) and Ibn al-Muqaffaʿ (d. 139/756) – are remembered as the founders of Arabic prose.

There are several important differences between the *qiyān* and the *kuttāb* that must be acknowledged. For instance, the *qiyān* were women, while most *kuttāb* were men; the *qiyān* were typically enslaved, while the *kuttāb* were typically freed persons; the *qiyān* used the oral medium of poetry, while the *kuttāb* used the written medium of prose.[5] However, both the *qiyān* and the *kuttāb* were essentially subaltern groups whose entire careers depended on the mastery of

Arabic. This linguistic expertise was a double-edged sword for both the *kuttāb* and the *qiyān*; while it allowed them a certain degree of social advancement and prestige, it also placed them in a constantly precarious position. If the *kuttāb* were suspected of using their language to challenge existing power structures, they were scapegoated or cast out as corrupters of society. Likewise, *qiyān* were damned to moral condemnation and ignominy if they composed provocative poems, and damned to poverty and obscurity if they did not. To toe this fine line, the language of both groups was mired in ambiguity; they relied heavily on allusions, stories and double entendres. Political theorist Jennifer London has shown how the secretary Ibn al-Muqaffaʿ translated animal fables and ancient wisdom in order to indirectly advise his ruler.[6] Likewise, historians Hilary Kilpatrick and Matthew Gordon have analysed the ways *qiyān* used poetry to express their emotions and voice their desires.[7] Such ambiguous speech may have been a way for the *qiyān* and *kuttāb* to communicate without attracting scrutiny or reproach, allowing them to balance oppression and expression.

Another similarity between the *qiyān* and the *kuttāb* is that modern scholars have typically treated both groups as 'foreigners' or 'non-Arabs'.[8] However, I suggest that the ethnic identity of both groups is more complicated. First, I find little or no evidence that the original Arabic-Islamic sources describe the *qiyān* as foreign. As Matthew Gordon has suggested, the term most often used to describe the *qiyān* is '*muwalladāt*' – women born into slavery in an Arabian household.[9] The early Arabic sources use ethnic markers to describe *other* kinds of female slaves, particularly the *umm walads* of notable men. Ibn Saʿd's *Ṭabaqāt* very occasionally provides ethnic markers for *umm walads* who bore famous members of the religio-political elite; for example, he notes that Salama ibn Abī Salama's daughter, Amat al-Wāḥid, was born of a Berber *umm walad.*[10] Ethnicity or place of origin seems to have been more of an issue for people grappling with the role of *motherhood* than with the notion of cultural production.[11] Even sources that do highlight the ethnicity of enslaved women, such as Ibn Buṭlān's (d. 458/1066) *Manual for the Purchase and Training of Slaves,* indicate that *qiyān* were procured at a young age and trained in Arabian centres such as Medina specifically so that they would not have foreign accents. In short, the *qiyān* appear to be Arabian natives in terms of birth, language and culture, even if they perhaps have foreign mothers or foreign 'blood'.[12]

As for the *kuttāb*, the issue of foreignness is more complicated. As the conclusion chapter will discuss in more detail, 'non-Arab' is a common definition for *mawlā*, but one which erases many historical complexities of the term. All *mawālī* are not the same, and they seem to have held different views about their own foreignness. Take ʿAbd al-Ḥamīd al-Kātib, for example. ʿAbd al-Ḥamīd was a third-generation Muslim for whom Arabic was a native language.[13] Wadad Kadi has argued that ʿAbd al-Ḥamīd wanted to de-emphasise his identity as a '*mawlā*' (which had connotations of inferiority) and instead to create for himself and his cohort a professional identity as 'scribes', valued for their particular skills and training.[14] Likewise, London has argued that ʿAbd al-Ḥamīd advocated for the supposedly 'Arab-chauvinist' Umayyad dynasty and warned against the dangers of Persian heretics who were corrupting Islam. He highlighted that the bureaucratic skills the secretaries adopted from the old Persian-Sasanian dynasty were valuable because they served the Islamic empire, not because they were 'Persian' *per se*.[15] In short, ʿAbd al-Ḥamīd took great pains to identify himself with his service to the Arabic-Islamic empire of the Umayyads, and he might be dismayed that scholars today continue to identify him as a 'non-Arab' secretary.

Similarly, many early-Abbasid-era scholars were technically *mawālī*, but these scholars appear to have not identified themselves as non-Arabs or to have championed their own '*mawlā*' identity. Rather, *mawlā*-scholars such as Ibn Isḥāq and Ibn Saʿd presented themselves first and foremost as good Muslims whose authority came from their expertise in early Arabic-Islamic history. To focus on the foreign ancestors of such scholars, or to define them as 'non-Arabs', is to focus on lineage-based forms of identity and to treat such identities as somehow natural or obvious, rather than as historically contingent and in need of deep analysis.[16] Lineage is only one, rather limited, way of reckoning ethnic identity; linguistic mastery and cultural production are more inclusive ways of reckoning identity which allow people to 'become' Arabs by choice, even if they are not Arabs by lineage.

To complicate matters, some early Islamic *kuttāb* do appear to have identified themselves with non-Arab cultural traditions, even as they translated such traditions into Arabic. For example, the late-Umayyad/early-Abbasid secretary, Ibn al-Muqaffaʿ, seems to have advocated forcefully for the value of his Persian heritage. Ibn al-Muqaffaʿ was a first-generation Muslim who seems to have styled himself as a bridge between Arabic-Islamic and Persian-Zoroastrian cultures. He translated Persian literature into Arabic, and he urged his caliph to adopt implicitly Persian notions of justice and good governance.[17] And yet, even Ibn al-Muqaffaʿ's case is complicated. Ibn al-Muqaffaʿ is remembered still today as one of the founders of Arabic prose style. He notoriously loved to correct Arab-Muslim leaders' grammar and vocabulary, in some sense 'out-Arabing' the native-born Arabs.[18] Should Ibn al-Muqaffaʿ be considered a Persian, an Arab, neither, or both? Such questions are not easy to answer, but *qiyān* and *kuttāb* challenge current scholars to carefully analyse Umayyad-era notions of ethnicity, and to avoid unthinkingly applying over-simplified, nationalistic notions of identity to the sources as a matter of course. The sources debate these issues precisely because they are blurry, complex, and difficult.

In order to investigate this complex intersection of language mastery, cultural identity, and political power in the Umayyad period, this chapter focuses on two case studies of Umayyad-era *qiyān* and *kuttāb*. The first section of the chapter analyses the career of Ḥabāba (d. 105/724), an Umayyad-era courtesan. Ḥabāba is a transitional figure who allows us to interrogate the way political structures were changing in late-Umayyad history, and to better understand the ways enslaved women could exercise political power in an increasingly centralised harem system. She also allows us to analyse the forms of power *qiyān* harnessed through their linguistic expertise, as well as the limits on this kind of linguistic power. While her linguistic expertise gave Ḥabāba some sway over the caliph Yazīd II ibn ʿAbd al-Malik (d. 105/724), her power was spontaneous and precarious; it was based entirely on the careful management of individual, personal relationships, rather than being a systematised and routinised part of the political structure.

The second section mines an individual text, al-Jahshiyārī's *Kitāb al-Wuzarāʾ wa-al-Kuttāb* (Book of Secretaries and Scribes), to trace the development of scribal practice throughout the Umayyad period. First, a brief prosopographical analysis of the scribes mentioned in al-Jahshiyārī's work suggests that there were debates in the late-Umayyad period about the advisability of using *mawālī* as secretaries. This finding complicates the usual narrative that *mawālī* slowly but surely came to dominate scribal practice during the period of 'Arabisation' (approximately 60–100/680–720).

Second, individual stories about *mawālī* scribes in al-Jahshiyārī's text corroborate this notion of contested scribal practices. *Mawālī* secretaries appear to have gone through a difficult learning period before they finally mastered the craft of Arabic prose. I suggest that they eventually emerged as the dominant scribal class not merely because of their bilingualism, but also because their linguistic power was tempered by their subaltern status. By looking at these two case studies together, we get a better picture of how the increasingly centralised Umayyad caliphate offered new opportunities for enslaved groups to participate in politics, and also the limits of their political participation.

Ḥabāba, the Qayna-Queen

Ḥabāba was a courtesan who reportedly 'completely dominated' the late-Umayyad caliph Yazīd II; Yazīd reportedly even offered to let her run the caliphate in his absence. While scholars such as Pellat and Lammens/Blankenship have noted that the descriptions of Ḥabāba's power are likely overblown, no one has done a careful, source-critical analysis of Ḥabāba's biography.[19] Upon closer inspection, it appears that Ḥabāba is in many ways a typical *qayna* – she sings, dances, plays the lute, is a local celebrity, seduces a caliph, and amasses wealth. However, Ḥabāba is remarkable in that she also appears to have wielded a considerable degree of political power, something later Abbasid *qiyān* are not known for doing. Instead, in her exercise of power, Ḥabāba resembles later concubine-queens such as al-Khayzurān and Shaghab, who gained their power not as *qiyān* but as queen mothers within a centralised harem system. As someone who bridges the roles of *qayna* and concubine-queen, Ḥabāba captures a transitional moment when slave women were beginning to exercise certain forms of power in an increasingly centralised Umayyad polity, but before that exercise of power had become fully routinised.

Many Arabic-Islamic narrative sources tell the tale of Ḥabāba, including Iṣbahānī's *Kitāb al-Aghānī* (Book of Songs), al-Mas'ūdī's *Murūj al-Dhahab* (Meadows of Gold), and al-Balādhurī's *Ansāb al-Ashrāf* (Genealogies of the Notables).[20] These sources provide many alternative versions of specific episodes in Ḥabāba's life, but they generally agree on the basic outlines. Ḥabāba's original name was al-'Āliya, and she was born into slavery as a *muwallada* in Medina. The exact identity of her owner is contested, but whoever he was, he seems to have taken a vested interest in her education; she reportedly trained with famous Medinese singers such as Ibn Surayj and Jamīla. Ḥabāba appears to have been a minor celebrity in the Hijaz, and her prospects skyrocketed when she attracted the attention of the young Umayyad prince, Yazīd ibn ʿAbd al-Malik, who was on his way to Mecca to perform the Hajj. Prince Yazīd bought al-ʿĀliya for a high price, but he appears soon to have doubted the wisdom of the purchase. Either his older brother – the reigning caliph Sulaymān – or his own doubts convinced him to sell al-ʿĀliya to a new owner, who took her to Egypt or North Africa. When Yazīd II finally became caliph in 101/720, he expressed the wish to re-unite with al-ʿĀliya. A female member of his household (usually presented as one of his wives) tracked down al-ʿĀliya, bought her, and gifted her to Yazīd. Yazīd re-named her Ḥabāba, 'Beloved', and thereafter enjoyed spending most of his time with her. She reportedly exerted much power and influence in his court. She died of a sudden illness in 105/724, and Yazīd himself died shortly thereafter, apparently of a broken heart.

Literary Analysis

While there appears nothing overtly suspicious about this basic biography, a closer examination of the accounts reveals the clear polemical and symbolic undertones of Ḥabāba's biography. The sources use Ḥabāba to represent Yazīd's poor rulership, his moral corruption, and the downward spiral of the late Umayyad caliphate. Two examples clearly illustrate this phenomenon. First, Yazīd reportedly tried to quit visiting Ḥabāba in order to emulate his famously pious predecessor and cousin, ʿUmar II ibn ʿAbd al-ʿAzīz (d. 101/720). ʿUmar II had reportedly enjoyed no courtesans, and he remarkably had only one *umm walad* before he attained the caliphate (and took no new concubines during his caliphate).[21] In the most common version of this account, Yazīd's older half-brother, Maslama ibn ʿAbd al-Malik, accosts him and accuses him of squandering Umar's legacy.[22] A repentant Yazīd decides to stop visiting Ḥabāba, who becomes troubled by her master's changed behaviour. She commissions the poet al-Aḥwaṣ to compose an alluring poem to win back Yazīd's affections. In some versions, al-Aḥwaṣ recites the poem to Yazīd, who rushes to reunite with Ḥabāba, while, in others, it is Ḥabāba who sways Yazīd by singing the poem to him.[23] Regardless, the lovers are reunited, and Yazīd returns to his inattentive and pleasure-loving ways. In another highly suspect story, a likely inebriated Yazīd declares that he wants to fly away. In one version, he declares, 'I want to fly away – so let me fly away to the curse of God and the most grievous punishment!'[24] In another version, Ḥabāba asks, 'To whom will you entrust the *umma* [if you fly away]?' and Yazīd responds, 'To you, by God!'[25]

Neither of these accounts should be taken at face value, as objective descriptions of Yazīd and Ḥabāba. The first account clearly serves to demonstrate that Yazīd did not deserve to hold the caliphate, and that his rule fell short of the Islamic ideal in terms of both moral vision and practical administration. In this account, Maslama challenges Yazīd in the name of ʿUmar II; as Antoine Borrut has shown, Maslama and ʿUmar II are the twin symbols of Umayyad legitimacy, respectively representing heroic jihad and moral rectitude.[26] Against the images of the world-conquering military hero and the world-renouncing caliph-saint,[27] Yazīd appears as nothing more than an easily distracted libertine. In one account, Yazīd even orders Maslama to lead the prayer while he runs off to dally with Ḥabāba, implying that Maslama himself should have been the leader of the *umma,* or that Maslama was more legitimate as the empire's 'quasi-caliph' than Yazīd was as its actual caliph.[28] If the Maslama/ʿUmar dyad is presented as the angel sitting on Yazīd's shoulder urging him to righteousness, Ḥabāba plays the role of the devil whispering words of temptation in his other ear.

The account about Yazīd's desire to fly serves much the same purpose, although instead of hearkening back to the romanticised reign of ʿUmar II, it prefigures the disastrous reign of Yazīd's son, al-Walīd II (d. 126/744). Al-Walīd is notorious in the Arabic-Islamic sources for drinking and carousing, for sleeping with his father's *umm walads*, and for sending a disguised concubine to lead the Friday prayer when he was too drunk to lead it himself. The 'flying Yazīd' account implies that it is a short and slippery slope from Yazīd II's fanciful promise to put a singing-girl in charge of the *umma,* to al-Walīd's allowing a singing-girl to perform the most important symbolic act of religious leadership. What is important here is not whether Yazīd or al-Walīd *actually* put slave women in charge of the *umma,* but the way these accounts use slave women to symbolise the degradation of the caliphate. The sources present the slave-concubine as the last person who should ever lead the *umma* – she represents an ironic inversion of power structures, like the clown who has become king for a day.

These accounts are likely examples of Abbasid-era recollections and reconfigurations of Umayyad history. As Tayeb El-Hibri has shown, Abbasid-era historians resuscitated select moments and figures from Umayyad history, in order to bolster the proto-Sunni claim that there had been a continuous legitimate chain of succession leading directly from the Muḥammad to the Abbasids.[29] Abbasid scholars could not completely denigrate the Umayyads without opening room for Alid counter-claims to the caliphate. Thus, they pointed to a few bright lights of morality and propriety shining in the Umayyad darkness, leading the way to the Abbasid golden age. Maslama and ʿUmar II serve as those bright spots in the accounts analysed above. (It is worth noting that Abbasid-era authors had a vested interest in treating the slave-born Maslama as the rightful caliph, for most Abbasid rulers were born of slave women.) However, these accounts also seem to indirectly critique the roles that women played in the Abbasid polity by denouncing Yazīd II's relationship with Ḥabāba. Hārūn al-Rashīd's mother was al-Khayzurān, a famously powerful concubine-queen who intervened in Abbasid politics, and whom the sources usually portray as a conniving villain. The accounts about Yazīd and Ḥabāba make it perfectly clear that slave women should have no role in politics. Thus, while these accounts about Yazīd are 'sites of memory' that bolster the legitimacy of the Abbasid dynasty as the heirs of Maslama and ʿUmar II, they also indirectly criticise certain aspects of Abbasid imperial practice.

Political Analysis

Unpacking the symbolic resonances of Ḥabāba's story helps us better analyse the actual historical context of her life. For example, we do not have to accept that Ḥabāba was the 'bad' influence while Maslama was the 'good' one, but it does seem that they accurately represent two different avenues to power, one more public and based on military might, and one more private and based on the centralised palace complex. The fact that Ḥabāba apparently won Yazīd's heart in the end might simply indicate a shift away from the military-oriented, conquest polity of the earlier Umayyads and towards the more sedentarised, palace-based polity that would emerge under the

Abbasids. As Peirce and others have already shown, such a shift away from a mobile conquest polity and towards a centralised, bureaucratised polity can provide ample opportunities for women and enslaved persons to access political power.[30] Ḥabāba appears to capture this transitional moment towards the classical Abbasid harem-based polity.

Ḥabāba initially seems to have gained her power as a *qayna*. In this, she seems to have wielded forms of power familiar from other *qiyān*; she was sexy, alluring and educated, and she attracted the interests of the literary caliph, Yazīd II. As a *qayna*, Ḥabāba was also allowed access to the male sphere, from which many free females and even umm *walad*s would have been excluded, and she seems to have had a fair degree of physical mobility.[31] Even though she often appears behind screens or in tents, she seems to have travelled fairly widely within the Hijaz, even after she entered Yazīd's service. For example, a group of travellers reportedly encountered her on the road from Medina to the nearby Dhū Khashab.[32] A *shaykh* of Dhū Khashab said, 'We set out heading for Dhū Khashab – we were walking – and there we saw a dome in which there was a slave (*jāriya*). She was singing: "They went into the interior of Māḥiṣ and then left, returning. / They brought down upon me, when they left, deep sadness and sighing."'[33] Later, they would learn that the *jāriya* in question was Ḥabāba, and that she had requested that Yazīd send each of the travellers one thousand dinars. Ḥabāba was also apparently familiar with the famous singers not only of her hometown of Medina, but also of Mecca. When Yazīd wanted a particular poem made into a song, she informed him that only a certain al-Aḥwal al-Makkī sang the poem, but that perhaps Fulān ibn Abī Lahab could also sing it.[34] While this account has its suspicious elements – Fulān ibn Abī Lahab is the grandson of the arch-villain of early Islamic history, Abū Lahab – it appears to signal that Ḥabāba maintained a wide network in the Hijaz. These porous gender boundaries allowed her to learn new poems and styles of singing, and possibly to maintain alliances outside the harem.

However, her education and mobility could only take Ḥabāba so far, for she had to ensure that she used her skills only to please Yazīd. If she began to please others with her skills, she could arouse the caliph's jealousy; indeed, her reputation in the Hijaz seems to have possibly caused Yazīd to sell her away to North Africa.[35] Renown was a double-edged sword: a *qayna* needed just enough of it to attract her master's attention, but not so much of it to arouse his suspicion. Her individual literary skill alone was not enough to give her a prominent position in Umayyad politics – it was too precarious, too personal, too dependent on the whims of the caliph. Instead, it was the intervention of some of the free women of Yazīd's household that secured a more permanent position for Ḥabāba in Yazīd's harem, indicating the increasingly prominent role of women (both enslaved and freeborn) in a slowly emerging harem system. While these accounts may be meant to blame some woman – and thus to absolve Yazīd – for introducing Ḥabāba into Umayyad politics, the accounts seem to accurately depict a complex relationship of cooperation and competition among the women of the harem. The most common account asserts that Yazīd's wife, Suʿdā bint ʿAbdallāh al-ʿUthmāniyya, bought Ḥabāba for him, in order to curry his favour. According to Al-Iṣbahānī, 'It is said that [Suʿdā] had begun, before she gave [Ḥabāba] to him, to prepare her son by him to become the crown prince; and [after she bought Ḥabāba for him], he gave her everything she wanted.'[36] However, this explanation seems to confuse some transmitters of this story, for Suʿdā's unnamed son did not actually become the crown prince; instead, the crown prince was al-Walīd II, whose mother was Umm al-Ḥajjāj. Perhaps to account for this discrepancy, al-Iṣbahānī also reports that 'it is said' that Umm al-Ḥajjāj bought Ḥabāba for Yazīd, and that Ḥabāba was thus beholden to Umm al-Ḥajjāj for her position in Yazīd's palace.[37] Alternatively, al-Masʿūdī indicates that it was Yazīd's grandmother, Umm Saʿīd al-ʿUthmāniyya, who bought Ḥabāba for him. This account would make sense in the light of later harem contexts, wherein the older women of the harem were allowed or even expected to decide the younger generation's sexual partners. However, I suggest that here in this early harem context, it rings true that one of Yazīd's free wives might have bought Ḥabāba for him, attempting to secure the caliphate for her own son. Neither Suʿdā nor Umm al-Ḥajjāj seems to have appreciated that Ḥabāba might have actually posed a political threat to them or their sons – the harem system was only just emerging, and these free wives could not foresee the opportunities that the centralised harem would afford to intimate slaves like Ḥabāba. The idea that the caliph's wives were beginning to push for their own sons as crown princes, instead of consulting the wider Umayyad family or leading tribal notables, also speaks for the increasing centralisation of the caliphate.[38]

Regardless of which free woman bought Ḥabāba for Yazīd, Ḥabāba seems soon to have created her own retinue of personal slaves and servants. Some of her female servants (*jawārī*) may themselves have been *qiyān*-in-training; when Ḥabāba died, a distraught Yazīd surrounded himself with her *jawārī*, who reminisced with him about Ḥabāba's life and sang him sad songs.[39] Al-Iṣbahānī also provides an account (on the authority of al-Madā'inī) in which Ḥabāba uses her slaves as her political agents. In this account, Yazīd approaches Khālid ibn ʿAbdallāh – the brother of his wife, Suʿdā – because of hopes to marry one of Khālid's nieces. Khālid reportedly mutters, 'It isn't enough that he has Suʿdā, that how he has to have one of my nieces?' Somehow, Yazīd hears about Khālid's facetious retort, and he banishes Khālid to his tent. While Khālid is sulking in his camp, Ḥabāba sends one of her female slaves to bring Khālid a message: 'I [Ḥabāba] have spoken to the Commander of the Faithful, and he is pleased with you.' The sources do not state outright the implications of this message, but Ḥabāba seems to be offering Khālid some kind of political deal – Ḥabāba is offering to return Khālid to Yazīd's good graces, and, in return, Khālid will owe Ḥabāba some kind of favour or loyalty. Khālid does not like the deal, and he tells the slave girl to reply to Ḥabāba, 'My favour in the caliph's eyes is none of your business.' Shortly thereafter, Ḥabāba's *jāriya* messenger returns with a band of servants who tear down Khālid's tent while he and his companions are still inside it. When he asks what has happened, they reply: 'Messengers of Ḥabāba. This is what you have done to yourself.'[40] If Khālid will not accept Ḥabāba as his patron and lifeline to the caliph, he will have no access to the caliph at all.

Ḥabāba's reach apparently extended beyond her enslaved retinue. The above account hints that Ḥabāba was trying to build her own political network. While her efforts failed with Khālid, they appear to have worked with ʿUmar ibn Hubayra (fl. 97–105/713–724), a late-Umayyad governor of Iraq.[41] According to al-Iṣbahānī (once again drawing upon al-Madā'inī): 'Ḥabāba dominated Yazīd. ʿUmar ibn Hubayra became her protégé and his position increased, such that he could enter into Yazīd's presence whenever he wanted . . . Ibn Hubayra worked in the governorship of Iraq because of (*min qibal*) Ḥabāba – she worked for him to get that.' One of Ibn Hubayra's rivals, al-Qaʿqāʿ ibn Khālid, reportedly learned that Ibn Hubayra's star was rising, and he asked who was empowering his opponent. An anonymous interlocutor answered: 'Ḥabāba by night, and her gifts by day.' It is unclear whether the implications of 'Ḥabāba by night' are that she was sleeping with Ibn Hubayra, or rather that she sang Ibn Hubayra's praises to the caliph Yazīd when they were alone together. In either case, Ḥabāba could apparently intervene politically on several levels: she could provide access to the caliph's inner circle, financially back her favourites and ultimately win high political positions for those who accepted her patronage.

Finally, the sources provide one last tantalising hint that Ḥabāba might have been on the cusp of securing political power as queen mother. In the account mentioned above, wherein Ḥabāba has her agents tear down the tent of Khālid bin ʿAbdallāh, the *jāriya* messenger announces that her message is from 'Umm Dāwūd'. When Khālid asks who Umm Dāwūd is, the *jāriya* responds, 'She is Ḥabāba.' The sources provide no other hints than this matronymic, but Ḥabāba may have tried to position herself not only as Yazīd's 'favourite', but also as the mother of the crown prince. We shall never know if Ḥabāba might have emerged as the first concubine-queen of Islamic history, however, for she pre-deceased Yazīd, and we hear no more of her son Dāwūd.[42]

Ultimately, Ḥabāba reveals both the power of the late-Umayyad *qiyān* and the limits of that power. Her education, skills and intelligence allowed her access to the caliph's inner circle – and, yet, these gifts did not prevent her from being bought and sold, from being reviled by her enemies and spurned by her caliph-lover, or from being remembered in Islamic history as a meddling villain. While the sources maintain that 'Ḥabāba dominated Yazīd' – invoking the tried-and-true trope of the slave girl who enslaves her master – it is clear upon further analysis that she only had certain, rather unstable forms of power in Yazīd's harem.[43] She began to exhibit some of the forms of power that later Abbasid queen-mothers would have, including having direct, intimate access to the caliph, dispersing wealth and building patronage networks. But we can also see that Ḥabāba did not yet have access to some of the later forms of power that concubine-queens exercised, such as funding public works, influencing court cases and managing the reproductive politics of the harem. Perhaps these forms of power were not open to her because she was not a queen mother, but merely a 'favourite' – in this, she appears to somewhat resemble the Abbassid al-Khayzurān or the Ottoman

Hurrem Sultan during the first stages of their careers, before they became queen-mothers. Ḥabāba thus captures a transitional moment in the development of the imperial harem; she lived at a time when the Umayyad empire was moving away from an expansive jihad state and towards a sedentary, centralised system that would allow for women and enslaved persons to have greater access to political power.

A final lesson that Ḥabāba conveys, which I suggest also applies to other *qiyān* of the Abbasid period, is that writers treat her as a liminal figure not because of her ethnicity but because of her behaviour. Writers do not worry that she is a 'foreigner' introducing foreign mores – they treat her as a native Hijazi and a monolingual Arabic speaker – but rather that she is an unsuitable representative of Arabic-Islamic culture. She seduces, distracts, cajoles and bullies in ways unbecoming of a 'good' Arab-Muslim woman. I suggest that authors spend so much time discussing and debating the role of *qiyān* such as Ḥabāba precisely because they defy easy categorisation, and they challenge author's conceptions of who counts as a 'true Arab' not in terms of lineage, but in terms of cultural production and moral comportment.

Mawālī Scribes

Just as Ḥabāba helps us discern changes in the structure of the late-Umayyad caliphate, *kuttāb* help us discern changes in wider Umayyad imperial practice. There are several Abbasid-era works that describe scribal practice in the early Islamic period, but this analysis focuses on only al-Jahshiyārī's *Kitāb al-Wuzarā' wa-al-Kuttāb*. This book is unique in the genre of secretarial writing, which mostly comprises style manuals and anthologies of eloquent scribal prose.[44] Al-Jahshiyārī (d. 331/942) instead tells a history of the Islamic community through scribes. He lists the scribes who worked for each caliph and governor, tells dramatic anecdotes about these scribes' relationships with their patrons, provides hints of developments in scribal practice and includes the texts of a few short letters. Some of this information can also be found scattered throughout other historical works, such as al-Ṭabarī's *Tārīkh al-Rusul wa-al-Mulūk* (History of Prophets and Kings) and the historical section of Ibn ʿAbd Rabbih's *Al-ʿIqd al-Farid* (The Unique Necklace), but only al-Jahshiyārī collects it all in one location and connects it entirely by the thread of scribal practice.[45] I focus on this unique historical work because it can provide a clear and coherent (if incomplete) snapshot of how scribal practice and social identity relate to each other. However, like all other works of early Islamic history, al-Jahshiyārī's text should not be taken as objective or unproblematic – his accounts need to be analysed using the critical methods outlined in other chapters.

The Bigger Picture: Prosopography

First, prosopography reveals some of the broader trends of Umayyad scribal practice, at least according to al-Jahshiyārī. To conduct this analysis, I compiled a list of all the secretaries al-Jahshiyārī mentions in the period spanning from the Prophet Muḥammad to the fall of the Umayyad caliphate – a data set comprising 117 entries. I then used other sources (such as al-Ṭabarī's *Tārīkh*, al-Balādhurī's *Ansāb al-Ashrāf* and Ibn ʿAsākir's *Tārīkh*) to further identify these scribes. I particularly focused on their tribal, religious and ethnic identities, as indicated by the sources. The sources usually describe the secretaries in one of the following terms: Qurashī, other (non-Qurashī) Arabian tribesman, *mawlā*, Christian/Nabatean and Persian. When the sources do not provide further information on these figures, I tried to identify them based on naming practices; for instance, if a scribe is named 'ʿAbdallāh ibn Muslim', with no other tribal identifier, I tentatively assume this person is a *mawlā*.[46] This method is not perfect, and I invite other scholars to contribute their own analysis and interpretation of the data.

Once thus compiled, the data can be broken down to analyse how tribal practice changed over time, as well as how it varied according to place and specific occupation. In terms of change over time, I find that the *mawālī*'s domination of the imperial bureaucracy reached a height in the mid-Marwanid period but actually experienced a decline in the late Umayyad period. In terms of geography, it appears that Iraq had only marginally more *mawālī* scribes than did Syria, and that both Iraq and Syria employed many more *mawālī* scribes than did Khurasan. Finally, it appears that *mawālī* participated prominently in the epistle-writing bureau (*dīwān al-rasāʾil*), the official-seal bureau (*dīwān al-khātim*) and the tax-collecting bureau (*dīwān al-kharāj*), but that they did not play as prominent a role in bureaus that provided direct access to the caliph (*dīwān al-khāṣṣ*) or that allowed them to make on-the-ground decisions about provincial administration. That is, *mawālī* scribes appear to be underlings following orders, not directly advising the caliph or making administrative decisions.

Change over Time

Al-Jahshiyārī organises his text roughly chronologically, as he moves caliph-by-caliph and explains which scribes worked for each caliph and his sub-governors. Like the Ibn Saʿd data set examined in Chapter 5, al-Jahshiyārī's chronology is imperfect, as he rarely provides specific dates for specific scribes or even specific sub-governors. I have once again placed a somewhat artificial chronological framework atop the data, seeking to compare time periods that are roughly the same size, and that also include roughly comparable sample sizes.[47] Finally, note that the timeline used in this chapter does not line up perfectly with that use in Chapter 5 for concubinage practice; the timeline in this chapter traces a political history of dynastic change, while the former traced a social history across generations of Muslims. However, with these caveats in mind, al-Jahshiyārī's text provides a rough picture of changing scribal practice throughout early Islamic history, which I provide here both in table form (see Table 6.1) and graph form (see Figure 6.1) for ease of analysis:

Certain of these findings are unremarkable. For example, Quraysh played a prominent scribal role under Muḥammad and his immediate successors, but they slowly declined until they became completely absent from scribal practice. This decline can perhaps be attributed to a growing sense that Quraysh were military elites who should not have to perform mundane bureaucratic jobs – or perhaps the Umayyad government increasingly excluded rival Qurashis from access to government posts, thus consolidating the government in the hands of the Umayyad house. Likewise, scholars have previously noted the large role that Syrian Christians played in the early Umayyad (Sufyanid) government,[48] as well as the increasing prevalence of *mawālī* in the Umayyad bureaucracy.

However, some of the findings are more surprising. First, during the final decades of the Marwanid period (roughly 725–745 CE), freeborn Arab-Muslim tribesmen experience a resurgence as scribes, while the *mawālī* experience a slight decline. Only a small majority of scribes are *mawālī* in this period, while *mawālī* had completely dominated the craft in the previous period. This finding suggests that Umayyad scribal practice was not

Table 6.1 Chronological change in scribal practice according to identity

Dates (political period)	**Sample Size**	**Quraysh #/%**	**Arabian #/%**	***mawlā* #/%**	**Christian #/%**	**Persian #/%**
610–632 CE (Muḥammad)	13	6/46%	6/46%	1/8%	0	0
632–661 CE (Rashidun)	24	7/29%	10/42%	6/25%	0/0%	1/4%
661–685 CE (Sufyanid)	19	3/16%	2/11%	6/32%	8/42%	0/0%
685–705 CE (Marwanid I)	18	0/0%	3/17%	10/36%	3/17%	2/11%
705–725 CE (Marwanid II)	24	0/0%	4/17%	19/79%	1/4%	0/0%
725–745 CE (Marwanid III)	44	0/0%	16/36%	24/55%	4/9%	0/0%

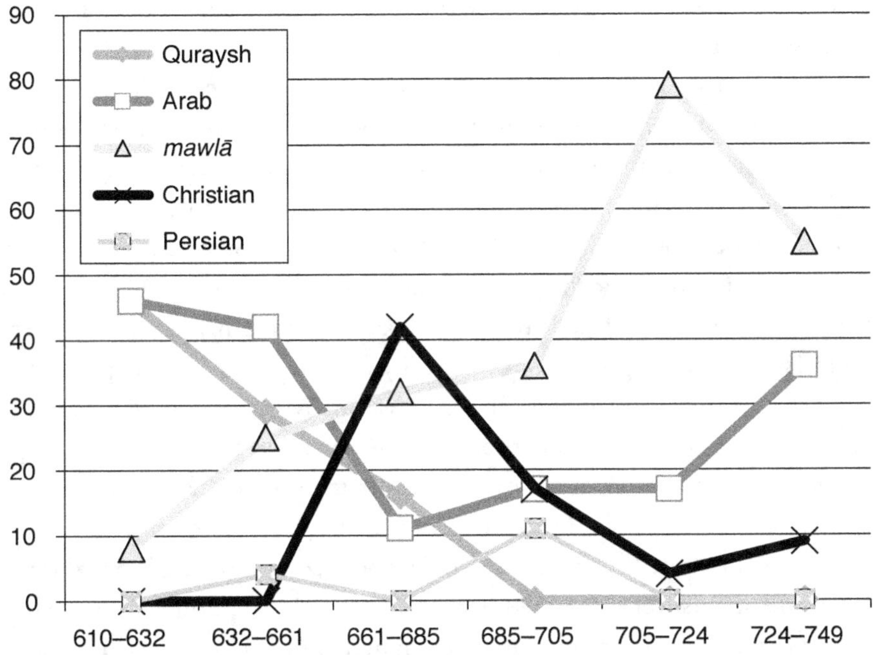

Figure 6.1 Changing percentages of scribal practice according to identity

characterised by a simple, linear trajectory of *mawālī* success; rather, scribal practice appears to have been a somewhat contested issue. This reaction roughly corresponds to a similar trend we saw in Chapter 5: after concubinage reached a height in generation four (*c.* 720–740 CE), it experienced a downturn in generation five (*c.* 740–760 CE). This slight pushback against the *mawālī* appears to have happened slightly earlier than the pushback against concubines, but it appears to capture a similar dialectic concerning the position of enslaved or unfree people in Islamic society. Perhaps the resurgence of Arab scribes was a ramification of the 'Arabisation' of the government; that is, perhaps the earlier Marwanids used *mawālī* as a temporary stopgap measure, to translate the bureaucracies into Arabic and provide some training on previous bureaucratic practice, so that Arabs could take over the bureaucracy for themselves. Or perhaps in the factionalised milieu of the late Umayyad period, caliphs were appointing Arabs from different tribal factions to bureaucratic positions in order to balance the factions, giving out political favours and to maintain an uneasy political balance. In any case, there seems to have been some fluctuation in the late Umayyad period in the employment of *mawālī* secretaries.

The other remarkable trend in this chart is that scribes explicitly identified as Persian never appear to play a prominent role in any of these periods. Persian scribes reach their greatest extent (of only 11 per cent of all scribes) during ʿAbd al-Malik's period, indicating that Persian scribes played a role in Arabising the bureaucracy and translating previous Sasanian bureaucratic practice. This low incidence of Persian scribes perhaps complicates Paul Heck's assertion that al-Jahshiyārī's purpose in writing his text was to dress up in Islamic clothing what was essentially Sasanian bureaucratic practice.[49] At least according to this prosopographical analysis, al-Jahshiyārī presents very few 'Persian' scribes as participating in Umayyad bureaucracy. Perhaps al-Jahshiyārī attempted to remove references to sustained Persian, Sasanian or Zoroastrian influence, in order to present the story as more Islamic. Or perhaps it simply tells us that the people who were translating these government documents were identified not by their ethnic or cultural heritage, but by their status as subaltern or *mawlā*. Many *mawālī* may in fact have been of Persian origins, but our authors do not identify them as such, and it is dangerous to make such ethnic assumptions in the absence of more explicit evidence.

Analyses according to Place and Occupation

In addition to allowing for chronological analysis, al-Jahshiyārī's text also allows for geographic analysis (see Table 6.2 and Figure 6.2). Once again, some of this data is fairly expected, like the dominance of Arabian tribesmen and Quraysh in Hijaz. However, it appears remarkable that Syria only has a slightly higher percentage of Arabian tribesmen, and slightly lower percent-

Table 6.2 Scribal identities according to place (numbers and percentages)

Region	Total #	Quraysh	Arab	*mawlā*	Christian	Persian
Hijaz	21	9/43%	7/33%	5/24%	0	0
Syria	57	1/2%	19/34%	29/51%	8/14%	0
Egypt	3	0	0	2/67%	1/33%	0
Iraq	33	1/3%	9/27%	20/61%	1/3%	2/6%
Khurasan	5	0	2/40%	2/40%	1/20%	0

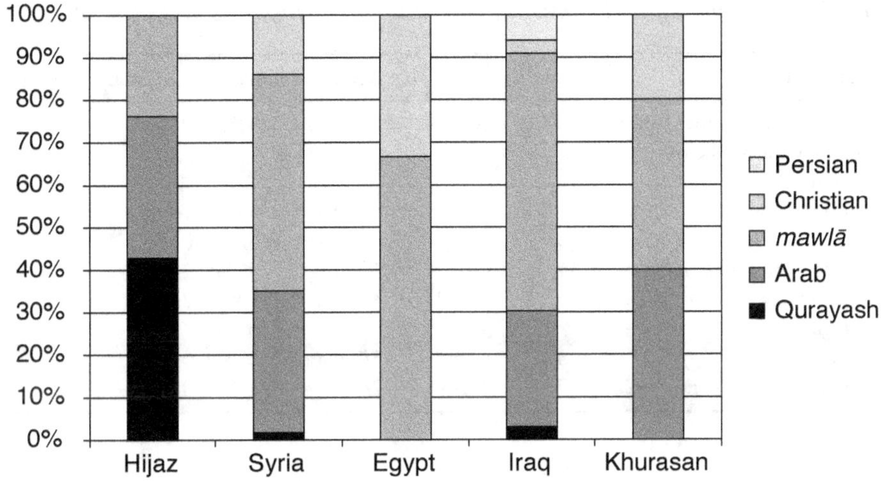

Figure 6.2 Percentage of scribal identities according to place

age of *mawālī*, than does Iraq. Additionally, Khurasan has a higher percentage of Arabian tribesmen and a lower percentage *mawālī* than either Syria or Iraq (although it must be noted that Khurasan's data set is quite small). These findings are somewhat surprising because the narrative sources often present Iraq and Khurasan as full of *mawālī*, peasants and other 'non-Arabs' seeking to join the Islamic community. However, I suggest that *mawālī* does not necessarily mean 'non-Arab Muslim' in this context, but rather subaltern or underling. Whether they were working in Syria, Iraq or Khurasan, the Umayyads and their governors apparently often relied on their own extended household networks – employing many scribes from among their own *mawālī,* that is, their personal servants and protégés.

Finally, al-Jahshiyārī provides specific occupational information for 64 out of his 117 scribes, providing a limited glimpse into what kinds of jobs different scribes were performing (see Table 6.3). These data indicate that the *mawālī* particularly dominated the epistolary bureau, as well as the tax-collection bureau. The *mawālī* also played a prominent role in the bureau of the official seal, which might have been used to seal official correspondence or to assess taxes.[50] Thus, as other scholars have suggested, the *mawālī* seem to have benefited from their previous knowledge of tax-collecting practices. However, the *mawālī* did not dominate all bureaucracies; they

Table 6.3 Scribal practice according to occupation (numbers and percentages)

Occupation	Total#	Quraysh	Arab	*mawlā*	Christian	Persian
Muḥammad's scribes (special roles, such as scribe of revelation)	13	6/46%	6/46%	1/8%	0	0
Epistles (*Rasā'il*)	16	0	4/25%	11/69%	1/6%	0
Official seal (*Khātim*)	9	0	3/33%	6/67%	0	0
Tax collection (*Kharāj*)	12	0	1/8%	7/58%	2/17%	2/17%
Bureaucracy (*Dīwān*) of a city or region	10	2/20%	4/40%	1/10%	2/20%	1/10%
Privy secretary (*Khāṣṣ*)	4	0	3/75%	1/25%	0	0
Other (incl. *Jund* and *Ṣadaqa*)	7	1/14%	2/29%	4/57%	0	0

play a distinctly minor role in running the administration of entire cities or regions. Instead, Arabian tribesmen dominated these bureaus.[51] Even more remarkably, Arabian tribesmen apparently dominated the position of privy secretary, the position that would have granted the most intimate access to the caliph or governor. It appears that caliphs sometimes granted the privy secretary position to their in-laws, in order to cement their tribal alliances. For example, ʿAbd al-Malik appointed his own brother-in-law, Qabīṣa ibn Dhu'ayb of Khuzāʿa, as his privy secretary; Qabīṣa's son, Isḥāq, served as privy secretary for ʿAbd al-Malik's son, Hishām. While my interpretation of this finding is tentative and requires further investigation, I suggest that these prestigious positions – privy secretary, and leadership of the bureaucracy of a city or region – were parcelled out to tribal allies as a way of cementing political alliances. On the other hand, *mawālī* secretaries did the nitty-gritty, day-to-day bureaucratic work such as writing letters and collecting taxes as a form of service to their masters' households.

The Smaller Picture: Case Studies of Scribal Scapegoats

Overall, al-Jahshiyārī's text suggests that bureaucracy was a complex and contested practice in the Umayyad period. Individual accounts in al-Jahshiyārī's text further illuminate the types of debates associated with changing scribal practices. Particularly, I suggest that stories about scribal scapegoats – scribes who were blamed for a problem or mistake in the bureaucracy – illustrate these debates. Focusing on scribal scapegoats helps us discern what forms of power scribes were able to exercise in certain contexts, and what were the limits of that power. More broadly, this analysis of scribal power then allows us to discern the shifting contours of the nascent Islamic polity as it slowly defined and defended its boundaries.[52] In particular, it appears that the early Umayyads removed Qurashis from the bureaucracy in order to limit their threat to the Umayyad dynasty.[53] Arab-Christians then experienced a heyday of bureaucratic prominence under the early Umayyads (Sufyanids), but they fell from prominence when the Marwanids attempted to more strictly define the empire as 'Islamic'. Finally, by the end of the Umayyad period, the *mawālī* had taken on the bulk of bureaucratic positions. As the previous prosopography suggests, however, this *mawālī* dominance was not without its fluctuations, and some *mawālī* appear to have provoked controversy because of their incomplete mastery of Arabic. Ultimately, I suggest that the *mawālī* emerged as the dominant scribal class not necessarily because of their bilingualism or bureaucratic expertise, but because they fit the right power balance in an increasingly centralised, autocratic late-Umayyad imperial system.

The most famous example of a Qurashi scribe who threatened the caliph's authority is Marwān ibn al-Ḥakam (d. 65/685). One account in al-Jahshiyārī's text blames Marwān for writing an inflammatory letter that ultimately resulted in the murder of caliph ʿUthmān and the outbreak of the devastating First Fitna.[54] Blaming Marwān for this letter absolves the 'Rightly Guided' caliph ʿUthmān from wrongdoing, and it instead places the blame on a representative of both the old-guard Qurashi polytheists and the much-maligned Umayyad dynasty. Marwān also illustrates the threat that a Qurashi scribe, in particular, poses to the standing caliph: a Qurashi scribe could plausibly manipulate the state right into his own hands, as Marwān eventually did.[55] Muslim rulers seem to have learned relatively quickly not to place Qurashis in such positions of power; the last Umayyad caliph to employ a Qurashi in any kind of bureaucratic position, according to al-Jahshiyārī, was Muʿāwiya (r. 41–60/661–680).[56] After that, the caliphs began hiring non-Qurashi Arabian tribesmen, Arab Christians and *mawālī* as their scribes, none of whom were perceived as a legitimate candidate for the caliphate.

After Qurashis stopped holding the position of scribe, stories of scribal scapegoats reveal different concerns for the health of the post-conquest *umma*. The Qurashi scribe might be a dangerous insider who could usurp the caliphate for himself, but Christian and *mawlā* scribes are semi-outsiders who might not fully understand the symbols and language of the Islamic community. These scribes might introduce corrupting foreign knowledge unbeknown to the mostly monolingual Arab-Muslim conquerors, or they might even deliberately torpedo the Islamic empire from the inside. Thus, stories about such scribes reveal broader concerns to define and defend the boundaries of 'Islam' as a religion and 'Arabness' as an ethnicity. As Fred Donner and others have suggested, ʿAbd al-Malik and his sons appear to have instituted a number of reforms intended to distinguish 'Islam' from other monotheistic traditions, and to distinguish the 'Arab' conqueror-elites from the conquered population. Many stories about Christian and *mawlā* scribal scapegoats appear to come from this period of Arabisation, and they reveal both the fears that Marwanid-era rulers had about employing Christian and *mawlā* scribes, as well as some of the problems they experienced in attempting to Arabise the bureaucracy.

The most prominent example of a religiously suspect scribe in al-Jahshiyārī's text is the Christian Sarjūn (Sergius) ibn Manṣūr (d. *c.* 73/693), whom al-Jahshiyārī subtly blames for some of the Umayyads' policies.[57] For example, in one account, Sarjūn appears responsible for hiring the infamous general ʿUbaydallāh ibn Ziyād as governor of Iraq. This ʿUbaydallāh is the son of Ziyād ibn Abīhi, the notorious Umayyad governor we met in Chapter 3; ʿUbaydallāh is also responsible for fighting against the Prophet Muḥammad's grandson, al-Ḥusayn. Just as blaming the Qurashi scribe Marwān ibn al-Ḥakam protected his caliph ʿUthmān from accusations of malfeasance, so blaming Sarjūn for hiring ʿUbaydallāh ibn Ziyād somewhat absolves the caliph Yazīd I of this travesty, protecting the legitimacy of the caliphal institution. However, unlike the Qurashi scribe, now the Christian scribe appears almost as a double agent, working to undermine the caliphate from the inside. The account implies that Sarjūn deliberately aimed to undermine the young Islamic community by getting the grandson of its Prophet killed.[58] Al-Jahshiyārī also famously blames Sarjūn for having caused ʿAbd al-Malik to Arabise the bureaucracy in the first place. Sarjūn was reportedly dragging his heels, slowing down the working of ʿAbd al-Malik's government, and essentially gloating that the Umayyad empire relied heavily upon his own expertise. As a result, so the story goes, ʿAbd al-Malik had the bureaucracy translated into Arabic.

While historians should not accept this simple story as explanation for a complex, empire-wide translation and reform project, they should analyse what the account implies about the changing contours of the *umma*. ʿAbd al-Malik does not identify Sarjūn's Christianity as the main problem, but rather his knowledge of Greek. Bilingualism is a form of power, one that was apparently beyond the grasp of the Umayyad caliph and apparently many of the other Arab-Muslim elites who had grown up in the Hijaz.[59] Because Sarjūn possessed this knowledge that was needed to run the empire, he gained a measure of personal independence – he could speed up or slow down production as he saw fit. Put in the theoretical language of unfreedom, Sarjūn's bilingualism allowed him to exercise individual agency, instead of the loyal inter-agency expected of a subaltern. Because the caliph realised that Sarjūn's power lay in his bilingualism, he strove to Arabise the diwans and to consolidate linguistic power inside the Arab-Islamic community. Although the Arabisation was certainly motivated by more factors than simple frustration with Sarjūn, this account appears plausible as a memory-marker of the end of the ecumenical Believers' movement and the beginning of a truly Islamic empire, as the empire adopted Arabic to articulate stronger religious and cultural boundaries.

It is remarkable that Sarjūn's bilingualism is cited here as a problem, as is that of Zādhān Farrūkh, Sarjūn's Zoroastrian contemporary working in Iraq.[60] Some scholars have presented bilingualism as the prime requisite for working in the bureaucracy during this period. These scholars have presented the bilingualism of the *mawālī* as a boon, as something that caused them to 'win out' as bureaucrats, and that also enhanced their position as translators, scholars and nodes of cultural transmission.[61] However, I am not convinced that bilingualism is in itself enough to explain the prevalence of *mawālī* in the bureucracy. Not only could Iraqi and Syrian Arabs be fully bilingual,[62] but al-Jahshiyārī also indicates that many *mawālī* struggled to become fully bilingual. Al-Jahshiyārī transmits several accounts of scribal error during the early and middle Umayyad periods wherein the scribes do not *deliberately* undermine the Islamic state, but *accidentally* do so. These scribal bloopers reveal fears about the increasing numbers of *mawālī* entering the Islamic polity, and fears that corruption of the Arabic language could lead to widespread corruption of state and society.

Some of al-Jahshiyārī's stories indicate that scribes were sometimes uncomfortable with written Arabic conventions and grammar. For example, Ziyād ibn Abīhi discovered a mistake in his bureaucracy (*dīwān*):

> Ziyād used to visit his diwans to oversee the work being done there. One day, Ziyād entered his diwan and found a piece of writing which contained the phrase: 'Three *dinān*.' He said, 'Who wrote this?' They said, 'That boy (*ghulām*) over there.' He said: 'Kick him out of the diwan so that he does not corrupt it. Erase this and write: "Three *adunn*."'[63]

The word in question is the plural of *dann,* an earthenware jug. The plural of abundance (more than ten) is *dinān,* and the plural of paucity (three to ten) is *adunn.* While the registry in question is clearly a tax registry and has nothing to do with the professional prose expected of state epistle-writers, the story nevertheless presents a perfect knowledge of Arabic and all its complicated broken plurals as a prerequisite for the job. On a purely practical level, writing '*dinān*' instead of '*adunn*' would probably have made no difference in the levying of the three earthenware jugs. But this account implies that levying taxes is only one facet of a larger cultural, religious and political project. The Muslim state could hardly present itself as a bastion of Arabic-Islamic values if it went around levying taxes in bastardised Arabic. Both the taxation and the letter-writing aspects of the secretarial craft are presented here as going hand in hand; both are equally important representations of the secretary's craft, and both require an equally excellent knowledge of Arabic. Whether or not this anecdote about Ziyād is historically true, it appears to capture a memory of the potentially 'corrupting' influence of *mawālī* in the bureaucracy. It does not reflect fears about the insertion of Persian values per se, but simply about the *mis*-understanding of Arabic, even in the bean-counting taxation bureau.

It was not only the Umayyads who apparently struggled with their scribes, but also the Zubayrids, the family that held much political power in the Hijaz and Iraq during the Second Fitna. The Zubayrid governor of Iraq, Muṣʿab ibn al-Zubayr (d. 72/92), reportedly read over a letter written by one of his scribes on his behalf. The letter began, 'From *al*-Muṣʿab'. Muṣʿab asked, 'What are these two additions here?' meaning the *alif* and *lam*, which spell the Arabic definite article *al.*[64] It seems likely that an Arabian tribesman and native Arabic speaker would innately know which Arabic names start with *al* (such as al-Ḥusayn, al-Walīd and al-Zubayr) and which ones do not (such as Muḥammad, Muṣʿab and Yazīd). However, this scribe seems to have struggled with this aspect of Arabic nomenclature. Although he is not named explicitly here, perhaps the struggling scribe was Muṣʿab's head letter-writer, who according to al-Jahshiyārī was called ʿAbdallāh ibn Abī Farwa.[65] This ʿAbdallāh's father, Kaysān, was a *mawlā* of al-Ḥārith al-Ḥuffār, who was himself a *mawlā* of ʿUthmān. That is, ʿAbdallāh was the *mawlā* of a *mawlā* – an incredibly lowly social position – and seemingly a first- or second-generation Muslim who might not have been completely comfortable with Arabic naming practices.

Finally, the Marwanids apparently continued to struggle with their secretaries. According to al-Jahshiyārī, caliph ʿUmar II (r. 99–101/717–720) dictated a letter to his (anonymous) scribe, to be sent to the governor of Medina, Abū Bakr ibn Ḥazm. ʿUmar's orders were to conduct a census (*aḥṣi*) of the 'effeminates' of Medina, a class of entertainers and matchmakers working in pre-Islamic and early Islamic Medina.[66] However, the scribe miswrote (*ṣaḥḥafa*) the letter and instead ordered the governor to castrate (*ikhṣi*) the effeminates of Medina – which he did.[67] While there are many plausible interpretations of this scribe's mistake, it is possible to understand it as a non-native Arabic speaker's mispronunciation of the difficult Arabic letter *ḥa*. Based on al-Jahshiyārī's data, six (or seven) out of eight of ʿUmar II's scribes were *mawālī*[68]; if they were first-generation *mawālī*, perhaps they were not completely fluent in Arabic. Moreover, ʿUmar II appears to have dictated his letters, which leaves room for listening-comprehension errors on the part of his scribes. If this account is understood as a 'mishearing' of the *ḥa* as a *kha* by a non-native speaker, it appears as a cautionary tale about the dangers of using first-generation *mawālī* as scribes. It implies that the conquered population should not have such great power over the fate of the Islamic community; it is potentially subversive and culturally disastrous to let such apparent foreigners work for the government. They are responsible not just for perpetrating this single, brutal act of castration, but also for figuratively castrating Arabic culture in its entirety with their foreign, corrupting ways.

Why did Marwanid caliphs continue to use *mawālī* scribes if they struggled to master Arabic? Especially if the Marwanids implemented reforms that sought to represent the caliphate as explicitly Arabic and Islamic, why did they allow struggling *mawālī* to write for them? To answer this question, I think we must recognise the tension between two Marwanid trends. On the one hand, the Marwanids had a desire to delineate the rulers from the ruled, the conquerors from the conquered. In seeking to define this boundary, they created new, starker definitions of 'Islam' and 'Arab' than had previously existed. I suggest that the *mawālī* become conflated with 'non-Arabs' (*ʿajam*) for the first time in the Marwanid period, and so the Marwanids seem to have had some fears about whether these *mawālī* could really represent the Arabic-Islamic empire. These fears are reflected in stories about *mawālī*-scribes who made linguistic errors and thus threatened the integrity of the caliphate.

But, on the other hand, the Marwanids had a desire to consolidate the empire in their own hands, to cut out rival Qurashi families such as the Hasanids, and to control rebels and revolutionaries. They also had to contend with increasing factionalism in the late-Umayyad period; late-Umayyad political history was dominated by a fierce and destructive rivalry between two military factions, the Qays and the Yaman. While the Umayyad caliph (and Quraysh more generally) was technically above these factions, the caliph nevertheless had to manage them. If one faction was becoming too powerful, the caliph might dismiss governors and generals from that faction and replace them with members of the other faction. As they attempted to balance these factional rivalries the Ummayads also came to rely heavily on their own extended households and personal cronies for loyal service – they accordingly became increasingly centralised and autocratic. (We have already seen this pattern in Chapter 5, as the Umayyads increasingly practised concubinage in order to exclude rivals from other families and clans.) That is, they seem to have relied heavily on their *mawālī* as subaltern, dependent members of their extended household, who were expected to have only their master's interests at heart. Such *mawālī* scribes were supposed to exist only as servants of the dynasty. If they made mistakes, they could be punished or dismissed without sparking a factional war. I thus suggest that the *mawālī* emerged as the dominant scribal class, not necessarily because they were experts in Sassanian bureaucratic practice, but because they were subalterns whose linguistic power could be controlled.

Conclusion

Early Arabic-Islamic authors wrote hundreds of pages on both the *qiyān* and the *kuttāb*. I suggest that they did so precisely because these groups are so liminal, debatable and difficult to place. Both groups raise intractable problems about the nature of ethnic identity and the meaning of 'cultural stuff' such as shared language and lore. Accordingly, the *qiyān* appear alternately as heroines of Arabic culture and as wicked, foreign corruptors. Likewise, *mawālī* secretaries appear alternately as founders of Arabic prose and as bumbling slaves and crypto-Manicheans. I suggest that these debates about cultural/linguistic definitions of 'Arabness', which would continue into the Abbasid period (indeed, they continue even today), began in the Umayyad period, largely as a result of the increasing prominence of educated, unfree groups such as the *qiyān* and the *kuttāb*.

Both groups apparently played an increasingly prominent political role as the Umayyad caliphate became more centralised and autocratic. Ḥabāba was able to wield power as Yazīd II's favourite, as a member of the harem network. *Mawālī* scribes served the dynasty as members of the imperial household, rising above factional politics. This finding suggests that there was no comprehensive, revolutionary sea-change between the Umayyad period and the Abbasid period. The late Umayyads were already developing the harem system that would later allow concubine-queens such as al-Khayzurān and Shaghab to exercise power. The Umayyads were already transitioning to an autocratic form of politics based on proximity and subservience to the ruler, not based on 'noble' Arabian lineage or tribal networks. In this context, *qiyān* and *kuttāb* could use their language mastery to access political power; love poetry and epistolary prose were potent tools that could secure patronage and political advancement.

However, these groups also allow us to see that education or expertise is not enough to liberate subordinated groups, if that education perpetuates unequal power structures. Both groups had to use their language mastery to satisfy their masters and to serve the needs of the empire. They were both ultimately subalterns, playing by the rules of someone else's game. Instead of blaming subalterns and slaves for corrupting Islamic politics, scholars should interrogate the wider political structures that allowed unfree people to access political power precisely so that their power could be monitored and controlled.

Notes

1. On the development of the term 'Arab' in the Umayyad period, see Peter Webb, *Imagining the Arabs*. I also speak more about this development in the conclusion chapter.
2. Fredrik Barth coined the term 'cultural stuff' in *Ethnic Groups and Boundaries: The Social Organization of Cultural Difference*, 15. See also Peter Webb, 'Identity and Social Formation in the Early Caliphate'.
3. For example, Hilary Kilpatrick reports an anecdote from al-Iṣbahānī's *Kitāb al-Aghānī* in which the caliph al-Mutawakkil rejects a *qayna* because she has freckles (which he apparently sees as a blemish). In response, the woman composes such a witty Arabic verse that he changes his mind and chooses her after all (Kilpatrick, 'Women as Poets and Chattels', 166).
4. Later, even concubine-queens such as al-Khayzurān would have their own *kuttāb*. On al-Khayzurān's privy secretary, ʿUmar ibn Mahrān, see Nabia Abbott, *Two Queens of Baghdad*, 121.
5. There are some exceptions to these general rules. For example, some enslaved females appear to have worked as *kuttāb*. Moreover, I thank Dwight Reynolds for reminding me that some prominent *qiyān* (such as Jamīla) were freed women (*mawlāt*) and no longer technically enslaved.
6. Jennifer London, 'How to Do Things with Fables'.
7. Kilpatrick, 'Women as Poets and Chattels'; Matthew Gordon, 'Abbasid Courtesans and the Question of Social Mobility'.
8. For instance, Abd al-Kareem al-Heitty explains that 'abandoned behaviour existed mainly among foreign *jawārī*' ('The Contrasting Spheres of Free Women and *Jawārī*', 34.) Similarly, Matthew Fuad Caswell argues that Abbasid poetry styles changed because of 'the influx of multi-national slave girls' (*The Slave Girls of Baghdad*, 207).
9. Gordon translates this term as 'of mixed parentage', born to a free Arab father and an enslaved mother (see 'Abbasid Courtesans and the Question of Social Mobility', 28–36). He finds many examples where fathers actually raised their own daughters as *qiyān*. Such fathers refused to acknowledge their paternity of the daughters they had with enslaved concubines – or sometimes even revoked their acknowledgement of paternity after previously giving it. While this mixed heritage is certainly possible for the *muwalladāt*, I do not find evidence that it

must always be the case. A *muwallada* might simply be born into a master's slave household, the offspring of his own slaves or of a marriage he has contracted between his female slave and another man.

10. Even in such cases, Ibn Saʿd provides information on ethnicity, geographic origin or colour only very rarely.
11. On the resolution to the problem of 'foreign' mothers in Islamic Spain, see D. Fairchild Ruggles, 'Mothers of a Hybrid Dynasty'; and Cristina de la Puente, 'The Ethnic Origins of Female Slaves in al-Andalus'.
12. Such a finding complicates the legal dictum, supposedly articulated by ʿUmar ibn al-Khaṭṭāb, that Arabs are not supposed to be enslaved (on this dictum, see Franz, 'Slavery in Islam', 87.)
13. On ʿAbd al-Ḥamīd's biography, see Wadad Kadi (al-Qadi), 'Identity Formation of the Bureaucracy of the Early Islamic State', 144–145.
14. Kadi, 'Identity Formation'.
15. Jennifer London argues that ʿAbd al-Ḥamīd adopted a strategy of 'assimilating' his knowledge to the Arabic-Islamic ruling class, while Ibn al-Muqaffaʿ was more forceful in arguing for preserving and adopting Persian values (personal correspondence with Jennifer London).
16. As Webb has argued in *Imagining the Arabs*, such proto-nationalistic definitions of 'Arabness' are advanced in Abbasid-era narratives and genealogies. The problem is only exacerbated by scholars working in the nineteenth and twentieth centuries, whose worldviews were dominated by nationalism. Such scholars tended to view categories such as 'Arab' and 'Persian' as timeless, essential categories, rather than historically contingent ones.
17. I thank Jennifer London for these insights and look forward to her future monograph on Ibn al-Muqaffaʿ.
18. For instance, when Ibn al-Muqaffaʿ overheard an Arabian tribesman describing a horse as 'black', he jumped in to point out that the correct term is actually 'bay'. On this and other examples of Ibn al-Muqaffaʿ's penchant for correcting people's grammar and usage, see Dominique Sourdel, 'La biographie d'Ibn al-Muqaffaʿ d'après les sources anciennes', 308.
19. Charles Pellat, 'Ḥabāba', *The Encyclopedia of Islam,* 2nd edition; H. Lammens and Kh. Y. Blankenship, 'Yazīd b. ʿAbd al-Malik', *The Encyclopedia of Islam,* 2nd edition.
20. See Al-Iṣbahānī, *Kitab al-Aghānī,* 15:85–90; al-Masʿūdī, *Murūj al-Dhahab,* 4:30–35; Ibn ʿAbd Rabbih, *Al-ʿIqd al-Farīd,* 4:441–445; al-Balādhurī, *Ansāb al-Ashrāf,* 7:201–206. Other sources, such as al-Ṭabarī's *Tārīkh,* Ibn Qutayba's

Maʿārif and al-Jaḥiẓ's *Al-Bayān wa-al-Tabyīn,* have shorter notices on Ḥabāba. The basic outlines of her life are also given in Pellat, 'Ḥabāba'; Lammens and Blankenship, 'Yazīd b. 'Abd al-Malik'; and Buthayna Bin Husayn, *Nisā' al-Khulafā' al-Umawīyīn,* 77–81.

21. This abstention from slave-girls fits ʿUmar II's biography as an ascetic, world-renouncing caliph. It also fits his presentation as an attentive caliph, the so-called fifth Rightly Guided caliph, who would never let himself be distracted from his office by the pleasure of courtesans. On ʿUmar II as the fifth of the 'Rāshidūn' caliphs, see Borrut, *Entre memoire et pouvoir,* Chapter 6; and Nancy Khalek, 'Early Islamic History Reimagined'.
22. Al-Iṣbahānī, *Kitāb al-Aghānī,* 15:89; al-Masʿūdī, *Murūj al-Dhahab,* 4:31; al-Balādhurī, *Ansāb al-Ashrāf,* 7:204. In another version, Yazīd simply wonders, 'What would ʿUmar ibn ʿAbd al-Azīz do?' (Al-Iṣbahānī, *Kitāb al-Aghānī,* 15:89). In a third version, ʿUmar ibn ʿAbd al-ʿAzīz himself sends letters to his governors – including Yazīd – warning them to avoid injustice (al-Masʿūdī, *Murūj al-Dhahab,* 4:33). While al-Balādhurī discusses the relationship between Maslama and Yazīd II, he does not include any accounts about Maslama chiding Yazīd for wasting ʿUmar II's legacy. Instead, in al-Balādhurī's account, Maslama intervenes to advise the grief-addled Yazīd after Ḥabāba's death. Yazīd reportedly refused to bury Ḥabāba's corpse for several days; Maslama encouraged Yazīd to bury her, offered to pray over her body and advised Yazīd not to exhume Ḥabāba's corpse (as he apparently later wanted to do). See al-Balādhurī, *Ansāb al-Ashrāf,* 7:204–205.
23. Al-Iṣbahānī, *Kitāb al-Aghānī,* 15:89–90; al-Masʿūdī, *Murūj al-Dhahab,* 4:31; al-Balādhurī, *Ansāb al-Ashrāf,* 7:205.
24. Al-Masʿūdī, *Murūj al-Dhahab,* 4:34.
25. Al-Balādhurī, *Ansāb al-Ashrāf,* 7:201.
26. On the shaping of the historical memory of Maslama and ʿUmar II, see Borrut, *Entre memoire et pouvoir,* chapters 5 and 6. Borrut unpacks the complicated (and sometimes conflicting) relationship between these two figures, unearths complex layers of historical writing about them and argues that both the Umayyads and later the Abbasids invoked these figures to legitimise their rule. Here, Maslama and ʿUmar do not appear in their messianic or apocalyptic guises, but merely as the symbolic 'military hero' and 'caliph-saint' who represent righteous rule.
27. I have adapted these phrasings from Borrut's felicitous French chapter titles, as well as his conclusion: 'Le calife du « renoncement au monde » fonctionne en complémentarité avec le « conquérant du monde ».' See also Aziz Al-Azmeh,

Muslim Kingship, 39, on the complementary roles of the World Conqueror and World Renouncer in political thought.

28. Al-Iṣbahānī, *Kitāb al-Aghānī*, 15:89. On the idea of Maslama as a 'quasi-caliph', see Borrut, *Entre memoire et pouvoir*, 264.
29. Tayeb El-Hibri, 'The Redemption of Umayyad Memory by the Abbasids'.
30. See Peirce, *Imperial Harem*, Chapters 1–2.
31. On enslaved women's access to public and semi-public spheres, see Abd al-Kareem al-Heitty, 'The Contrasting Spheres of Free Women and *Jawārī*'.
32. Al-Iṣbahānī, *Kitāb al-Aghānī*, 15:86.
33. Al-Mas'ūdī, *Murūj al-Dhahab*, 4:32. Mahis is a place near Medina.
34. Al-Mas'ūdī, *Murūj al-Dhahab*, 4:32.
35. The sources usually say that this is because Sulaymān made Yazīd sell Ḥabāba. Alternatively, Al-Iṣbahānī reports this account (on the authority of Isḥāq ibn Ibrāhīm al-Mawṣilī): 'Many poets composed words about her, and the male singers of Mecca sang their poems. That reached Yazīd and it horrified him, and he said: 'This is before we have even left [Mecca] and we are already worried – so how will it be when we depart?' The people mentioned the pain of separation, and it also reached him that Sulaymān was talking about that, so he rejected her'. Al-Iṣbahānī, *Kitāb al-Aghānī*, 15:88.
36. Al-Iṣbahānī, *Kitāb al-Aghānī*, 15:86.
37. *Ibid.*
38. The fact that Yazīd II's wives seem to have been advocating for their own sons as crown princes also seems to accord with Abdulhadi Alajmi's reading of the famous letter of al-Walīd II (Yazīd II's son). Alajmi argues that, by insisting on his right as caliph to name his own crown princes without consulting the other Umayyad elders, al-Walīd II was trying to consolidate power in his own direct lineage (Abdulhadi Alajmi, 'Ascribed vs. Popular Legitimacy: The Case of al-Walīd II and Umayyad 'ahd').
39. Al-Mas'ūdī, *Murūj al-Dhahab*, 4:33–34; al-Balādhurī, *Ansāb al-Ashrāf*, 7:204–205.
40. Al-Iṣbahānī, *Kitāb al-Aghānī*, 15:86–87; al-Balādhurī, *Ansāb al-Ashrāf*, 7:201–202.
41. On him, see J. C. Vadet, 'Ibn Hubayra', *EI2*.
42. Al-Balādhurī does not mention any Dāwūd among Yazīd II's children. Instead, he presents an account in which Ḥabāba's servant merely claims she has a message from 'my mistress', rather than from 'Umm Dāwūd' (Al-Balādhurī, *Ansāb al-Ashrāf*, 7:201).

43. On the trope of the slave who enslaves her master, see Aram Shahin, 'The Slave-Girls Who Enslaved the Free-Born'. Julia Bray has warned scholars to read such accounts carefully, as reflections of male slave-owners' fantasies rather than historical reality. See Bray, 'Men, Women and Slaves in Abbasid Society'.
44. For the categorisation of different works on the secretarial craft, see s.v. 'Risāla', *EI2*. In addition to the usual style manuals and literary anthologies, there exists another unusual work, al-Baghdādī's *Kitāb al-Kuttāb*, which provides several different lists of scribes. The lists include categories such as 'scribes for the Messenger of God (s.a.w.)', 'scribes who later became caliphs', 'scribes who excelled at rhetoric' and 'female scribes'. However, al-Baghdādī merely lists these scribes, providing no other historical information, anecdotes or examples of their writing. For an analysis and translation of al-Baghdādī's work, see D. Sourdel, 'Le « Livre des Secrétaires » de 'Abdallāh al-Baġdādī'.
45. On the working method of al-Jahshiyārī, particularly in comparison to other historians such as al-Ṭabarī and al-Tanūkhī, see D. Sourdel, 'Le valeur littéraire et documentaire du *Livre des Vizirs* d'al-Jahshiyārī'. While Sourdel's article focuses on Jahshiyārī's coverage of the Abbasid caliph Hārūn al-Rashīd and the Barmakid family of viziers, his remarks on the psychologising and moralising tendencies of al-Jahshiyārī are nevertheless applicable here.
46. On typical *mawlā* naming practices, see Motzki, 'The Role of Non-Arab Converts in the Development of Early Islamic Law', 308–310.
47. A notable exception here is Muḥammad's time period, which has fewer scribes than the usual sample, and the final Marwanid period, which has more scribes than usual.
48. On the contested role of Christians in the Umayyad government, see now Borrut and Donner, eds, *Christians and Others in the Umayyad State*.
49. Paul Heck, *The Construction of Knowledge in Islamic Civilization*, 12.
50. On the use of seals in assessing taxes, see Chase Robinson, 'Neck Sealing in Early Islam'.
51. For example, ʿAbd al-Malik ibn Marwān ran the *dīwān* of Medina for ʿUthmān, and Ḥabīb ibn ʿAbd al-Malik ran it for Muʿāwiya (al-Jahshiyārī, *Kitāb al-Wuzarāʾ*, 13–16); Abū Jubayra ibn al-Ḍaḥḥāk al-Anṣārī led the *dīwān* of Kufa for ʿUmar and ʿUthmān (*ibid.*, 11–12); Sulaymān al-Mishjāʿī of Quḍāʿa ran the *dīwān* of Palestine for Muʿāwiya (*ibid.*, 16); and Muḥammad ibn al-Muntashir ibn Akhī Masrūq ibn al-Ajdaʿ of Hamadān ran the *dīwān* of Iraq for Hishām (*ibid.*, 38).
52. A wealth of previous scholarship on the development of early Islamic scribal

practice informs my reading of the 'scribe-as-scapegoat' phenomenon and its relationship to social identities. The pre-eminent scholar working on early Islamic scribal practice today, and particularly how scribal practice relates to social identity, is Wadad Kadi. See Kadi, 'Identity Formation of the Bureaucracy of the Early Islamic State' and 'The Names of Estates in State Registers Before and After the Arabisation of the "Dīwāns"' and 'Early Islamic State Letters: The Question of Authenticity'.

Other scholarship on the development of early Islamic scribal practice includes the foundational M. Sprengling, 'From Persian to Arabic'. See also M. Carter, 'The *Kātib* in Fact and Fiction'; Bo Holmberg, 'Christian Scribes in the Arabic Empire'; Amidu Sanni, 'The Secretary (*Kātib*) and his Tool in Medieval Islam'; Klaus Hachmeier, 'Die Entwicklung Der Epistolographie Vom Frühen Islam Bis Zum 4./10. Jahrhundert'; and Hussain Ali Mahafzah, 'The Development of the Job of the Secretaries of State and Their Role in the Early Period of Islam'. While the last item in this list has a promising title, its contents unfortunately do not adhere to rigorous academic standards.

53. We saw a similar trend in Chapter 5 regarding marital practices; what began as a rather broad network of Qurashi-noble elites soon became an intra-Quraysh competition for power.
54. Al-Jahshiyārī, *Kitāb al-Wuzarā'*, 14. See also the extended narrative of ʿUthmān's unpopularity and eventual murder in al-Ṭabarī's *Tārīkh*, I:2980–3025. For a recent analysis of ʿUthmān's legacy in history and memory, see Heather Keaney, *Medieval Islamic Historiography: Remembering Rebellion*.
55. Belonging to the Quraysh tribe is one of the basic qualifications for the caliphate in works of classical Islamic thought, such as al-Māwardī's (d. 450/1058) *al-Aḥkām al-Sulṭāniyya* (Ordinances of Government).
56. Muʿāwiya placed the Qurashi ʿAmr ibn Saʿīd ibn al-ʿĀṣ in charge of the army and Ḥabīb ibn ʿAbd al-Malik ibn Marwān in charge of the *dīwān* of Medina (al-Jahshiyārī, *Kitāb al-Wuzarā'*, 15–16).
57. On Sarjūn and his family, see Sidney H. Griffith, 'The Mansur Family and St. John of Damascus', and the sources cited therein.
58. For a deeper analysis of this particular incident, see Nancy Khalek, 'Some Notes on the Representation of Non-Muslim Officials', 507–509.
59. Sprengling points out that that early leaders such as Muʿāwiya and Ziyād ibn Abīhi had lived most of their lives in places such as Syria and Basra, and they were likely to be bilingual themselves or at least to be comfortable in a milieu where people spoke Greek, Aramaic and Persian. Conversely, the next generation

of leaders, such as ʿAbd al-Malik and al-Ḥajjāj, had lived most of their life in the Hijaz before being sent out to rule in Syria and Iraq (Sprengling, 'From Persian to Arabic', 196). Perhaps this cultural upbringing is why ʿAbd al-Malik and al-Ḥajjāj resented their bilingual scribes (Sarjūn and Zādhān Farrūkh, respectively) more than Muʿāwiya and Ziyād had done.

60. Al-Jahshiyārī transmits a similar account wherein Zādhān Farrūkh brags that al-Ḥajjāj needed him, which led another scribe to suggest that al-Ḥajjāj should Arabise the dīwāns (al-Jahshiyārī, *Kitāb al-Wuzarāʾ*, 23). For deeper analysis of this story, see Khalek, 'Some Notes on the Representation of Non-Muslim Officials', 510–512.
61. On the *mawālī*'s domination of the bureaucracy, see Kadi, 'Identity Formation', 141–144.
62. Michael G. Morony mentions that many sedentary Arabs from among the conquered populations were likely bilingual (*Iraq After the Muslim Conquest*, 222), and that 'the second generation of the garrison cities after the conquest tended to be of mixed parentage and were bilingual' (*ibid.*, 255).
63. Al-Jahshiyārī, *Kitāb al-Wuzarāʾ*, 16.
64. *Ibid.*, 29.
65. *Ibid.*, 28.
66. Everett K. Rowson, 'The Effeminates of Early Medina'.
67. Rowson provides convincing evidence that this mass castration did actually take place. Rowson finds the 'clerical error' explanation to be feeble, while I find it to be more plausible. Rowson instead understands this incident to mean that the scribe dropped an accidental blob of ink over the letter in question (changing it from a *ḥa* to a *kha*), and he reads it as a straightforward example of scapegoating the scribe to protect the caliph from the accusation of having perpetrated this brutality. Whatever actually happened, it is interesting simply to consider how different authors in different genres try to understand this disaster from their particular perspectives. The literary anthologist al-Iṣbahānī says the castration happened because of love, jealousy and the power of poetry (Rowson, 'Effeminates', 690–693). The scribal historian al-Jahshiyārī frames it as bad bureaucratic practice and uses it to highlight the importance of scribes. Both authors are trying in their own way to make sense of linguistic power, whether it is the power of the poet or of the scribe.
68. According to al-Jahshiyārī, *Kitab al-Wuzarāʾ*, 33–34, the scribes of ʿUmar II were: 1) Layth ibn Ruqayya, the *mawlā* of Umm al-Ḥakam bint Abī Sufyān 2) Rajāʾ bin Ḥaywa ibn Jandal (al-Kindī); 3) Ismaʿīl ibn Abī Ḥukaym, the *mawlā*

of al-Zubayr; 4) Sulaymān ibn Sa'd al-Khushanī, *mawlā* of the Khushan tribe (according to Ibn 'Asākīr, *Tārīkh Madīnat Dimashq,* 22:317); 5) Maymūn ibn Mihrān, *mawlā* of Naḍr ibn Mu'āwiya of Hawazin (see Parvaneh Pourshariati, 'The Mihrans and the Articulation of Islamic Dogma'); 6) his son 'Amr ibn Maymūn ibn Mihrān; 7) Ibn Abī al-Zinād (maybe) or his father Abū al-Zinād, in either case, a *mawlā* of 'Uthmān's family, and 8) someone called al-Ṣabbāḥ ibn al-Muthannā, about whom I can find no information.

7

Conclusions

This book has posited that enslaved and freed persons provide a fruitful window on to Islamic history precisely because of their liminality. As liminal figures, they sparked debates about the political, social and religious boundaries of the *umma*: who belongs to the *umma,* and how do they demonstrate that belonging? How can Muslims navigate the tension between more egalitarian and more hierarchical readings of religious texts? Who should have access to political power and cultural authority? By tracing how such debates unfolded in the first two centuries of Islam, this book has hoped to shed some light on how Islam transformed from a small Arabian reform movement into the official doctrine of a world-spanning empire. It has also hoped to combat essentialising narratives that present the first century of Islam as a static age that represents some ideal, 'true' Islam. Instead, by revealing how early Muslims constructed and re-constructed their identities to fit changing contexts, this book has celebrated the flexibility and creativity of early Islamic history.

For example, we have seen how '*mawlā*' was simply a marker of shared faith for Abū Bakra, while later authors used his *mawlā* identity as an anti-Umayyad political symbol. We have seen how enslaved prostitutes in Medina advocated for their own interpretation of Q 24:33, even as later Iraqi exegetes downplayed or discounted these women's actions. We have seen how many Arabian tribal notables – and not only the Umayyads – had a vested interest in excluding 'half-blood' children from attaining the imamate; but these children of mixed parentage eventually successfully advocated for their own 'Arab' identity by invoking prophetic precedent. Finally, we have seen how *muwalladāt* courtesans and *mawālī* scribes teetered on the precipice of power in the Marwanid polity. They used their mastery of Arabic language and lore to enter the caliph's inner circle, but their unfreedom placed great limits on the power that their language mastery afforded them.

In addition to these findings, several larger conclusions emerge from the research presented here. First, enslaved and freed persons shaped Islamic society in myriad ways. From their subaltern positions, they negotiated the meaning of the Quran; helped create a collaborative (if still not completely egalitarian) community in Medina; changed definitions of lineage and ethnicity; produced great works of Arabic-Islamic culture; and acted as powerful courtiers and queens. Scholars have previously noted the intellectual contributions of non-Arab Muslims, often as a subtle way of trumpeting the superiority of Romans and Persians over the barbarian Arabs.[1] Here, instead of engaging in polemics about which 'civilisation' is superior, I have instead viewed unfree people as participating in a complex network of dependencies and power relationships. For example, I suggest that the courtesans might have sung in double-entendres because they were unfree, not because they were 'foreign'. I likewise suggest that *mawālī* scholars might have contributed so greatly to Islamic scholarship not because of their foreign educations, but because they were trying to resolve their liminality and prove their true belonging to the Arabic-Islamic world. Unfreedom, and not merely 'foreignness', is a crucial component in understanding these cultural and intellectual contributions.

Second, women have been too often overlooked as agents of historical change. Here, I have argued that enslaved and freed women were integral to debates about sexual ethics, motherhood, proximity politics and ethnicity. Enslaved prostitutes advocated for their own readings of Q 24:33, playing an active part in the earliest *umma*. Enslaved mothers changed the demographics of the Umayyad empire and indirectly changed the conception of 'Arab' lineage. Enslaved musicians participated in Umayyad politics as courtesans, producers of Arabic culture and would-be queens. We cannot understand the rise of the slave-born caliph in the late Umayyad period without understanding the impact of slave mothers themselves. We cannot understand how the increasingly centralised Umayyad caliphate worked without analysing the career of women such as Ḥabāba. If we fail to study women, we will necessarily only see half the picture.

Third, ethnicity is not a timeless category, but a historical and contested one. In the Umayyad period, unfree people sparked debates about whether Arab identity is based on blood/lineage or language/culture. Even as the 'half-bloods' re-defined themselves as full Arabs based on their fathers' lineage, so the ostensibly non-Arab courtesans and scribes gained power through their mastery of Arabic language and lore. These subaltern groups also reveal many ambiguities and ironies inherent in trying to resolve the intractable question of ethnicity. For example, while 'half-blood' men eventually successfully argued for their status as full Arabs, female *muwalladāt* (who were often also technically 'half-bloods') remained enslaved and excluded from the category of Arab. In short, Muslims of slave origins throw the debates about the meaning of ethnic categories into sharp relief.

Future Trajectories

There is still much left to do to explore the role of unfreedom and the status of unfree people in early Islamic history. In particular, many ambiguities remain in the identity and meaning of the early Islamic *mawālī*. In order to continue to explicate the meaning of this term, I suggest that scholars should avoid adopting 'non-Arab Muslims' as their primary definition, but instead adopt the lens of unfreedom. One of the pitfalls of glossing *mawālī* as 'non-Arab Muslims' is that it has sometimes led scholars to see *mawālī* where they do not actually appear in the sources. For example, in the year 83/702–703, the Umayyad governor al-Ḥajjāj famously returned the peasants of Iraq to their farms and forced them to pay the land tax. Otherwise insightful and careful scholars use the term '*mawālī*' when describing this incident. For example, Chase Robinson writes of 'al-Ḥajjāj returning the *mawālī* to the garrison cities of Iraq',[2] while Gerald Hawting describes how al-Ḥajjāj responded to decreasing tax revenues by 'rounding up the *mawālī* in the towns, driving them out, and forcing them to pay their taxes'.[3] However, the primary sources for this event do not use the word *mawālī*. The account in al-Ṭabarī's *Tārīkh* simply calls them the 'protected population (*ahl al-dhimma*) who had submitted (*aslamū*)'.[4]

Al-Jāḥiẓ also gives a version of this same episode in his 'al-Risāla fī al-Nābita', in which says, 'He [al-Ḥajjāj] decreed tattooing the hands of the male Muslims and painting on the hands of the female Muslims, and he returned them after their *hijra* back to the villages.'[5] The word *mawālī* here is absent, and the issue at stake here is that people are trying to become Muslims by making *hijra* (emigrating to the cities), not by becoming *mawālī*. In fact, al-Jāḥiẓ mentions the *mawālī* later in this same letter, as a group of upstarts in Jāḥiẓ's own day who claimed to combine the characteristics of the Arabs and Persians.[6] That is, al-Jāḥiẓ is perfectly aware of the term *mawālī*, but he does not use it here in this account about al-Ḥajjāj. The most obvious conclusion is that the people fleeing to the garrison towns are not *mawālī*.[7]

In another famous incident, the pious ʿUmar II (r. 99–101/717–720) reportedly sacked his governor, al-Jarrāḥ, for perpetrating injustices against the people of Iraq. According to the historian al-Yaʿqūbī, ''Umar heard of matters concerning al-Jarrāḥ which he found reprehensible, such as his collecting the poll-tax from people who had converted to Islam, sending *mawālī* on campaigns without granting them stipends, and displaying factionalism'.[8] Similarly, al-Ṭabarī reports that a *mawlā* named Ṣāliḥ or Saʿīd complained to ʿUmar II, 'There are twenty thousand *mawālī* who make raids without receiving any stipend or spoils, and there are a similar number of *ahl al-dhimma* who have converted to Islam, yet are still made to pay the tribute.'[9] Such accounts actually treat 'converts to Islam' and *mawālī* as two different groups facing two different economic problems. Those who converted are not called *mawālī* here, but 'protected peoples' (*ahl al-dhimma*) who had 'submitted' (*aslamū*); the problem is that they are being unfairly taxed. Those who are called *mawālī* here are not explicitly described as converts, and they seem to be dependent military contingents; the problem is that they are not being paid for their military service. Moreover, as Gibb has shown, the fiscal rescript of Umar II, found in Ibn ʿAbd al-Ḥakam's *Sīrat ʿUmar,* does not use the term '*mawālī*' at all when discussing the caliph's agrarian tax policies.[10] Accounts such as these suggest that the *mawālī* and serfs are not exactly the same thing. More work needs to be done to explicate the relationship between *mawālī* and serfs, and 'unfreedom' might prove a fruitful lens for analysing these different statuses.

Finally, several notable scholars, including H. A. R. Gibb, M. A. Shaban and Hawting, describe the late-Umayyad rebel al-Ḥārith ibn Surayj as a champion of the *mawālī*.[11] Al-Harith certainly used religious slogans that may have appealed to many groups, including unfree and disenfranchised groups. However, al-Ṭabarī describes al-Ḥārith's followers not as '*mawālī*' but as a 'numerous assemblage' made up of Tamīmīs, *dihqāns* and others. Al-Ḥārith also flees to the lands of the non-Arabs (*ʿajam*), fights using Persian weapons and allies with a Turkish *khāqān*. That is, the primary sources do not call him a champion of 'the *mawālī*', but rather associate him with terms such as *dihqāns*, *ʿajam* and Turks.[12] Such non-Arab groups only become synonymous with 'the *mawālī*' in the minds of modern scholars who assume that *mawālī* and non-Arabs must be the same thing, an assumption that our primary sources do not always support. As previously mentioned, according to al-Jāḥiẓ, the *mawālī* of the third/ninth century actually presented themselves as something of a hybrid between Arabs and Ajam; they even claimed that their hybrid identity made them superior to both the Arabs and the Ajam, for 'he who displays the characteristics of both is superior to he who displays only one'.[13] To place the *mawālī* firmly in the 'non-Arab' camp is to miss a large part of the tension or debate that they caused. It is also to ignore the fact that many *mawālī* seem to have rejected the ascription of 'non-Arab' identity and, instead, to have identified themselves strongly as Muslims and masters of Arabic-Islamic learning. Additionally, recent scholars such as Peter Webb and Fred Donner have argued that terms such as 'Arab' and 'Muslim' are second-/eighth--century constructions that do not reflect earlier history.[14] For these many reasons, it seems unwarranted to insist on continuing to gloss *mawālī* automatically as 'non-Arab Muslims'.

Assuming we read our primary sources carefully, it remains quite unclear what the relationship is between individual *mawālī*-freedmen, and the collective or group called 'the *mawālī*'. Many previous scholars have compiled evidence on individual *mawālī*.[15] The most comprehensive of these is Jamal Juda's work, detailing numerous references to different *mawālī* in various different sources. One of his most important findings is that the *mawālī* were not a coherent social class; any individual *mawlā*'s social standing depended on that of his master. That is, they were in unfree relationships with their masters. In Juda's analysis, *mawālī* seem to have been embedded in relationships of dependency on the level of the individual household or extended family – they were domestic servants or personal retainers. But what happens to the term '*mawālī*' when it becomes stripped of this personal, relational quality? For it does seem that, by the end of the Umayyad period and into the early Abbasid period, the sources begin to use the collective term 'the *mawālī* with more frequency. Who are these collective *mawālī*, as opposed to the individual *mawālī of* individual masters or patrons?

A few texts provide tantalising hints, but no hard-and-fast answers. For example, one version of the peace treaty the Arabian armies made with the people of Tiflis (Tblisi) contains the Quranic paraphrase: 'If you submit (*aslamtum*) and perform the prayer, [you are] our brothers in religion and our *mawālī*.'[16] While an in-depth analysis of this Quranic phrasing is beyond the scope of this concluding chapter, I find this sentence curious. It slightly alters and conflates two different Quranic verses (9:11 and 33:5), and the purpose of its conditional clause 'if . . . then' is ambiguous. On the one hand, the text could be saying to the people of Tiflis: 'You are currently Christians, and you owe us these forms of service. But *if* you become Muslims, *then* you will become one of us – you will then no longer owe us service.' However, there is another way of reading the text, which accords more with Donner's 'Believers' Movement' thesis. This text could be saying to the people of Tiflis: 'You are Christians and owe us these forms of service *because* God said: "If you submit, perform the prayer, and uphold the tax, you are our brothers in religion and our *mawālī*."' That is, it could be confirming the people of Tiflis as monotheistic brethren and helpers (*mawālī*), which is precisely why the people of Tiflis should provide the conquering armies faithful service. Military service is a sign of their shared piety. In this case '*mawālī*' would mean something like 'vassals', or conquered populations who receive protection in return for acts of service. Could '*mawālī*' in other contexts indicate such collective vassalage agreements? If so, it might help explain the Umayyad-era debates about whether or not military *mawālī* should be paid.[17] Perhaps 'the *mawālī*' were not paid because military service was part of their vassalage agreement.

The treaty of Tiflis seems to present *mawālī* as having more of a communal agreement of political dependency, rather than a domestic relationship of personal dependency. But the accounts of the rebellion of al-Mukhtār destroy this relational character altogether. Several accounts of al-Mukhtār's rebellion in 66–67/685–687 present 'the *mawālī*' as a stand-alone group, disconnected from any communal or personal relationships. Many scholars have noted that these *mawālī* are probably freed slaves. This may well be true, but some of the accounts of al-Mukhtār's rebellion treat slaves and *mawālī* as slightly different groups. For instance, al-Madā'inī transmits an account that treats *mawālī* and slaves as performing different social roles. In this account, al-Mukhtār's army has been defeated, and a Kufan notable demands that the victorious Umayyad general 'should return our slaves to us, for they are for our widowers and our weak ones. But the *mawālī* should have their necks struck, for their disbelief (*kufr*), the magnitude of their arrogance, and the paucity of their thankfulness have become apparent. I do not trust them with religion.'[18] According to this account, slaves are still needed for personal service; they are apparently still considered members of the household, albeit disobedient ones. The *mawālī* appear to be more detached from the familiar household. It is noteworthy that this account uses the term 'our' slaves as a relational term, in contrast to 'the' *mawālī* as a collective. Other accounts also refer to 'the' *mawālī*, as when the poet Aʿshā Hamdān says, 'There gathered against you the *mawālī* and their betwitcher [al-Mukhtār].'[19] Similarly, Abū Mikhnaf transmits a report asserting that 'nothing was worse than al-Mukhtār assigning the *fay'* to the *mawālī*'.

In short, the identity of the *mawālī* who joined al-Mukhtār's rebellion remains somewhat uncertain. Were they masses of freedmen who now existed in such numbers, or at such a generational distance from their original conquerors, that their bonds of dependency had begun to disintegrate? Or were they masses of vassals who had become resentful enough, and powerful enough, to re-negotiate the terms of their original vassalage agreement? Or were they perhaps a combination of both? In either case, the *mawālī* in al-Mukhtār's rebellion seem to signal the inadequacy of the individual household, or ad-hoc vassalage agreements, for cementing the expanding Islamic state into a cohesive religio-political unit. The Umayyad state would need to create more systematic, centralised political institutions to achieve unity.

And yet, even as the sources begin to speak of 'the *mawālī*' as participating in al-Mukhtār's revolt, or forming a class of *qayna*-trainers in Medina, or taking over the reins of Umayyad-era scholarship, it is clear that many individual *mawālī* continued to be enmeshed in personal, domestic relationships of dependency. How did individual *mawālī* involved in such relationships relate to 'the *mawālī*' as a political or social collective? Perhaps the lens of unfreedom would prove useful in teasing out the nuances of these questions.

Finally, it seems possible that *mawālī*, converts, peasants and other subalterns played a role in the increasing dominance of the terms 'Islam' and 'Muslim' in the Umayyad period. Several scholars have previously noted that the early followers of Muḥammad did not call themselves 'Muslimūn' (Submitters) but rather 'Mu'minūn' (Believers). Contemporary non-Arabic sources also describe the conquerors not as 'Muslimūn' but as 'Muhajirūn' (Emigrants). In the Quran, it appears that these two terms, Believers and Emigrants, are conceptually related: belief entailed emigration, and emigration demonstrated belief. According to Q 49:14–15, failing to emigrate in this way rendered one merely a 'Submitter', not a true 'Believer'.[20] Documentary evidence makes it clear that, by the 2nd/8th century, the terms 'Arab' and 'Muslim' were starting to supersede the terms 'Believers' and 'Emigrants'. However, documentary evidence does little to explain *why* and *how* such a terminological shift occurred.

In trying to determine why the conquerors dropped the term 'Emigrants' for themselves, and adopted instead the term 'Arabs' in the second/eighth century, Peter Webb points out that the descendants of the original conquerors had stopped emigrating to new frontier towns to wage jihad; instead, many of them had settled permanently in the original Iraqi garrison towns and had taken up civilian occupations. That is, they were no longer technically 'Emigrants'. At the same time, as we have seen, the conquered peasants of the countryside apparently attempted to make themselves 'Emigrants' by moving to the garrison towns in the early second/eighth century.[21] Because the Quran appears to conflate Emigration with Belief, when al-Ḥajjāj barred these Emigrants from entering Basra, he was not merely demonstrating his ethnic prejudice or his political injustice, but he was also potentially barring people from attaining salvation. That is, *hijra* may have been just as important as a marker of belief for these peasants as, say, prayer or almsgiving. Thus, perhaps the Umayyads needed to find a compromise – a name for the religion that would allow for all people to achieve salvation, while also maintaining a subordinated population of tax-paying peasants. 'Islam' seems to strike such a compromise, as it implies submission to God, but it can also imply submission to worldly authority figures. Likewise, the aforementioned treaty of Tiflis might imply that good 'Muslims' submit to the conquering armies, pay their taxes to the state and offer their services. That is, 'Muslim' might be a useful term in incorporating new Believers, but also subordinating them to the increasingly centralised Islamic state.

I do not wish to overstate my case. I do not mean to say that the Umayyads invented the term 'Muslim', or that it must necessarily have insidious, autocratic overtones, or that the incorporation of subalterns is the *only* way to explain the change towards 'Muslim'. Islam is clearly a Quranic term that may be a proper name for the religion, as in Q 5:3: 'On this day I have perfected your religion for you, and completed my favour onto you – I have chosen Islam for you as your religion.'[22] It also seems that the Umayyads might have advocated for the term 'Muslim' in order to exclude revolutionaries and rebels such as ʿAbdallāh Ibn al-Zubayr or the Kharijites – one can only attain salvation if one 'submits' to the caliph, God's viceregent on earth. Instead, I merely suggest that the relatively more hierarchical or authoritarian ring of 'Muslims' (Submitters), as opposed to the relatively more egalitarian-sounding term 'Believers' or the more activist term 'Emigrants', may have represented a satisfactory compromise between the needs of an orderly, hierarchical empire and the moral imperative of a universalising religion.

Final Remarks

In the end, I hope future studies of the *mawālī, muwalladāt* and other unfree groups will not attempt to posit some hard-and-fast definition of who these groups 'were', but instead explore the debates and tensions these groups created. These groups linger at the blurred edges of a religio-political community that needs to be defined and controlled, but never really can be. These groups inhabit the grey area between Arab and non-Arab, slave and free, conqueror and conquered, elite and commoner, insider and outsider. Therein lies their incredible richness and value.

One might wonder, what is the continued relevance or fruitfulness of studying such groups in today's ostensibly post-slavery world? The term *hujanā'*, ('half-bloods') seems to have died out by the end of the Umayyad period; the term *mawālī* ceased describing a distinct social class by the mid-Abbasid period.[23] *Umm walads* no longer inhabit the homes of the urban elite; famous singers of the Arab world today are free, not enslaved. However, 'unfreedom' clearly does still exist in many different guises in today's world, from exploitative labour practices to sex trafficking. Moreover, questions persist about the meaning of 'Arab' and 'Islam', and the relationship between the two. The obsolescence of some of the terms investigated in this book does not signal the disappearance of debates about who belongs to the *umma* or how they belong. This book merely provides a glimpse into one chapter of how some people have attempted to find meaning, belonging and sense of self on a swiftly tilting planet.

Notes

1. On this subtext of discussions of the *mawālī* scholars, see Motzki, 'The Role of Non-Arab Converts', 295, fn. 8.
2. Robinson, 'Neck-Sealing', 431.
3. Hawting, *First Dynasty*, 70.
4. Al-Ṭabarī, *Tārīkh*, II:1,123.
5. Al-Jāḥiẓ, *Rasā'il al-Jāḥiẓ*, 2:14. Note how the male peasants have a permanent mark tattooed on their hands, while the female peasants only have a temporary mark painted on their hands. This seems to indicate that the boundaries between the communities were more porous for women than for men.
6. Al-Jāḥiẓ, *Rasā'il al-Jāḥiẓ*, 2:17.
7. Patricia Crone has been more careful in saying that these people were *trying* (but failing) to become *mawālī* (Crone, *Slaves on Horses*, 52), but the sources do not state this explicitly. Instead of trying to become '*mawālī*', they may have been trying to become '*muhājirūn*' or Emigrants.
8. Al-Yaʿqūbī, *Tārīkh*, 2:362.
9. Al-Ṭabarī, *Tārīkh*, II:1,354. See Robinson, 'Neck Sealing', 416. Robinson indicates that *dhimma* at this time does not necessarily refer to People of the Book (protected monotheistic communities) but any conquered people put under the 'protection' of their conquerors.
10. Gibb, 'The Fiscal Rescript of Umar II', *Arabica*, 2, no. 1 (January 1955): 1–16. That particular text raises many questions, such as why it fails to mention peasants seeking to make *hijra* to the garrison towns. This text mentions peasants fleeing from their lands into other lands, and it specifically mentions *bedouin* (*aʿrāb*) being allowed to make *hijra*.
11. See, for example, Hawting, *First Dynasty*, 86.
12. They also strongly associate him with intra-Arab factionalism. As Wadad Kadi notes, most of al-Ḥārith's followers were Arabs, not *mawālī* (Kadi, 'The Earliest "Nabita" and the Paradigmatic "Nawabit"', 37, fn. 32.)
13. Al-Jāḥiẓ, *Rasā'il al-Jāḥiẓ*, 2:17. Al-Jāḥiẓ, who identified strongly with the 'Arab' camp, found the *mawālī*'s claims to be ludicrous.
14. Donner has argued that Muhammad's earliest followers called themselves

'Believers', not 'Muslims'; see Fred Donner, *Muhammad and the Believers*, especially pp. 39–144. Peter Webb has argued that 'Arab' as an ethonym only first appeared in the second/eighth century; see Peter Webb, *Imagining the Arabs,* especially pp. 110–239.

15. For example, Motzki, 'The Role of Non-Arab Converts', compiles information on *mawālī* scholars from al-Shīrāzī's (d. 476/1083) *Ṭabaqāt al-Fuqahā'*. Bernards and Nawas have compiled information from many more sources for their Netherlands Ulama Project. See Bernards and Nawas, 'A Preliminary Report of the Netherlands Ulama Project (NUP)'; Bernards and Nawas, eds, *Patronate and Patronage in Early and Classical Islam*; Nawas, 'The Birth of an Elite: Mawālī and Arab ʿUlamāʾ'; Nawas, 'The Contribution of the Mawālī to the Six Sunnite Canonical Ḥadīth Collections'; and Nawas, 'The Emergence of Fiqh as a Distinct Discipline'. It should be noted that these scholars' findings pertain only to *mawālī* intellectuals and scholars (particularly, jurists), and thus their findings cannot be extrapolated to *all mawālī*.
16. Al-Ṭabarī, *Tārīkh*, I:2,675; al-Balādhurī, *Futūḥ al-Buldān*, 201–202. For an in-depth analysis of this text, see Noth, *The Early Arabic Historical Tradition*, 64–76.
17. Earlier scholars such as Wellhausen have suggested that *mawālī* were left unpaid because the Arab commanders were prejudiced against non-Arabs; Crone has conversely suggested that these *mawālī* were peasant volunteer foot-soldiers (*Slaves on Horses*, 52–53).
18. Al-Ṭabarī, *Tārīkh*, II:750; al-Balādhurī, *Ansāb al-Ashrāf*, 6:135.
19. Al-Ṭabarī, *Tārīkh*, II:730.
20. Q 49:14–15 read: 'The bedouin say, "We believe." Say: You do not believe, so say, "We submit." For faith has not entered your hearts. But if you obey God and his Messenger, He will not belittle any of your deeds, for God is forgiving and merciful. Believers are only those who believe in God and His messenger, and thereafter have never doubted – they strive with their possessions and selves in the path of God. Those are the sincere ones.'
21. Webb, *Imagining the Arabs*, 143–144; see also Ilkka Lindstedt, '*Muhājirūn* as a Name for the First/Seventh Century Muslims'.
22. See also Q 2:131–132: 'Lo, God said to Abraham: "Submit." Abraham said: "I submit to the Lord of the Worlds." And Abraham bequeathed this to his sons, and Jacob: "O my children, God has purified your religion. Do not die unless you are Muslims."'
23. For the decline of the term '*mawlā*' as a salient social indicator in the biographi-

cal dictionaries, see Donner, 'Tribal Settlement'; Richard Bulliet, 'Conversion-Based Patronage and Onomastic Evidence'; and Nawas, 'A Profile of the *Mawālī Ulama*'. However, the term always persisted in legal circles to mean freed slave, and it persisted also in its 'upper' form meaning master or lord. For example, the Mevlevis (*mawlāwīs*) of Turkey are known as such because they follow the path of their '*mawlā*' or founder, Jalal al-Din Rumi. It also is worth mentioning that in modern Bollywood films, there are still stock characters known as *mawaali*, who are usually seedy Muslims associated with the criminal underworld. (I thank Dr Shailaja Paik for drawing this final point to my attention.)

Bibliography

Primary Sources

ʿAbd al-Razzāq ibn Ḥammām al-Ḥimyarī. *Al-Muṣannaf.* Edited by Ḥabīb al-Raḥmān al-ʿAẓamī. 11 vols. Beirut: al-Maktab al-Islāmī, 1970–1972.

——. *Tafsīr Al-Qur'ān.* 3 vols. Riyadh: Maktabat al-Rushd, 1989.

Abū Dā'ūd, Sulaymān ibn al-Ashʿath al-Sijistānī. *Sunan.* Edited by Muḥammad Muḥyī al-Dīn ʿAbd al-Ḥamīd. 4 vols. n.p.: Dār Iḥyā' al-Sunna al-Tabawiyya, 1970.

al-Azharī, Muḥammad ibn Aḥmad. *Tahdhīb al-Lugha.* Edited by Aḥmad ʿAbd al-Raḥmān Mukhaymar. 11 vols plus indices. Beirut: Dār al-Kutub al-Ilmiyya, 2004.

al-Balādhurī, Aḥmad ibn Yaḥyā. *Liber expugnationis regionum (= Futūḥ al-Buldān).* Edited by M. J. de Goeje. Leiden: Brill, 1968.

——. *Ansāb al-Ashrāf.* Edited by Maḥmūd al-Fardaws al-ʿAẓm. 26 vols. Damascus: Dār al-Yaqaẓa al-ʿArabiyya, 1997–.

al-Bayḍāwī, ʿAbdallāh ibn ʿUmar. *Tafsīr Qāḍī Bayḍāwī al-musammá bi-Anwār al-tanzīl wa-asrār al-ta'wīl.* 2 vols. [Istanbul?]: Dār al-Ṭibāʿa al-ʿĀmira, 1285 [1868]. Accessed on 28 July 2017 at Hathi Trust. https://catalog.hathitrust.org/Record/001926422

al-Bazzār, Abū Bakr Aḥmad ibn ʿAmr. *Al-Baḥr al-Zakhkhār al-Maʿrūf bi-Musnad al-Bazzār.* Edited by Maḥfūẓ al-Raḥmān Zayn Allāh. 20 vols. Medina: Maktabat al-ʿUlūm wa-Ḥikam, 2003–2009.

al-Bukhārī, Muḥammad ibn Ismāʿīl. *Kitāb al-Tārīkh al-Kabīr.* 4 vols. Hyderabad: Maṭbaʿat Jamʿiyyat Dāʾirat al-Maʿārif al-Uthmāniyya, 1941–1958.

——. *Ṣaḥīḥ al-Bukhārī.* Edited by Muḥammad Muḥsin Khān. 9 vols. Gujranwala: Taleem-ul-Quran Trust, 1971.

al-Dārimī, ʿAbd Allāh ibn ʿAbd al-Raḥmān. *Musnad al-Dārimī, al-maʿrūf bi-Sunan al-Dārimī*. Edited by Ḥusayn Salīm Asad al-Dārānī. 4 vols. Riyadh: Dār al-Mughnī; Beirut: Dār Ibn Ḥazm, 2000.

al-Dhahabī, Muḥammad ibn Aḥmad. *Siyar Aʿlam al-Nubalāʾ*. Edited by Muṣṭafā ʿAbd al-Qādir ʿAṭā. 17 vols. Beirut: Manshūrāt Muḥammad ʿAlī Bayḍūn, Dār al-Kutub al-ʿIlmiyya, 2004.

al-Ḥamawī, Yāqūt ibn ʿAbdallāh. *Muʿjam al-Buldān*. 7 vols. Beirut: Dār Ṣādir, 1991–2010.

al-Hawwārī, Hūd ibn Muḥakkam. *Tafsīr Kitāb Allāh Al-ʿAzīz*. 4 vols. Beirut: Dār al-Gharb al-Islāmī, 1990.

Ibn ʿAbd al-Ḥakam, ʿAbd al-Raḥmān. *The History of the Conquest of Egypt, North Africa and Spain (Futūḥ Miṣr)*. Edited by Charles C. Torrey. New Haven: Yale University Press, 1922.

Ibn ʿAbd Rabbih. *Al-ʿIqd al-Farīd*. Edited by Aḥmad Amīn. 7 vols. Cairo: Maṭbaʿat Lajnat al-Taʾlīf wa-al-Tarjama wa-al-Nashr, 1940–1953.

Ibn Abī Shayba, ʿAbd Allāh ibn Muḥammad. *Al-Kitāb al-Muṣannaf*. Edited by Ḥamad ibn ʿAbd Allāh al-Jumʿa and Muḥammad ibn Ibrāhīm al-Laḥīdān. 16 vols. Riyadh: Maktabat al-Rushd Nāshirūn, 2004.

Ibn ʿAsākir, ʿAlī ibn al-Ḥasan. *Tārīkh Madīnat Dimashq*. Edited by ʿUmar ibn Gharāma al-ʿAmrawī. 80 vols. Beirut: Dār al-Fikr, 1995–2000.

Ibn Aʿtham al-Kūfī. *Kitāb al-Futūḥ*. 8 vols. Hyderabad: Maṭbaʿat Majlis Dāʾirat al-Maʿārif al-ʿUthmāniyya, 1968–.

Ibn Ḥabīb, ʿAbd al-Malik. *Kitāb al-Taʾrīj (La Historia)*. Edited by Jorge Aguadé. Madrid: Consejo Superior de Investigaciones Científicas, Instituto de Cooperación con el Mundo Arabe, 1991.

Ibn Ḥajar al-ʿAsqalānī, Aḥmad ibn ʿAlī. *Tahdhīb al-Tahdhīb fī Rijāl al-Ḥadīth*. Edited by ʿĀdil Aḥmad ʿAbd al-Mawjūd and ʿAlī Muḥammd Muʿawwaḍ. 7 vols. Beirut: Dār al-Kutub al-ʿIlmiyya, 2004.

Ibn Ḥanbal, Aḥmad. *Al-Musnad lil-Imām Aḥmad ibn Muḥammad ibn Ḥanbal*. 2nd edition. Edited by Aḥmad Muḥammad Shākir. 15 vols. Cairo: Dār al-Maʿārif, 1946–1956.

——. *Kitāb al-Asāmī wa-al-Kunā*. Edited by ʿAbd Allāh ibn Yūsuf al-Judayʿ. Kuwait: Maktabat Dār al-Aqṣá, 1985.

Ibn Hishām, ʿAbd al-Malik. *Al-Sīra al-Nabawiyya*. Edited by Muṣṭafā al-Saqqā Ibrāhīm al-Ibyārī and ʿAbd al-Ḥafīẓ Shalabī. 2 vols. Cairo: Maktabat wa-Maṭbaʿat al-Bābī al-Ḥalabī, 1955.

Ibn Isḥāq, Muḥammad. *Sīrat Rasūl Allāh*. Edited by Ferdinand Wüstenfeld. 2 vols. Göttingen: Dieterich, 1858–1860.

Ibn al-Jawzī, Abū al-Faraj ʿAbd al-Raḥmān ibn ʿAlī. *Zād Al-Masīr Fī ʿIlm Al-Tafsīr*. 8 vols. Beirut: Dār al-Kutub al-ʿIlmiyya, 1994.

Ibn al-Kalbī, Muhammad. *Jamharat Al-Nasab*. Edited by Nājī Ḥasan. Beirut: ʿĀlam al-Kutub, 1986.

Ibn Kathīr, Ismāʿīl ibn ʿUmar. *Tafsīr Al-Qur'ān Al-ʿAẓīm*. 15 vols. Giza: Mu'assasat Qurṭuba, 2000.

Ibn Māja, Muḥammad ibn Yazīd. *Sunan al-Ḥāfiẓ Abī ʿAbd Allāh Muḥammad ibn Yazīd al-Qazwīnī ibn Māja*. Edited by Muḥammad Fuʾād ʿAbd al-Bāqī. 2 vols. Cairo: Dār Iḥyāʾ al-Kutub al-ʿArabiyya, 1952–1953.

Ibn Qayyim al-Jawziyya, Muḥammad ibn Abī Bakr. *Zād al-Maʿād fī Hady Khayr al-ʿIbād*. Edited by Muṣṭafā ʿAbd al-Qādir ʿAṭā. 6 vols. Beirut: Manshūrāt Muḥammad ʿAlī Bayḍūn, Dār al-Kutub al-ʿIlmiyya, 1998.

Ibn Qutayba, ʿAbd Allāh ibn Muslim. *Kitāb al-Maʿārif*. 2nd edition. Cairo: Dār al-Maʿārif, [1969].

——. *The Excellence of the Arabs*. Edited by James E. Montgomery et al. New York: New York University Press, 2017.

Ibn Saʿd, Muḥammad. *Ibn Saad: Biographien Muhammeds, seiner Gefährten und der späteren Träger des Islams, bis zum Jahre 230 der Flucht* (= *al-Ṭabaqāt al-Kubrā*). Edited by Eduard Sachau. 9 vols. Leiden: Brill, 1904–1940.

——. *Al-Ṭabaqāt al-Kubrā*. Edited by Muḥammad ʿAbd al-Qadīr ʿAṭā. 9 vols. Beirut: Dār al-Kutub al-'Ilmiyya, 1990.

Ibn Sīda, ʿAbd al-Ḥamīd Hindāwī. *Al-Muḥkam wa-al-Muḥīṭ al-Aʿẓam*. Edited by ʿAbd al-Ḥamīd Hindāwī. 11 vols. Beirut: Manshūrāt Muḥammad ʿAlī Bayḍūn; Dār al-Kutub al-Ilmiyya, 2000.

Ibn Ṭiqṭaqā, Muḥammad ibn ʿAlī. *Al-Fakhrī fī al-Ādāb al-Sulṭāniyya wa-l-Duwal al-Islāmiyya*. n.p.: n.p., 1966.

al-Iṣbahānī, Abū al-Faraj. *Kitāb al-Aghānī*. Edited by Iḥsān ʿAbbās. 25 vols. Beirut: Dar Ṣādir, 2002–2015.

al-Jāḥiẓ, ʿAmr ibn Baḥr. *Al-Bayān wa-al-Tabyīn*. 3rd edition. Edited by ʿAbd al-Sallām Muḥammad Hārūn. 4 vols. Cairo: Maktabat al-Khānjī, 1968.

——. 'Al-Risāla fī al-Nābita'. In *Rasāʾil al-Jāḥiẓ*, edited by Muḥammad Bāsil ʿUyūn al-Sūd and ʿUbayd Allāh ibn Ḥassān, 2: 3–18. Beirut: Dār al-Kutub al-Ilmiyya, 2013.

——. *Rasāʾil al-Jāḥiẓ*. Edited by Muḥammad Bāsil ʿUyūn al-Sūd and ʿUbayd Allāh ibn Ḥassān. 4 vols in 2. Beirut: Dār al-Kutub al-Ilmiyya, 2013.

al-Jahshiyārī, Muḥammad ibn ʿAbdūs. *Kitāb al-Wuzarāʾ wa-al-Kuttāb*. n.p.: n.p., 1938.

Khalīl ibn Aḥmad. *Kitāb al-Jumal fī al-Naḥw*. 2nd edition. Edited by Fakhr al-Dīn Qabāwa. Beirut: Mu'assasat al-Risāla, 1987.

Makkī ibn Abī Ṭālib. *Tafsīr al-Hidāya ilā Bulūgh al-Nihāya*. Edited by Muḥammad 'Uthmān. 7 vols. Beirut: Dār al-Kutub al-'Ilmiyya, 2011.

Mālik ibn Anas. *Al-Muwaṭṭa'*. Edited by Muḥammad Fawwād 'Abd al-Bāqī. 2 vols. [Cairo]: Dār Iḥyā' al-Kutub al-'Arabiyya, 1951.

Marwān ibn Abī Ḥafṣa. *Shi'r Marwān ibn Abī Ḥaf,a (105–172 H.)*. Edited by Ḥusayn 'Aṭwān. Cairo: Dār al-Ma'ārif.

al-Mas'ūdī, 'Alī ibn Ḥusayn. *Murūj al-Dhahab wa-Ma'ādin al-Jawhar*. Edited by Charles Pellat. 7 vols. Beirut: American University of Beirut Press, 1965–1979.

al-Māturīdī, Muḥammad ibn Muḥammad. *Tafsīr al-Qur'ān al-'Aẓīm, al-Musammá, Ta'wīlāt Ahl al-Sunna*. 5 vols. Beirut: Mu'assasat al-Risāla Nāshirūn, 2004.

Mubarrad, Muḥammad ibn Yazīd. *Al-Kāmil fī al-Lugha*. Edited by Muḥammad Abū al-Faḍl Ibrāhīm. 4 vols. Cairo: Maktabat Nahḍat Miṣr, [1956].

Mujāhid ibn Jabr. *Tafsīr Mujāhid*. 2 vols. Beirut: al-Manshūrāt al-'Ilmiyya, [197–?].

Muqātil ibn Sulaymān. *Tafsīr Muqātil ibn Sulaymān*. Edited by 'Abd Allāh Maḥmūd Shiḥāta. [Cairo]: al-Hay'a al-Miṣriyya al-'Āmma lil-Kitāb, 1979–1989.

al-Murtaḍā al-Zabīdī, Muḥammad ibn Muḥammad. *Tāj al-'Arūs min Jawāhir al-Qāmūs*. Edited by 'Alī Shīrī. 20 vols. Beirut: Dār al-Fikr, 1994.

Muslim ibn Ḥajjāj al-Qushayrī. *Kitāb al-Kunā wa-al-Asmā'*. With an introduction by Muṭā' al-Ṭarābīshī. Damascus: Dār al-Fikr, 1984.

——. *Ṣaḥīḥ Muslim*. Vol. 4 of *Jam' Jawāmi' al-Aḥādīth wa-al-Asānīd wa-Maknaz al-Ṣaḥāḥ wa-al-Sunan wa-al-Masānī*. Vaduz: Jam'iyyat al-Maknaz al-Islāmī, 2000–2001.

al-Nasā'ī, Aḥmad ibn Shu'ayb. *Tafsīr al-Nasā'ī*. 2 vols. Cairo: Maktabat al-Sunna, 1990.

——. *Sunan*. Edited by Abu Tahir Zubayr 'Ali Za'i. 6 vols. Riyadh: Darussalam, 2008.

Naṣr ibn Muzāḥim. *Kitāb Waq'at Ṣiffīn*. 2nd edition. Edited by 'Abd al-Sallām Muḥammad Hārūn. Cairo: Al-Mu'assasa al-'Arabiyya al-Ḥadītha, 1962.

Nu'aym ibn Ḥammād al-Marwazī. *Kitāb al-Fitan*. Edited by Suhayl Zakkār. Beirut: Dār al-Fikr, 1991.

al-Qummī, 'Alī ibn Ibrāhīm. *Tafsīr Al-Qummī*. 2 vols. Najaf: Maktabat al-Hudá, 1967.

al-Qurṭubī, Muḥammad ibn Aḥmad. *Al-Jāmi' Li-Aḥkām Al-Qur'ān: Wa-Al-Mubayyin Li-Mā Taḍammanahu Min Al-Sunna Wa-Āy Al-Furqān*. 24 vols. Beirut: Mu'assasat al-Risāla, 2006.

Qutb, Sayyid. *Fī Ẓilāl al-Qur'ān*. 6 vols. Beirut: Dār al-Shurūq, 1992.

al-Rāzī, Fakhr al-Dīn Muḥammad ibn ʿUmar. *Al-Tafsīr al-Kabīr* [*Mafātīḥ al-Ghayb*]. 32 vols in 16. Cairo: Al-Maṭba'a al-Bahiyya al-Miṣriyya, [1934–1962].

al-Shaʿrāwī, Muḥammad Mutawallī. *Tafsīr Al-Shaʿrāwī*. 24 vols. [Cairo]: Akhbār al-Yawm, Qiṭāʿ al-Thaqāfa wa-al-Kutub wa-al-Maktabāt, [1991].

al-Shawkānī, Muḥammad ibn ʿAlī. *Fatḥ Al-Qadīr: Al-Jāmiʿ Bayna Fannay Al-Riwāya Wa-Al-Dirāya Min ʿIlm Al-Tafsīr*. 6 vols. Al-Mansura [Egypt]: Dār al-Wafā' lil-Ṭibāʿa wa-al-Nashr wa-al-Tawzīʿ, 1994.

Sibawayhī, ʿAmr ibn ʿUthmān. *Al-Kitāb*. Edited by Muḥammad Kāẓim al-Bakkāʾ. 5 vols. Beirut: Muʾassasat al-Risāla, 2004.

al-Suddī, Ismāʿīl ibn ʿAbd al-Raḥmān. *Tafsīr Al-Suddī Al-Kabīr*. Al-Mansura, Egypt: Dār al-Wafā', 1993.

al-Ṭabarānī, Sulaymān ibn Aḥmad. *Al-Tafsīr al-Kabīr: Tafsīr Al-Qur'ān Al-ʿAẓīm*. 6 vols. Irbid, Jordan: Dār al-Kitāb al-Thaqāfī: Dār al-Mutanabbī, 2008.

al-Ṭabarī, Muḥammad ibn Jarīr. *Annales quos scripsit Abu Djafar Mohammed ibn Djarir al-Tabari (= Tārīkh al-Rusul wa-al-Mulūk)*. Edited by M. J. De Goeje. 15 vols. Leiden: Brill, 1879–1901.

——. *The History of al-Ṭabarī: An Annotated Translation*. Ehsan Yar-Shater, general editor. 40 vols. Albany: State University of New York Press, 1985–2007.

——. *Tafsīr al-Ṭabarī: Jāmiʿ al-Bayān ʿan Ta 'wīl Āy al-Qur'an*. 26 vols. Riyadh: Dār ʿĀlam al-Kutub, 2003.

al-Ṭūsī, Muḥammad ibn al-Ḥasan. *Al-Tibyān Fī Tafsīr Al-Qur'ān*. 10 vols. Beirut: Al-Amīra lil-Ṭibāʿa wa-al-Nashr wa-al-Tawzīʿ, 2010.

al-ʿUṣfūrī, Khalīfa ibn Khayyāṭ. *Kitāb al-Ṭabaqāt*. Edited by Suhayl Zakkār. 2 vols. Damascus: Maṭābiʿ Wizārat al-Thaqāfa wa-al-Siyāḥa wa-al-Irshād al-Qawmī, 1966.

——. *Tārīkh Khalīfa ibn Khayyāṭ*. 2nd edition. Edited by Akram Ḍiyāʾ al-ʿUmarī. Damascus and Beirut: Dār al-Qalam; Beirut: Muʾassasat al-Risāla, 1977.

al-Yaʿqūbī, Aḥmad ibn Abī Yaʿqūb. *Tārīkh Aḥmad ibn Abī Yaʿqūb ibn Jaʿfar ibn Wahab ibn Wāḍiḥ al-Maʿrūf bi-al-Yaʿqūbī*. Edited by M. Th. Houtsma. 2 vols. Leiden: Brill, 1969.

al-Wāḥidī al-Nīshābūrī, Abū al-Ḥasan ʿAlī. *Asbāb Al-Nuzūl*. Cairo: Mu'assasat al-Ḥalabī, 1968.

al-Wāqidī, Muḥammad ibn ʿUmar. *Kitāb al-Maghāzī*. Edited by Marsden Jones. 3 vols. Oxford: Oxford University Press, 1966.

al-Zamakhsharī, Maḥmūd ibn ʿUmar. *Al-Kashshāf ʿan Ḥaqā'iq Ghawāmiḍ*

Al-Tanzīl Wa-ʿUyūn Al-Aqāwīl Fī Wujūh Al-Taʾwīl. 4 vols. Beirut: Dār al-Kutub al-ʿIlmiyya, 2009.

Secondary Sources

Abbott, Nabia. *Two Queens of Baghdad: Mother and Wife of Hārūn Al Rashīd.* Chicago: University of Chicago Press, 1991.

Abou El Fadl, Khaled. *Speaking in God's Name: Islamic Law, Authority, and Women.* New York: OneWorld, 2014.

Abū Zayd, Naṣr Ḥāmid. *Mafhūm al-Naṣṣ: Dirāsa fī ʿUlūm al-Qurʾān.* [Cairo]: Al-Hayʾa al-Miṣriyya al-ʿĀmma lil-Kitāb, 1990.

Afsaruddin, Asma. 'Literature, Scholarship, and Piety: Negotiating Gender and Authority in the Medieval Muslim World', *Religion & Literature*, 42, nos 1/2 (2010): 111–131.

Agha, Saleh Said. *The Revolution which Toppled the Umayyads: Neither Arab nor ʿAbbāsid.* Leiden and Boston: Brill, 2003.

Ahmed, Asad Q. *The Religious Elite of the Early Islamic Ḥijāz: Five Prosopographical Case Studies.* Oxford: Oxford University Press, 2011.

Alajmi, Abdulhadi. 'Ascribed vs. Popular Legitimacy: The Case of al-Walīd II and Umayyad *ʿahd*', *Journal of Near Eastern Studies*, 72, no. 1 (April 2013): 25–33.

Al-Azmeh, Aziz. *Muslim Kingship: Power and the Sacred in Muslim, Christian and Pagan Polities.* London: Tauris, 2001.

——. *The Arabs and Islam in Late Antiquity: A Critique of Approaches to Arabic Sources.* Berlin: Gerlach Press, 2014.

——. *The Emergence of Islam in Late Antiquity.* Cambridge: Cambridge University Press, 2017.

Al-Heitty, Abd al-Kareem. 'The Contrasting Spheres of Free Women and *Jawārī* in Literary Life of the early'Abbasid Caliphate', *Al-Masaq*, 3 (1990): 31–51.

Ali, Kecia. *Sexual Ethics and Islam.* Oxford: Oneworld, 2006.

——. *Marriage and Slavery in Early Islam.* Cambridge, MA: Harvard University Press, 2010.

——. 'Review of Matthew S. Gordon and Kathryn Hain, eds., Concubines and Courtesans: Women and Slavery in Islamic History', *Al-Usur al-Wusta*, 26 (2018). Accessed on 12 March 2019. https://islamichistorycommons.org/mem/wp-content/uploads/sites/55/2018/11/UW-26-Ali.pdf.

Al-Naimat, Salameh and Aysha al-Sweidat. 'Al-Bighā' ʿinda al-ʿArab qabla al-Islām', *Al-Majalla al-Urduniyya lil-ʿUlūm al-Ijtimāʿiyya*, 7, no. 1 (2014): 1–8.

Amir-Moezzi, Mohammed Ali. *The Divine Guide in Early Shiʿism: The Sources of*

Esotericism in Islam. Translated by David Streight. Albany: State University of New York Press, 1994.

——. 'Šahrbanu'. In *Encyclopaedia Iranica,* edited by Ehsan Yarshater. London: Routledge, 1982–. Accessed on 22 May 2019. http://www.iranicaonline.org/articles/sahrbanu.

Amitai, Reuven. 'The Mamlūk Institution, or One Thousand Years of Military Slavery in the Islamic World'. In *Arming Slaves: From Classical Times to the Modern Age,* edited by Christopher Leslie Brown and Philip D. Morgan, 40–78. New Haven: Yale University Press, 2006.

Arazi, A. and H. Ben-Shammay. 'Risāla'. In *The Encyclopaedia of Islam,* 2nd edition. Accessed on 22 May 2019. http://dx.doi.org/10.1163/1573-3912_islam_COM_0926.

Archer, Léonie J., ed. *Slavery and Other Forms of Unfree Labour.* London: Routledge, 1988.

Arjomand, Said Amir. 'The Constitution of Medina: A Sociolegal Interpretation of Muhammad's Acts of Foundation of the *Umma*', *International Journal of Middle East Studies,* 41 (2009): 555–575.

Athamina, Khalil. 'How did Islam Contribute to Change the Legal Status of Women: The Case of the *Jawārī* or the *Female Slaves*', *Al-Qantara,* 28, no. 2 (2007). Accessed on 22 May 2019. http://al-qantara.revistas.csic.es/index.php/al-qantara/article/view/42/36.

Badawi, El-Said and M. A. Haleem. *Arabic-English Dictionary of Qur'anic Usage.* Leiden and Boston: Brill, 2008.

Barker, Hannah. 'Purchasing a Slave in Fourteenth-Century Cairo: Ibn al-Akfānī's *Book of Observation and Inspection in the Examination of Slaves*', *Mamluk Studies Review,* 19 (2016): 1–23. Accessed on 22 May 2019. https://knowledge.uchicago.edu/record/1183.

Barlas, Asma. *'Believing Women' in Islam: Unreading Patriarchal Interpretations of the Qur'ān.* 1st edition. Austin: University of Texas Press, 2002.

Barth, Fredrik. *Ethnic Groups and Boundaries: The Social Organization of Cultural Difference.* Boston: Little, Brown, [1969].

Barton, Simon. *Conquerors, Brides, and Concubines: Interfaith Relations and Social Power in Medieval Iberia.* Philadelphia: University of Pennsylvania Press, 2015.

Bennett, Judith. 'Feminism and History', *Gender & History,* 1, no. 3 (1989): 251–272.

Berg, Herbert. 'The Scepticism and Literary Analysis of J. Wansbrough, A. Rippin, *et al*'. In *The Development of Exegesis in Early Islam: The Authenticity of Muslim Literature from the Formative Period*, 78–83. Richmond: Curzon, 2000.

——. 'The "*Isnād*" and the Production of Cultural Memory: Ibn ʿAbbās as a Case Study', *Numen*, 58, nos 2–3 (2011): 259–283.

Bernards, Monique and John Nawas, eds. 'A Preliminary Report of the Netherlands Ulama Project (NUP): The Evolution of the Class of ʿ*Ulamā* in Islam with Special Emphasis on the non-Arab Converts (*Mawālī*) from the First through Fourth Century A.H'. In *Law, Christianity, and Modernism in Islamic Society: Proceedings of the Eighteenth Congress of the UEAI held at the Katholieke Universiteit Leuven*, edited by U. Vermeulen and J. M. F. van Reeth, 97–107. Peeters: Leuven, 1998.

——. *Patronate and Patronage in Early and Classical Islam*. Leiden: Brill, 2005.

Bin Husayn, Buthayna. *Nisā' al-Khulafā' al-Umawiyyīn: Dirāsa Jadīda*. Beirut: Manshūrat al-Jamal, 2014.

Blachère, R. "Antara'. In *The Encyclopaedia of Islam*. 2nd edition. Accessed on 22 May 2019. http://dx.doi.org/10.1163/1573-3912_islam_SIM_0685.

Blankinship, Khalid Yahya. *The End of the Jihād State: The Reign of Hishām Ibn 'Abd Al-Malik and the Collapse of the Umayyads*. Albany: State University of New York Press, 1994.

Bock, Gisela. 'Women's History and Gender History: Aspects of an International Debate', *Gender & History*, 1, no. 1 (1989): 7–30.

Bordieu, Pierre. *The Logic of Practice*. Cambridge: Polity, 1990.

Borrut, Antoine. *Entre mémoire et pouvoir: l'espace syrien sous les derniers Ommeyades et les premiers Abbassides (v. 72–193/692–809)*. Leiden: Brill, 2011.

Borrut, Antoine and Fred McGraw Donner, eds. *Christians and Others in the Umayyad State*. Chicago: Oriental Institute, 2016.

Bosworth, C. E. 'Tulaḳāʾ'. In *The Encyclopaedia of Islam*. 2nd edition. Accessed on 22 May 2019. http://dx.doi.org/10.1163/1573-3912_islam_SIM_7614.

Bouhdiba, Abdelwahab. *Sexuality in Islam*. London: Routledge, 1975.

Bray, Julia. 'Men, Women and Slaves in Abbasid Society'. In *Gender in the Early Medieval World: East and West, 300–900*, edited by Leslie Brubaker and Julia H. M. Smith, 121–146. Cambridge: Cambridge University Press, 2004.

Brockopp, Jonathan. *Early Mālikī Law: Ibn 'Abd al-Ḥakam and His Major Compendium of Jurisprudence*. Leiden: Brill, 2000.

Brock, S. P. 'North Mesopotamia in the Late Seventh Century: Book XV of John Bar Penkāyē's *Rīš Mellē*', *Jerusalem Studies in Arabic and Islam*, 9 (1987): 51–75.

Brown, Jonathan. *The Canonization of Al-Bukhārī and Muslim: The Formation and Function of the Sunnī Ḥadīth Canon*. Leiden: Brill, 2007.

Bulliet, Richard. *Conversion to Islam in the Medieval Period.* Cambridge, MA: Harvard University Press, 1979.

——. 'Conversion-Based Patronage and Onomastic Evidence in Early Islam'. In *Patronate and Patronage in Early and Classical Islam*, edited by Monique Bernards and John Nawas, 246–262. Leiden: Brill, 2005.

Burton, J. 'The Meaning of "Ihsan"', *Journal of Semitic Studies*, 19, no. 1 (1974): 47–75.

Calder, Norman. '*Tafsīr* from Ṭabarī to Ibn Kathīr'. In *Approaches to the Qur'an*, edited by G. R. Hawting and Abdul-Kader A. Shareef, 101–140. London: Routledge, 1993.

Campbell, Donald T. 'Common Fate, Similarity, and Other Indices of the Status of Aggregates of Persons as Social Entities', *Behavioral Science*, 3 (1958): 14–25.

Cannuyer, Christian. 'Māriya, la concubine copte de Muḥammad. Réalité ou mythe?' *Acta Orientalia Belgica*, 21 (2008): 251–264.

Carter, M. 'The *Kātib* in Fact and Fiction', *Abr Nahrain*, 11 (1971): 42–55.

Caswell, Matthew Fuad. *The Slave Girls of Baghdad: The* Qiyān *in the Early Abbasid Era*. London: Tauris, 2011.

Cobb, Paul. 'The Empire in Syria'. Chapter 6 in *The New Cambridge History of Islam*, Part I, edited by Chase Robinson, 226–268. Cambridge: Cambridge University Press, 2010.

Conrad, L. I. 'Arabic Plague Chronologies and Treatises: Social and Historical Factors in the Formation of a Literary Genre', *Studia Islamica*, 54 (1981): 51–93.

Constant-Martin, Denis. 'The Choices of Identity', *Social Identities*, 1 (1995): 5–20.

Conte, Edouard. 'Agnatic Illusions: The Element of Choice in Arab Kinship'. Chapter 1 in *Tribes and Power: Nationalism and Ethnicity in the Middle East*, edited by Faleh Abdul-Jabar and Hosham Dawod, 15–49. London: Saqi, 2001.

Cook, Michael. 'Eschatology, History, and the Dating of Traditions', *Princeton Papers in Near Eastern Studies*, 1 (1992): 23–48.

Cook, Michael and Patricia Crone. *Hagarism: The Making of the Islamic World.* Cambridge: Cambridge University Press, 1977.

Cooper, David. *The Measure of Things: Humanism, Humility, and Mystery.* Oxford: Clarendon, 2002.

Cornell, Rkia. 'Rabiʿah al-ʿAdawiyyah (circa 720-801)'. In *Dictionary of Literary Biography: Arabic Literary Culture, 500–925*, edited by Michael Cooperson and Shawkat Toorawa, 292–298. Farmington Hills: Gale, 2005.

Crone, Patricia. 'Mawlā'. In *The Encyclopaedia of Islam.* 2nd edition. Accessed on 22 May 2019. http://dx.doi.org/10.1163/1573-3912_islam_COM_0714.

——. *Slaves on Horses: The Evolution of the Islamic Polity*. Cambridge and New York: Cambridge University Press, 1980.

——. *Meccan Trade and the Rise of Islam*. Princeton: Princeton University Press, 1987.

——. *Roman, Provincial and Islamic Law: The Origins of the Islamic Patronate*. Cambridge and New York: Cambridge University Press, 1987.

——. 'The Significance of Wooden Weapons in Al-Mukhtār's Revolt and the `Abbāsid Revolution'. In *Studies in Honour of Clifford Edmund Bosworth*. Volume I: *Hunter of the East: Arabic and Semitic Studies*, edited by I. R. Netton, 174–187. Leiden: Brill, 2000.

——. '*Mawālī* and the Prophet's Family: An Early Shi'ite View'. Chapter 5 in *Patronate and Patronage in Early and Classical Islam,* edited by Monique Bernards and John Nawas, 167–194. Leiden and Boston: Brill, 2005.

Crone, Patricia and Martin Hinds. *God's Caliph: Religious Authority in the First Centuries of Islam*. Cambridge: Cambridge University Press, 1986.

Dakake, Maria Massi. *The Charismatic Community: Shi'ite Identity in Early Islam*. Albany: State University of New York Press, 2007.

Debié, Muriel. 'Christians in the Service of the Caliph: Through the Looking Glass of Communal Identities'. Chapter 3 in *Christians and Others in the Umayyad State,* edited by Antoine Borrut and Fred Donner, 53–72. Chicago: Oriental Institute, 2016.

Denny, F. M. 'The Meaning of *Ummah* in the Qur'ān', *History of Religions*, 15 (August 1975): 34–70. Reprinted in *The Koran: Critical Concepts in Islamic Studies,* edited by Colin Turner, Vol. 2, *Themes and Doctrines*, Chapter 15, 19–53.

——. '*Ummah* in the Constitution of Medina', *Journal of Near East Studies*, 36, no. 1 (1977): 39–47.

Dixon, 'Abd al-Ameer 'Abd. *The Umayyad Caliphate, 65–86/684–705: A Political Study*. London: Luzac, 1971.

Donner, Fred M. 'Tribal Settlement in Basra during the First Century A.H'. In *Land Tenure and Social Transformation in the Middle East*, edited by Tarif Khalidi, 97–120. Beirut: American University of Beirut, 1984.

——. *Narratives of Islamic Origins: The Beginnings of Islamic Historical Writing*. Princeton: Darwin, 1998.

——. 'Modern Nationalism and Medieval Islamic History', *Al-Uṣūr al-Wusṭā*, 13, no. 1 (2001): 21–22.

——. *Muhammad and the Believers at the Origins of Islam*. Cambridge, MA: Harvard University Press, 2012.

Drory, Rina. 'The Abbasid Construction of the Jahiliyya: Cultural Authority in the Making', *Studia Islamica*, 83 (1996): 33–49.

El Cheikh, Nadia M. 'Describing the Other to Get at the Self: Byzantine Women in Arabic Sources (8th–11th Centuries)', *Journal of the Economic and Social History of the Orient*, 40, no. 2 (1997): 239–250.

El-Hibri, Tayeb. 'The Redemption of Umayyad Memory by the Abbasids', *Journal of Near Eastern Studies*, 61, no. 4 (2002): 241–265.

——. *Parable and Politics in Early Islamic History: The Rashidun Caliphs*. New York: Columbia University Press, 2010.

The Encyclopaedia of Islam. 2nd edition. Edited by P. Bearman, Th. Bianquis, C. E. Bosworth, E. van Donzel and W. P. Heinrichs. Leiden: Brill, 2010. Accessed at www.brillonline.com.

Ess, Josef van. *Theologie und Gesellschaft im 2. und 3. Jahrhundert Hidschra: eine Geschichte des religiösen Denkens im frühen Islam*. Berlin and New York: de Gruyter, 1991–1997.

Fahd, T. 'Ibn Sīrīn, Abū Bakr Muḥammad'. In *The Encyclopaedia of Islam*. 2nd edition. Accessed on 22 May 2019. http://dx.doi.org/10.1163/1573-3912_islam_SIM_7614.

Faizer, Rizwi S. 'The Issue of Authenticity Regarding the Traditions of al-Wāqidī as Established in His *Kitāb al-Maghāzī*', *Journal of Near Eastern Studies*, 58, no. 2 (April 1999): 97–106.

al-Faruqi, Maysam J. '*Umma*: The Orientalists and the Qur'anic Concept of Identity', *Journal of Islamic Studies*, 16, no. 1 (2005): 1–34.

Fierro, Maribel. 'Los mawali de Abd al-Rahman I', *Al-Qantara*, 20 (1999): 66–97.

——. '*Mawālī* and *muwalladūn* in al-Andalus'. Chapter 6 in *Patronate and Patronage in Early and Classical Islam,* edited by Monique Bernards and John Nawas, 195–245. Leiden and Boston: Brill, 2005.

Finley, M. I. 'Between Slavery and Freedom', *Comparative Studies in Society and History*, 6, no. 3 (April 1964): 233–249.

Firestone, Reuven. *Journeys in Holy Lands: The Evolution of the Abraham-Ishmael Legends in Islamic Exegesis*. Albany: State University of New York Press, 1990.

Fishbein, Michael. 'The Life of al-Mukhtar b. Abi 'Ubayd in Some Early Arabic Historians'. PhD dissertation, UCLA, 1988.

Forand, P. G. 'The Relation of the Slave and Client to the Master or Patron in Medieval Islam', *International Journal of Middle East Studies*, 2 (1971): 59–66.

Franz, Kurt. 'Slavery in Islam: Legal Norms and Social Practice'. In *Slavery and the*

Slave Trade in the Eastern Mediterranean (c. 1000–1500 CE), edited by R. Amitai and C. Cluse, 51–141. Turnhout: Prepols, 2017.

Gibb, H. A. R. *The Arab Conquests in Central Asia*. London: The Royal Asiatic Society, 1923.

——. 'The Fiscal Rescript of Umar II', *Arabica*, 2, no. 1 (January 1955): 1–16.

Gil, Moshe. 'The Constitution of Medina: A Reconsideration', *Israeli Oriental Studies*, 4 (1974): 44–66.

Gilliot, Claude. 'The Beginnings of Qur'anic Exegesis'. In *The Qur'an: Formative Interpretation*, edited by Andrew Rippin, 1–27. Aldershot: Ashgate, 1999.

Gilliot, Claude. 'Mujāhid's Exegesis: Origins, Paths of Transmission and Development of a Meccan Exegetical Tradition in its Human, Spiritual and Theological Environment.' In *Tafsīr and Islamic Intellectual History: Exploring the Boundaries of a Genre*, edited by Andreas Görke and Johanna Pink, 63–111. Oxford: Oxford University Press, in association with the Institute of Ismaili Studies, 2014.

Glancy, Jennifer A. *Slavery in Early Christianity*. Oxford: Oxford University Press, 2011.

Gleave, Robert. 'Patronate in Early Shi'ite Law'. Chapter 4 in *Patronate and Patronage in Early and Classical Islam*, edited by Monique Bernards and John Nawas, 134–166. Leiden and Boston: Brill, 2005.

Goitein, S. D. 'Slaves and Slavegirls in the Cairo Geniza Records', *Arabica*, 9 (1962): 1–20.

Goldziher, Ignác. *Muslim Studies*. Edited by S. M. Stern. Translated by C. R. Barber and S. M. Stern. London: Allen & Unwin, [1967–1971].

Gordon, Matthew. 'Preliminary Remarks on Slaves and Slave Labor in the Third/Ninth Century ʿAbbāsid Empire'. In *Slaves and Households in the Near East*, edited by Laura Culbertson, 71–84. Chicago: Oriental Institute, 2011.

——. 'Abbasid Courtesans and the Question of Social Mobility'. Chapter 2 in *Concubines and Courtesans*, edited by Gordon and Hain. Oxford: Oxford University Press, 2017.

——. 'Introduction'. In *Concubines and Courtesans: Women and Slavery in Islamic History*, edited by Matthew S. Gordon and Kathryn A. Hain, 1–10. Oxford: Oxford University Press, 2017.

Gordon, Matthew S. and Kathryn A. Hain, eds. *Concubines and Courtesans: Women and Slavery in Islamic History*. Oxford: Oxford University Press, 2017.

Griffith, Sidney H. 'The Mansur Family and St. John of Damascus'. Chapter 2 in

Christians and Others in the Umayyad State, edited by Antoine Borrut and Fred Donner, 29–52. Chicago: Oriental Institute, 2016.

Günther, Sebastian. 'Clients and Clientage'. In *Encyclopaedia of the Qur'ān*, edited by Jane McAuliffe. Leiden: Brill, 2005. Accessed on 22 May 2019. http://dx.doi.org/10.1163/1875-3922_q3_EQSIM_00082.

Hachmeier, Klaus. 'Die Entwicklung Der Epistolographie Vom Frühen Islam Bis Zum 4./10. Jahrhundert', *Journal of Arabic Literature*, 33, no. 2 (2002): 131–155.

Haddad, Yvonne Yazbeck. 'Conception of the Term *Dīn* in the Qur'ān', *The Muslim World*, 64 (April 1974): 114–123. Reprinted in *The Koran: Critical Concepts in Islamic Studies*, edited by Colin Turner, Vol. 2, *Themes and Doctrines*, Chapter 16, 54–62.

Hawting, G. R. *The First Dynasty of Islam: The Umayyad Caliphate* A.D. *661–750.* Carbondale: Southern Illinois University Press, 1987.

——. 'Saʿd b. Abī Waḳḳāṣ'. In *The Encyclopaedia of Islam.* 2nd edition. Accessed on 22 May 2019. http://dx.doi.org/10.1163/1573-3912_islam_SIM_6393.

Heck, Paul. *The Construction of Knowledge in Islamic Civilization: Qudāma B. Ja'far and His Kitāb Al-Kharāj Wa-Ṣinā' at Al-Kitāba.* Leiden: Brill, 2002.

Hidayatullah, Aysha. 'Māriyya the Copt: Gender, Sex and Heritage in the Legacy of Muhammad's *umm walad*', *Islam and Christian–Muslim Relations*, 21, no. 3 (July 2010): 221–243.

Hinds, Martin. 'Kufan Political Alignments and Their Background in the Mid-Seventh Century A.D', *International Journal of Middle East Studies*, 2, no. 4 (October 1971): 346–367.

Holmberg, Bo. 'Christian Scribes in the Arabic Empire'. In *The Middle East: Unity and Diversity*, edited by Heikki Palva and Knut Vikør, 103–114. Copenhagen: NIAS, 1993.

Hoyland, Robert. *Seeing Islam As Others Saw It: A Survey and Evaluation of Christian, Jewish, and Zoroastrian Writings on Early Islam.* Princeton: Darwin, 2007.

Hurvitz, Nimrod. *The Formation of Hanbalism: Piety into Power.* London and New York: RoutledgeCurzon, 2002.

Isom-Verhaaren, Christine. 'Royal French Women in the Ottoman Sultans' Harem: The Political Uses of Fabricated Accounts from the Sixteenth to the Twenty-first Century', *Journal of World History*, 17, no. 2 (June 2006): 159–196.

Izutsu, Toshihiko. *God and Man in the Koran: Semantics of the Koranic Weltanschauung.* Tokyo: Keio Institute of Cultural and Linguistics Studies, 1964.

Johansen, Baber. 'The Valorization of the Human Body in Muslim Sunni Law', *Princeton Papers in Near Eastern Studies*, 4 (1996): 71–112.

Juda, Jamal. 'Die sozialen und wirtschaftlichen Aspekte der Mawālī in frühislamischer Zeit'. PhD dissertation, Tübingen, 1983.

——. 'The Economic Status of the *Mawālī* in Early Islam'. Chapter 7 in *Patronate and Patronage in Early and Classical Islam,* edited by Monique Bernards and John Nawas, 263–277. Leiden and Boston: Brill, 2005.

Juynboll, G. H. A. 'Shu'ba b. al-Ḥadjdjādj'. In *The Encyclopaedia of Islam*. 2nd edition. Accessed on 22 May 2019. http://dx.doi.org/10.1163/1573-3912_islam_SIM_6973.

——. 'Some *Isnād*-Analytical Methods Illustrated on the Basis of Several Woman-Demeaning Sayings from Ḥadīth Literature', *Al-Qanṭara,* 10 (1989): 343–384. Reprinted in his *Studies,* 343–383. Reprinted in Motzki, *Ḥadīth,* Chapter 10.

——. 'Nāfi', the *mawlā* of Ibn 'Umar and his Position in Muslim *Ḥadīth* Literature', *Der Islam,* 70 (1993): 207–244. Reprinted in his *Studies,* 207–244.

——. *Studies on the Origins and Uses of Islamic Ḥadīth*. Brookfield: Variorum, 1996.

Kadi, Wadad. 'Early Islamic State Letters: The Question of Authenticity'. In *The Byzantine and Early Islamic Near East I: Problems in the Literary Source Material,* edited by Averil Cameron and Lawrence Conrad, 215–275. Princeton: Darwin, 1992.

——. 'The Earliest "Nābita" and the Paradigmatic "Nawābit"', *Studia Islamica,* 78 (1993): 27–61.

——. 'The Names of Estates in State Registers Before and After the Arabization of the "Diwāns".' In *Umayyad Legacies: Medieval Memories from Syria to Spain,* edited by Antoine Borrut and Paul Cobb, 255–280. Leiden: Brill, 2010.

——. 'Identity Formation of the Bureaucracy of the Early Islamic State: 'Abd Al-Ḥamīd's "Letter to the Secretaries"'. In *Mediterranean Identities in the Premodern Era: Entrepôts, Islands, Empires,* edited by John Watkins and Kathryn Reyerson, 141–154. London: Taylor and Francis, 2016.

Katz, Marion. 'Concubinage, in Islamic Law'. In *Encyclopedia of Islam THREE.* Accessed on 22 May 2019. http://dx.doi.org/10.1163/1573-3912_ei3_COM_25564.

Keaney, Heather N. *Medieval Islamic Historiography: Remembering Rebellion.* London: Routledge, 2013.

Khalek, Nancy. 'Early Islamic History Reimagined', *Journal of the American Oriental Society,* 134, no. 3 (July–September 2014): 431–451.

——. 'Some Notes on the Representation of Non-Muslim Officials in al-Ǧahšiyārī's

(d. 331/942) *Kitāb al-Wuzarā' wa-l-kuttāb*', *Arabica,* 62, no. 4 (2015): 503–520.

Kilpatrick, Hilary. 'Women as Poets and Chattels: Abū l-farağ al-Iṣbahānī's 'Al-Imā' al-Šawā'ir', *Quaderni Di Studi Arabi*, 9 (1991): 161–176.

Kimmage, D. 'Sūra 106 In *tafsīrs*: Qur'ānic Commentary as a Historical Source', *Manuscripta Orientalia*, 6, no. 4 (2000): 34–43.

Kister, M. J. 'Some Reports Concerning al-Ṭā'if', *Jerusalem Studies in Arabic and Islam*, 1 (1979): 2–12.

Klar, Marianna. 'Between *History* and *Tafsīr*: Notes on Al-Ṭabarī's Methodological Strategies', *Journal of Qur'anic Studies*, 18, no. 2 (2016): 89–129.

Lammens, H. and Kh. Y. Blankenship. 'Yazīd b. 'Abd al-Malik'. In *The Encyclopedia of Islam*. 2nd edition. Accessed on 22 May 2019. http://dx.doi.org/10.1163/1573-3912_islam_SIM_8001.

Landau-Tasseron, Ella. 'Adoption, Acknowledgment of Paternity, and False Genealogical Claims in Arabian and Islamic Societies', *Bulletin of the School of Oriental and African Studies, University of London*, 66, no. 2 (2003): 169–192.

Lane, Edward William. *Arabic-English Lexicon: Derived from the Best and the Most Copious Eastern Sources*. London: Williams and Norgate.

Lecker, Michael. *The 'Constitution of Medina': Muhammad's First Legal Document.* Princeton: Darwin, 2004.

Leiser, Gary. *Prostitution in the Eastern Mediterranean World*. London: Tauris, 2017.

Levy-Rubin, Milka. *Non-Muslims in the Early Islamic Empire: From Empire to Co-Existence.* Cambridge: Cambridge University Press, 2011.

Lewis, Bernard. *Race and Slavery in the Middle East: An Historical Enquiry*. New York: Oxford University Press, 1990.

Lichtenstaedter, I. 'Fraternization (*Mu'ākhāt*) in Early Islamic Society', *Islamic Culture*, 16 (1942): 47–52.

Lindsay, James E. 'Sarah and Hagar in Ibn 'Asākir's *History of Damascus*', *Medieval Encounters*, 14, no. 1 (2008): 1–14.

Lindstedt, Ilkka. '*Muhājirūn* as a Name for the First/Seventh Century Muslims', *Journal of Near Eastern Studies*, 74, no. 1 (2015): 67–73.

London, Jennifer. 'How to Do Things with Fables: Ibn Al-Muqaffa''s Frank Speech in Stories from *Kalila Wa Dimna*', *History of Political Thought*, 29, no. 2 (2008): 189–212.

Madelung, W. 'Murdji'a'. In *The Encyclopaedia of Islam*. 2nd edition. Accessed on 22 May 2019. http://dx.doi.org/10.1163/1573-3912_islam_COM_0801.

——. 'Sunbādh'. In *The Encyclopaedia of Islam*. 2nd edition. Accessed on 22 May 2019. http://dx.doi.org/10.1163/1573-3912_islam_SIM_7194.

Mahafzah, Hussain Ali. 'The Development of the Job of the Secretaries of State and Their Role in the Early Period of Islam', *European Scientific Journal*, 8 (2012): 106–126.

Mahmood, Saba. *Politics of Piety: The Islamic Revival and the Feminist Subject*. Princeton: Princeton University Press, 2005.

Marmon, Shaun. 'Concubinage, Islamic'. In *Dictionary of the Middle Ages*, Volume 3, 527–529. New York: Charles Scribner and Sons, 1982–1987.

——. *Eunuchs and Sacred Boundaries in Islamic Society*. New York: Oxford University Press, 1995.

Matthee, Rudi. 'Prostitutes, Courtesans, and Dancing Girls: Women Entertainers in Safavid Iran'. In *Iran and Beyond: Essays in Middle Eastern History in Honor of Nikki R. Keddie*, edited by Rudi Matthee and Beth Baron, 121–150. Costa Mesa: Mazda, 2000.

Matthews, Jill. 'Feminist History', *Labour History*, 50 (1986): 147–153.

Mattson, Ingrid. 'A Believing Slave Is Better than an Unbeliever: Status and Community in Early Islamic Society and Law'. Unpublished PhD dissertation, The University of Chicago, 1999.

Mernissi, Fatima. *The Veil and the Male Elite: A Feminist Interpretation of Women's Rights in Islam*. Translated by Mary Jo Lakeland. Reading, MA: Addison-Wesley, 1991.

Miqdād, Maḥmūd. *Al-Mawālī wa-Niẓām al-Walāʾ min al-Jāhiliyya ilá Awākhir al-ʿAṣr al-Umawī*. Damascus: Dār al-Fikr, 1988.

Mirza, Younus. 'Remembering the *Umm al-Walad*: Ibn Kathir's Treatise on the Sale of the Concubine'. Chapter 15 in *Concubines and Courtesans: Women and Slavery in Islamic History*, edited by Matthew Gordon and Kathryn Hain, 297–323. Oxford: Oxford University Press, 2017.

Mitter, Ulrike. 'Unconditional Manumission of Slaves in Early Islamic Law: A *Ḥadīth* Analysis', *Der Islam*, 78 (2001): 35–72.

——. *Das frühislamische Patronat*. Würzburg: Ergon, 2006.

Morales, Camilo Álvarez de. 'Transgresiones sexuales en el Islam medieval', *Cuadernos del CEMYR*, 16 (2008): 47–70.

Morony, Michael G. *Iraq After the Muslim Conquest*. Princeton: Princeton University Press, 1984.

Mottahedeh, Roy P. *Loyalty and Leadership in Early Islamic Society*. Princeton: Princeton University Press, 1980.

Motzki, Harald. 'Wal-Muḥṣanātu Mina N-Nisā'i Illā Mā Malakat Aimānukum (Koran 4:24) Und Die Koranische Sexualethik', *Der Islam*, 63 (1986): 192–218.

——. 'The Role of Non-Arab Converts in the Development of Early Islamic Law', *Islamic Law and Society*, 6, no. 3 (1999): 293–317.

——. *Hadith: Origins and Developments*. Aldershot: Ashgate, 2004.

Musallam, Basim. *Sex and Society in Islam: Birth Control Before the Nineteenth Century*. Cambridge and New York: Cambridge University Press, 1983.

Najjār, Muḥammad al-Ṭayyib. *Al-Mawālī fī al-ʿAṣr al-Umawī: wa-Mudhayyal bi-Baḥth 'an al-Riqq wa-al-Walāʾ fī al-Islām*. [Cairo]: Dār al-Nīl lil-Ṭibā'a, 1949.

——. *Al-Dawla al-Umawiyya fī al-Sharq bayna ʿawāmil al-bināʾ wa-maʿāwil al-fanā*. [Cairo]: Tawzīʿ Dār al-Iʿtiṣām, 1977.

Nawas, John. 'The Emergence of *Fiqh* as a Distinct Discipline and the Ethnic Identity of the *Fuqaha* in Early and Classical Islam'. Chapter 43 in *Studies in Arabic and Islam: Proceedings of the 19th Congress, Union Européenne des Arabisants et Islamisants: Halle 1998*, edited by Stefan Leder, 491–500. Sterling, VA: U. Peeters, 2002.

——. 'A Profile of the *Mawālī ʿUlāmā*'. In *Patronate and Patronage in Early and Classical Islam*, edited by Monique Bernards and John Nawas, 454–480. Leiden: Brill, 2005.

——. 'The Contribution of the *Mawālī* to the Six Sunnite Canonical Ḥadīth Collections'. Chapter 7 in *Ideas, Images, and Methods of Portrayal*, edited by Sebastian Günther, 141–151. Leiden and Boston: Brill, 2005.

——. 'The Birth of an Elite: *Mawālī* and Arab *ʿUlamā*", *Jerusalem Studies in Arabic and Islam*, 31 (2006): 74–91.

Neuwirth, Angelika. 'Negotiating Justice: A Pre-Canonical Reading of the Qur'anic Creation Accounts (Parts I and II)', *Journal of Qur'anic Studies*, 2 (2000): 1–18, 25–41.

——. 'Referentiality and Textuality in *Surat al-Hijr*. Some Observations on the Qur'anic "Canonical Process" and the Emergence of a Community'. Chapter 7 in *Literary Structures of Religious Meaning in the Qur'ān*, edited by Issa J. Boullata, 143–172. Richmond: Curzon, 2000.

——. 'Qur'an and History – A Disputed Relationship: Some Reflections on Qur'anic History and History in the Qur'an', *Journal of Quranic Studies*, 5, no. 1 (2003): 1–18.

——. *Studien zur Komposition der Mekkanischen Suren: die literarische Form des Koran – ein Zeugnis seiner Historität?* 2nd edition. Berlin: De Gruyter, 2007.

Neuwirth, Angelika and Michael Anthony Sells. *Qur'ānic Studies Today*. London: Routledge, 2016.

Neuwirth, Angelika, Nikolai Sinai and Michael Marx, eds. *The Qur'ān in Context: Historical and Literary Investigations into the Qur'ānic Milieu*. Leiden and Boston: Brill, 2010.

Nora, Pierre. *Les lieux de mémoire*. 3 vols. Paris: Gallimard, 1984.

Noth, Albrecht. *The Early Arabic Historical Tradition: A Source-Critical Study*. Translated by Michael Bonner. Princeton: Darwin, 1994.

Öhrnberg, K. 'Mariya al-Qibtiyya Unveiled'. *Studia Orientalia*, 55 (1983–1984): 295–303.

Oliver Pérez, Dolores. 'Sobre el significado de mawlà en la historia omeya de al-Andalus', *Al-Qantara*, 22, no. 2 (2001): 321–344.

Paret, Rudi. *Der Koran: Übersetzung von Rudi Paret.* Stuttgart: Kohlhammer, 1979.

Patterson, Orlando. *Slavery and Social Death*. Cambridge, MA: Harvard University Press, 1982.

Peirce, Leslie. *The Imperial Harem: Women and Sovereignty in the Ottoman Empire.* New York: Oxford University Press, 1993.

Pellat, Charles. 'Ḥabāba'. In *The Encyclopaedia of Islam*. 2nd edition. Accessed on 22 May 2019. http://dx.doi.org/10.1163/1573-3912_islam_SIM_2571.

——. 'Isti'rāḍ'. In *The Encyclopaedia of Islam*. 2nd edition. Accessed on 22 May 2019. http://dx.doi.org/10.1163/1573-3912_islam_SIM_3691.

——. *Le milieu baṣrien et la formation de Ǧāḥiẓ*. Paris: Librairie d'Amérique et d'Orient Adrien-Maisonneuve, 1953.

Peters, F. E. 'The Quest of the Historical Muhammad', *International Journal of Middle East Studies*, 23, no. 3 (August 1991): 291–315.

Pipes, Daniel. '*Mawlās*: Freed Slaves and Converts in Early Islam'. Chapter 13 in *Muslims and Others in Early Islamic Society*, edited by Robert Hoyland, 277–322. Farnham: Ashgate Variorum, 2004. (Originally published in *Slavery & Abolition: A Journal of Slave and Post-Slave Studies*, 1 (1980): 132–177.)

——. *Slave Soldiers and Islam.* New Haven: Yale University Press, 1981.

Pohl, Walter. 'Conceptions of Ethnicity in Early Medieval Studies'. In *Debating the Middle Ages: Issues and Readings*, edited by Lester K. Little and Barbara H. Rosenwein, 13–24. Malden: Blackwell Publishers, 1998.

Pourshariati, Parvaneh. 'The Mihrans and the Articulation of Islamic Dogma: A Preliminary Prosopographical Analysis'. Chapter 16 in *Tresors d'orient: Mélanges offerts à Rika* Gyselen, 283–315. Paris: Association pour l'avancement des études iraniennes, 2009.

Powers, David S. *Muḥammad is Not the Father of Any of Your Men: The Making of the Last Prophet*. Philadelphia: University of Pennsylvania Press, 2009.

Puente, Cristina de la. 'The Ethnic Origins of Female Slaves in al-Andalus'. Chapter 6 in *Concubines and Courtesans,* edited by Matthew Gordon and Kathryn Hain, 124–142. Oxford: Oxford University Press, 2017.

Qaṭṭāṭ, Ḥayāt. *Al-'Arab fī al-Jāhiliyya al-Akhīra wa-al-Islām al-Mubakkir*. Tunis: Dār al-'Amal, 2006.

Raddatz, H. P. 'Sufyān al-Thawrī'. In *The Encyclopaedia of Islam*. 2nd edition. Accessed on 22 May 2019. http://dx.doi.org/10.1163/1573-3912_islam_SIM_7130.

Rahman, Fazlur. *Major Themes of the Quran*. Minneapolis: Bibliotheca Islamica, 1980.

Retsö, Jan. *The Arabs in Antiquity: Their History from the Assyrians to the Umayyads*. London and New York: RoutledgeCurzon, 2003.

Reynolds, Gabriel Said, ed. *New Perspectives on the Qur'an: The Qur'an in Its Historical Context 2*. New York: Routledge, 2011.

Rihan, Mohamad. *The Politics and Culture of an Umayyad Tribe: Conflict and Factionalism in the Early Islamic Period*. London: Tauris, 2014.

Rio, Alice. 'Freedom and Unfreedom in Early Medieval Francia: The Evidence of the Legal Formulae', *Past & Present*, 193 (November 2006): 7–40.

——. 'Self-sale and Voluntary Entry into Unfreedom, 300–1100', *Journal of Social History*, 45, no. 3 (Spring 2012): 661–685.

Rippin, A. 'The Exegetical Genre *Asbāb Al-Nuzūl*: A Bibliographical and Terminological Survey', *Bulletin of the School of Oriental and African Studies, University of London*, 48, no. 1 (1 January 1985): 1–15.

——. 'The Function of *Asbāb Al-Nuzūl* in Qur'ānic Exegesis', *Bulletin of the School of Oriental and African Studies, University of London*, 51, no. 1 (1 January 1988): 1–20.

Robertson Smith, William. *Kinship and Marriage in Early Arabia*. New Edition. London: Adam and Charles Black, 1903.

Robinson, Chase. *Empire and Elites After the Muslim Conquest: The Transformation of Northern Mesopotamia*. Cambridge: Cambridge University Press, 2003.

——. 'Neck-Sealing in Early Islam', *Journal of the Economic and Social History of the Orient*, 48, no. 3 (2005): 404–441.

——. 'Slavery in the Conquest Period', *International Journal of Middle East Studies*, 49 (2017): 158–163.

Robinson, Majied. 'Statistical Approaches to the Rise of Concubinage in Islam'. In *Concubines and Courtesans: Women and Slavery in Islamic History*, edited by

Matthew Gordon and Kathryn Hain, 11–26. Oxford: Oxford University Press, 2017.

Robinson, Neal. *Discovering the Qur'ān: A Contemporary Approach to a Veiled Text.* 2nd edition. Washington, DC: Georgetown University Press, 2003.

Rowson, Everett K. 'The Effeminates of Early Medina', *Journal of the American Oriental Society*, 111, no. 4 (October–December 1991): 671–693.

Rubin, Uri. 'The "Constitution of Medina" Some Notes', *Studia Islamica*, 62 (1985): 5–23.

——. '"Al-walad li-l-firāsh": On the Islamic Campaign against "Zinā"', *Studia Islamica*, 78 (1993): 5–26.

Ruggles, D. Fairchild. 'Mothers of a Hybrid Dynasty: Race, Genealogy, and Acculturation in al-Andalus', *Journal of Medieval and Early Modern Studies*, 34, no. 1 (Winter 2004): 65–94.

Sanni, Amidu. 'The Secretary (*Kātib*) and his Tool in Medieval Islam: Prosification as a Professional Technique', *Journal for Islamic Studies*, 21 (2001): 85–112.

Savant, Sarah Bowen. *The New Muslims of Post-Conquest Iran: Tradition, Memory, and Conversion*. New York: Cambridge University Press, 2015.

Sayeed, Asma. *Women and the Transmission of Religious Knowledge in Islam.* Cambridge: Cambridge University Press, 2013.

Schacht, Joseph. *Introduction to Islamic Law.* Oxford: Oxford University Press, 1964.

——. *The Origins of Muhammadan Jurisprudence*. Oxford: Clarendon, 1967.

——. 'Umm al-Walad'. In *The Encyclopaedia of Islam.* 2nd edition. http://dx.doi.org/10.1163/1573-3912_islam_COM_1290.

Schillinger, Jaimie. 'Intellectual Humility and Interreligious Dialogue between Christians and Muslims', *Islam and Christian–Muslim Relations*, 23, no. 3 (2013): 363–380.

Serjeant, R. B. 'The "Constitution of Medina"', *Islamic Quarterly*, 8 (1964): 3–16.

——. 'The *Sunnah Jāmi'ah*, Pacts with the Yathrib Jews and the "Tahrim" of Yathrib: Analysis and Translation Comprised in the So-Called "Constitution of Medina"', *Bulletin of the School of Oriental and African Studies, University of London* 41, no. 1 (1978): 1–42.

Shaban, M. A. *The 'Abbasid Revolution*. Cambridge: Cambridge University Press, 1970.

Shahin, Aram. 'The Slave-Girls Who Enslaved the Free-Born: Slave-Girls and Their Masters in Islamic Literature', *Revista de Humanidades*, 23 (2014): 16–30.

Sharon, Moshe. *Black Banners from the East: The Establishment of the 'Abbāsid State.* Jerusalem: Magnes Press, Hebrew University; Leiden: Brill, 1983.

——. 'The Development of the Debate around the Legitimacy of Authority in Early Islam', *Jerusalem Studies in Arabic and Islam*, 5 (1984): 121–141.

——. 'The Umayyads as *Ahl al-Bayt*', *Jerusalem Studies in Arabic and Islam*, 14 (1991): 115–152.

Sizgorich, Thomas. *Violence and Belief in Late Antiquity: Militant Devotion in Christianity and Islam*. Philadelphia: University of Pennsylvania Press, 2014.

Sonbol, Amira Azhary. 'Adoption in Islamic Society: A Historical Survey'. In *Children in the Muslim Middle East*, edited by Elizabeth Warnock Fernea, 45–67. Austin: University of Texas Press, 1995.

Sourdel, Dominique. 'Le « Livre des Secrétaires » de 'Abdallāh al-Baġdādī', *Bulletin d'études orientales*, 14 (1952–1954): 115–153.

——. 'La biographie d'Ibn al-Muqaffaʿ d'après les sources anciennes', *Arabica*, 1 (1954): 308.

——. 'Le valeur littéraire et documentaire du *Livre des Vizirs* d'al-Jahshiyārī', *Arabica*, 2 (1955): 193–210.

Spellberg, Denise A. *Politics, Gender, and the Islamic Past: The Legacy of 'A'isha Bint Abi Bakr*. New York: Columbia University Press, 2012.

Sprengling, M. 'From Persian to Arabic', *The American Journal of Semitic Languages and Literatures*, 56, no. 2 (April 1939): 175–224.

Stewart, Devin J. 'Consensus, Authority, and the Interpretive Community in the Thought of Muḥammad B. Jarīr Al-Ṭabarī', *Journal of Qur'anic Studies*, 18, no. 2 (2016): 130–179.

Stowasser, Barbara F. 'Die Wurtzel j-h-l im Koran'. In *Necati Lugal armağanı*, 571–575. Ankara: Tarih Kurumu Basımevi, 1968.

——. *Women in the Qur'an, Traditions, and Interpretation*. New York: Oxford University Press, 1994.

Stroumsa, Sarah. 'The Beginnings of the Muʿtazila Reconsidered', *Jerusalem Studies in Arabic and Islam*, 13 (1990): 265–293.

Syed, Mairaj U. 'The Construction of Historical Memory in the Exegesis of Kor 16, 106', *Arabica*, 62 (2015): 607–651.

Szombathy, Zoltán. 'Genealogy in Medieval Muslim Societies', *Studia Islamica*, 95 (2002): 5–35.

——. *The Roots of Arabic Genealogy: A Study in Historical Anthropology*. Piliscsaba: The Avicenna Institute of Middle Eastern Studies, 2003.

Taylor, Alice. '*Homo Ligius* and Unfreedom in Medieval Scotland'. In *New Perspectives on Medieval Scotland, 1093–1286*, edited by Matthew Hammond, 85–116. Woodbridge: Boydell, 2013.

Tillschneider, Hans-Thomas. 'Les *Asbāb an-Nuzūl*: Une Branche de La Tradition Prophétique', *Studia Islamica*, 108, no. 2 (2013): 175–188.

Toledano, Ehud R. *Slavery and Abolition in the Ottoman Middle East*. Seattle: University of Washington Press, 1998.

——. *As If Silent and Absent: Bonds of Enslavement in the Islamic Middle East*. New Haven: Yale University Press, 2017.

Turner, Colin, ed., *The Koran: Critical Concepts in Islamic Studies*. London and New York: Routledge, 2004.

Urban, Elizabeth. 'Humble in Word and Body: Abu Bakra as an Early Islamic Exemplar', *Interdisciplinary Humanities*, 30, no. 1 (Spring 2013): 42–58.

——. 'The Foundations of Islamic Society as Expressed by the Qur'anic Term *mawlā*', *Journal of Quranic Studies*, 15, no. 1 (April 2013): 23–45.

——. 'Gender and Slavery in Islamic Political Thought'. In *Oxford Handbook of Comparative Political Theory*, forthcoming.

Vacca, Alison. 'Conference Report: Navigating Language in the Early Islamic World (The Marco Institute for Medieval and Renaissance Studies, The University of Tennessee, Knoxville, 6–7 April 2018)', *Al-Usur al-Wusta*, 26 (2018). Accessed on 12 March 2019. https://islamichistorycommons.org/mem/wp-content/uploads/sites/55/2018/11/UW-26-Vacca.pdf.

Vadet, J. C. 'Ibn Hubayra'. In *The Encyclopaedia of Islam*. 2nd edition. Accessed on 22 May 2019. http://dx.doi.org/10.1163/1573-3912_islam_SIM_3205.

Varisco, Daniel Martin. 'Metaphors and Sacred History: The Genealogy of Muhammad and the Arab "Tribe"', *Anthropological Quarterly*, 68, no. 3 (July 1995): 139–156.

Wadud, Amina. *Qur'an and Woman Rereading the Sacred Text from a Woman's Perspective*. Oxford: Oxford University Press, 1999.

Wansbrough, John. *Quranic Studies: Sources and Methods of Scriptural Interpretation*. Oxford: Oxford University Press, 1977.

Watt, William Montgomery. *Muhammad at Medina*. Oxford: Clarendon, 1956.

Webb, Peter. 'Identity and Social Formation in the Early Caliphate'. In *Routledge Handbook on Early Islam*, edited by Herbert Berg, 129–158. Abingdon: Routledge, 2017.

——. *Imagining the Arabs: Arab Identity and the Rise of Islam*. Edinburgh: Edinburgh University Press, 2017.

Wellhausen, Julius. *The Arab Kingdom and its Fall*. Translated by Margaret Graham Weir. Calcutta: University of Calcutta, 1927.

Wensinck, A. J. and Patricia Crone. 'Mawlā'. In *The Encyclopaedia of Islam*. 2nd edition. Accessed on 22 May 2019. http://dx.doi.org/10.1163/1573-3912_islam_COM_0714.

Wright, W. *A Grammar of the Arabic Language.* 3rd edition. Beirut: Librairie du Liban, 1996.

Yarbrough, Luke. 'Did 'Umar b. 'Abd al-'Azīz Issue an Edict Concerning Non-Muslim Officials?' Chapter 8 in *Christians and Others in the Umayyad State,* edited by Antoine Borrut and Fred Donner, 173–206. Chicago: Oriental Institute, 2016.

Zakkar, S. 'Ibn Khayyāṭ al-Uṣfurī, Khalīfa'. In *The Encyclopaedia of Islam.* 2nd edition. Accessed on 22 May 2019. http://dx.doi.org/10.1163/1573-3912_islam_SIM_3256.

Ziadeh, Farhat. 'Equality (*kafā'ah*) in the Muslim Law of Marriage', *American Journal of Comparative Law*, 6 (1957): 503–517.

Index

'Abat', 81–2, 85–6, 96
Abbasid Revolution, 34, 112, 167
Abbasids
  as a historical era, 34–5, 77–8, 141, 143, 148, 152–3, 184
  as a political dynasty, 53, 119, 129–30
  reproductive practices of, 112, 115, 119, 125, 127
ʿAbd al-Ḥamīd al-Kātib, 141, 143
ʿAbd al-Malik ibn Marwān, 5, 107, 158, 160, 162–3
ʿAbd al-Razzāq al-Ṣanʿānī, 90–1
ʿAbd Shams, 116–18
ʿAbdallāh ibn Abī Farwa, 165
ʿAbdallāh ibn al-Zubayr, 4, 184
ʿAbdallāh ibn Khālid ibn Usayd ibn Abī al-ʿĀṣ, 119–20
ʿAbdallāh ibn Nātil, 89
ʿAbdallāh ibn Ubayy ibn Salūl, 84, 87–9, 92
Abou El Fadl, Khaled, 64
Abraham, 26, 120, 122, 128–9
Abū Bakr, 88–9, 124
Abū Bakr ibn Ḥazm, 165
Abū Bakra
  as Arabian tribesman, 61–4
  as contrasted with Ziyād ibn Abīhi, 56–65
  as mawla of the Prophet, 56–61
  as *ṭalīq allāh*, 50–6
  basic biography of, 23, 48–50, 95
  legal reputation of, 63–8
Abū Ḥanīfa, 34
Abū Sufyān, 57, 60, 62, 94
Abū ʿUthmān al-Nahdī, 60–1
ʿAdnān, 126
adoption *see diʿwa*
adultery, 25, 50, 64–5
Afsaruddin, Asma, 93
agency, 25, 29–30, 35, 63, 79, 89–95, 163
Ahmed, Asad Q., 108, 123, 127
Aḥwaṣ, al-, 146
ʿĀʾisha bint Abī Bakr, 50, 65, 81
ʿajam, 122, 166, 180; *see also* non-Arab
Al-Azmeh, Aziz, 4, 79
ʿAlī ibn Abī Ṭālib, 57, 67, 95, 124
ʿAlī ibn al-Ḥusayn Zayn al-ʿĀbidīn, 123, 130
Alids, 130, 148
ʿĀliya, al- *see* Ḥabāba
analysis, feminist, 2, 78–82
Anas ibn Mālik, 58
ʿAnbasa ibn Saʿīd ibn al-ʿĀṣ, 119
Anṣār (Helpers), 32, 54, 82–3, 92, 109, 116–17
apocalyptic, 120, 122–3
Arabia, 37, 54, 56, 81, 96, 141–2
Arabians
  early Islamic 55–8, 61–2, 116–18, 123, 126, 154–61
  pre-Islamic 22, 49–50, 55, 57, 94
Arabisation, 5, 144, 157, 162–3
Arabness, 5, 54–5, 62–3, 128–30, 140–4, 162–6, 180–4
asbāb al-nuzūl (occasions of revelation), 36, 81–2, 90–2
Aʿshā Hamdān, 182
ʿĀṣim al-Aḥwal, 60
Aws, 53, 116–18

Balādhurī, al-, 58, 64, 66–8, 108, 119, 129, 145
Basra, 50, 55–6, 58–61, 64, 87, 183
Battle of the Camel, 50

Bayḍāwī, al-, 35, 92
believers, 4, 19–33, 37, 51, 92, 183–4
'Believers' Movement', 3–4, 163, 181
Bennett, Judith, 79–80
bighā' (illicit sex), 26–9, 31, 82
bilingualism, 145, 161, 163
biographical dictionary *see ṭabaqāt*
biography *see sīra*
Bint Jarīr ibn 'Abdallāh, 119
Bock, Gisela, 79–80
bodies, 22, 31–2, 64, 67, 93
Borrut, Antoine, 147
Brockopp, Jonathan, 8
brotherhood
  figurative, (*mu'*ākhah), 32, 34, 54
  genetic, 49–50, 54–60, 62–4, 108, 126, 146, 151
  in religion, 19–23, 33, 48, 181
Bukhārī, al-, 61
bureaucracy, 5, 141, 143, 149, 154–66
Byzantines, 4–5, 61–2, 122–3

caliphate
  changing bureaucratic practices of, 153–66
  changing reproductive politics of, 106, 108, 119, 125–8, 177
  ideology of, 89, 107, 120–1, 128–30, 146–8
  transition from military to bureaucratic, 5–6, 145, 149–52, 167, 177
  see also names of individual caliphs
chastity, 24–31, 34–5, 81–2, 86, 88, 91, 94
Christianity, 31–2, 86, 91, 163
Christians
  as conquered populations, 107, 181
  associated with vice, 97
  in relationships with Muslims, 123, 127
  in the Quran, 21
  in the Umayyad government, 154–63
civil war *see fitna*
clients *see mawālī*
Companions, 59–60, 80, 82, 109, 124
concubinage
  and chastity, 29–30, 83
  as imperial reproductive strategy, 127
  as sanctioned in the Quran and Islamic law, 7, 29–30
  compared to marriage, 113–15
  rates of, 111–18
  see also umm walads
concubines *see umm walads*
conquests, Islamic, 3–7, 51, 108, 112–14, 121, 148–9, 161–2
'Constitution of Medina', 21
courtesans *see qiyān*
Crone, Patricia, 3, 55

*dhimmī*s (protected people), 178–9
di'wa (adoption), 22, 32, 54–5, 63
*dīwān*s (government bureaus), 154, 160, 163–4
Donner, Fred, 4, 162, 180–1

education, 140–4, 146, 149, 152, 161–2, 167, 177
'effeminates' of Medina, 165
egalitarianism
  attributed to the Abbasids, 125, 130
  in tension with hierarchy, 19–20, 23, 37, 48, 77, 176–7, 184
  in the earliest *umma*, 23, 37, 85–6, 124, 93
El-Hibri, Tayeb, 67, 148
Emigrants *see* Muhājirūn
emigration *see hijra*
empire-building, 3–5, 56, 107, 140–3, 153, 161–7, 176–7, 184
endogamy, 127
ethics, sexual, 19, 24–5, 27–33, 78, 83, 94, 177
ethnicity, 123, 140–4, 153–4, 158, 162, 177–8, 183
exegesis *see tafsīr*

factionalism, 50, 65, 126–7, 166–7, 179
Fakhr al-Dīn al-Rāzī, 90, 92
family
  and slavery, 7, 9, 85, 130, 180
  as a political unit, 48, 108, 118, 125–7, 150, 164
  in the Quran, 21, 24, 27
  see also household
fatayāt (young slave women), 26–8, 30
feminism *see* analysis, feminist
Fitna, First, 3, 50, 65, 67, 161
Fitna, Second (Great), 4–5, 97, 107, 164
Fitna, Third, 112
foreigners, 19, 22, 54, 78, 119, 122, 165
foreignness, 96, 128, 130, 142–3, 153, 177
fornication *see zinā*
Franz, Kurt 6 , 8
'freedman of God' *see ṭalīq allāh*
freedmen *see mawālī*
freedom, 6–9, 28, 51–5, 58

gender, 50, 77–9, 149
genealogy, 19, 22–4, 34, 37, 54–6, 61, 108–9, 129–30
generations, 59–61, 108–16, 121, 143, 150, 155–7, 165
genre, 36, 56, 63, 81, 86, 153
Glancy, Jennifer, 31
Gordon, Matthew, 142
Great Fitna *see* Second (Great) Fitna

Ḥabāba, 144–53, 167, 177
hadiths
  about paternity, 59–63
  about ʿUmar ibn al-Khaṭṭāb, 67
  scholars of (*muḥaddithūn*), 56, 61–3, 82, 92, 109, 124
  transmitted by Abū Bakra, 49–50, 58–61, 63–4, 68
  transmitted by women, 80
Hagar, 120, 128–31
Ḥajjaj ibn Yūsuf, al-, 52, 178–9, 183
Ḥakam ibn al-Walīd II, al-, 126
Ḥamawī, al- *see* Yāqūt al-Ḥamawī
ḥamrā' (reds), 122
harem, 128, 144–5, 149–53, 167
Ḥārith ibn Kalada, al-, 49, 51, 57, 62, 95
Ḥasan al-Baṣrī, al-, 55, 58, 61
Ḥasan ibn al-Ḥasan, al-, 128
Ḥasanids, 119, 125, 127–9
Hāshim, 108, 112–13, 116–17, 129
Hawting, Gerald, 178–9
Heck, Paul, 158
Helpers *see* Anṣār
hierarchy, 2–3, 5, 10, 20, 23, 36–7, 131, 184
hijāb (veiling/seclusion), 7, 81
Hijaz, 3–4, 108, 146, 149, 153, 158–9, 163–4
hijra, 32, 178–9, 183
Hishām ibn ʿAbd al-Malik, 112, 128–9, 160
historiography *see tārīkh*
household, 6, 9, 83–5, 142, 150, 159–60, 166–7, 181–2
Hūd ibn Muḥakkam, 9
hujanā ('half-bloods'), 118, 122–6, 178, 184; *see also umm walads*, children of
humility, 58, 66–8
Ḥusayn ibn ʿAlī, al-, 85, 162
Ḥusaynids, 119, 130

Ibn ʿAbd al-Ḥakam, 179
Ibn ʿAbd Rabbih, 94, 153
Ibn Abī Lahab, Fulān, 149
Ibn Abī Shayba, 61
Ibn al-Jawzī, 92
Ibn al-Kalbī, 109, 119
Ibn al-Muqaffaʿ, 141–4
Ibn al-Saʿī, 78
Ibn ʿAsākir, 123–4, 129, 154
Ibn Buṭlān, 142
Ibn Ḥanbal, 61
Ibn Ḥazm *see* Abū Bakr ibn Ḥazm
Ibn Hishām, 51
Ibn Isḥāq, 143
Ibn Jurayj, 82
Ibn Kathīr, 90–3
Ibn Qutayba, 129
Ibn Saʿd, 51, 54–5, 67, 93, 108–16, 121, 142
Ibn Shihāb al-Zuhrī *see* Zuhrī, al
Ibrāhīm ibn Muḥammad, 130
ideology, 50, 53, 57–61, 86–9, 106–7, 126, 128–31
iḥṣān, 25–6, 30–1
imamate *see* caliphate
inheritance, 7, 22, 24, 32–3, 62, 117
inter-agency, 9, 163
Iraq, 86–7, 97, 151, 154, 158–64, 178–9
Isaac, 122, 128
Iṣbahānī, al-, 145, 150–1
Isḥāq ibn Qabīṣa, 160
Ishmael, 128–9
Islam (technical term), 12, 182–4
isnād analysis, 59, 61, 80

Jābir ibn ʿAbdallāh, 82
jāhiliyya, 22, 27–9, 78, 85–7, 94, 96
Jāḥiz, al-, 178–80
Jahshiyārī, al-, 144–5, 153–5, 158–65
Jalālayn, al-, 90
Jarrāḥ, al-, 179
jihad state, 112, 147, 153, 183
Joseph, 26
Juda, Jamal, 8, 180
justice, 36, 52, 67–8, 81–7, 92–7, 144, 179, 183

Kadi, Wadad, 143
Kalb, 33, 126–7
Khālid al-Ḥadhdhā', 61
Khālid ibn ʿAbdallāh, 151–2
Khālid ibn Sumayr, 55
Khālid ibn Yazīd I, 126
Khalīfa ibn Khayyāṭ, 61
Kharijites, 55, 58, 184
Khayzurān, al-, 145, 148, 152, 167
Khazraj, 53, 111, 116–17
Khurasan, 154, 158–9

Kilpatrick, Hilary, 142
Kinda, 126
kinship, 7, 21, 32, 125–6
Kufa, 55–6, 59, 88–9, 183
kuttāb (bureaucrats, secretaries)
  Arabian tribesmen, 154–61
  as scapegoats, 160–5
  basic description of, 141
  Christian, 154–7
  mawālī, 143–5, 153–60, 167
  Persian, 154, 156–8
  Qurashi, 154–61
  resonances with the *qiyān* (courtesans), 141–2
  see also bureaucracy

law
  early Islamic (pre-canonical), 6–8, 66, 116, 120
  in the Quran and *tafsīr*, 22–3, 33
  relationship with historiography, 68–9
  Shii, 117
  Sunni, 55, 62, 66, 89–90, 97–8, 119
Levy-Rubin, Milka, 5
London, Jennifer, 142–3
loyalty, 8, 11, 107, 119, 123, 151, 163, 166

mā malakat al-aymān (Quranic term for slave), 6, 26, 30
Madā'inī, al-, 181–2
Mahdī, al-, 53
Mālik ibn Anas, 54
Maʿmar ibn Rāshid, al-, 86–7
Manṣūr, al-, 129–30
manumission, 6–7, 28, 51, 53–4
Māriya the Copt, 128, 130–1
marriage, 22–3, 27–9, 81, 113–17, 125–7
Marwān ibn Abī Ḥafṣa, 53
Marwān ibn al-Ḥakam, 128, 161–2
Marwanids, 5–6, 106–8, 118–19, 124–5, 154–7, 161–6
Mary, mother of Jesus, 27
Mary Magdalene, 86, 91
Maslama ibn ʿAbd al-Malik, 123–4, 146–8
Masrūḥ, 49, 54, 58, 60
Masʿūdī, al-, 57, 94–5, 145, 150
Māturīdī, al-, 91
mawālī (clients, freedmen)
  as a Quranic term, 19–23, 34, 48
  as a social group or collective, 180–2
  as distinct from serfs/peasants, 178–9
  as *kuttāb* (bureaucrats), 141–2, 153–66
  as political subalterns, 165–6
  as related to *hujanā'* (half-bloods), 122
  as subordinate members of households, 8–9, 180
  compared to *ṭalīq allāh*, 51–5
  ethnic identity of, 143–4, 178–80
  in classical exegeses of Q 33:5, 32–6
  in Islamic law, 7
  naming practices of, 35, 154
  services provided by, 8, 180
  symbolic resonances of, 54–61, 66, 68
  see also Abū Bakra
Mecca, 49, 51, 84, 87, 141, 146, 149
Medina, 64, 81–7, 109–11, 123–4, 127, 141–2, 149, 165
memory, 78, 94, 148, 163–4
Mernissi, Fatima, 63
mobility, 149
morality, 19, 28–9, 57, 61, 85, 91–4, 148
motherhood
  and ethnicity, 142
  as connected to child's identity, 95, 106–7, 123
  as path to freedom for enslaved women, 7
  demographics of, 111–18
  enslaved women's impact through, 97–8, 106
  ideologies of, 128–30
  importance of in tribal societies, 108, 123, 125–6
  in imperial politics, 125, 127–8, 145, 148, 150, 152–3
  in Muqātil's exegesis of Q 24:33, 89–90
  in Q 33:5, 22
  see also umm walads
Motzki, Harald, 25
Muʿādha, 82, 86–95
Muʿāwiya I ibn Abī Sufyān, 4, 57, 61, 120, 161
Mughīra ibn Shuʿba, al-, 64–6
Muhājirūn (Emigrants), 5, 22–3, 32, 54, 183–4
Muḥammad, prophet, 3–5, 22–3, 32–3, 49–51, 56–67, 88–9, 128–30 184
Muḥammad ibn ʿAbdallāh al-Nafs al-Zakiyya, 129–30
muḥṣina see *iḥṣān*
Mujāhid ibn Jabr, 82, 84, 91
Mukhtār, al-, 181–2
muʾminūn see believers
Muqātil ibn Sulaymān, 33, 89–90
Muṣʿab ibn al-Zubayr, 164–5
music, 141, 177

Muslim (technical term), 182–4
Muslim ibn Ḥajjāj, 62
muwalladāt, 142, 176–8

Nabateans *see* Christians
Nāfiʿ ibn al-Ḥārith, 49, 56–7
Nafs al-Zakiyya, al- *see* Muḥammad ibn ʿAbdallāh
Nasāʾī, al-, 81, 90, 92
non-Arabs, 55, 67, 120–2, 130, 140–3, 159, 166, 177–80; *see also* ʿ*ajam*
Nuʿaym ibn Ḥammād, 122–4
Nufayʿ ibn al-Ḥārith *see* Abū Bakra
Numayrī, al-, Imām ibn Aqram, 52

occasions of revelation *see asbab al-nuzūl*

paternity, 34, 59, 61–3, 97
patriarchy, 80–1, 92–3, 131
patrilineage, 119, 127, 130–1
Paul, Christian apostle, 31–2
Peirce, Leslie, 149
Persians, 5, 52, 129, 143–4, 156–60, 177, 179–80
poetry, Arabic, 52–3, 56–7, 97, 141–2, 146, 149, 167
prejudice, 107–8, 118–19, 124–5, 143, 183
prosopography, 80, 107–18, 124, 154–61
prostitutes
  as impelling *al-walad lil-firāsh* laws, 62, 97–8
  as peripheral to Islamic society, 96–8
  as reformed or 'saved', 86–93
  in classical Quranic exegesis, 35–6
  in early Islamic Medina, 77–8, 81–6
  in the Quran, 27–8
  negative historical portrayals of, 86, 93–6
prostitution, 24–37, 81–7, 91–4, 97–8

Qabīṣa ibn Dhu'ayb, 160
qadhf (slander), 50, 63–6
Qaḥṭān, 126
Qaʿqāʿ ibn Khālid, al-, 151
Qāsim ibn Muḥammad ibn Abī Bakr, al-, 123–4
Qays, 126, 166
qiyān (courtesans)
  and ethnic identity, 140, 142, 144, 153, 167, 178
  as absent in Quran, exegesis, and Islamic law, 8, 35
  as distinct from concubine queen-mothers, 145
  as distinct from prostitutes, 77–8
  as Ḥabāba's protégés, 151
  basic description of, 141
  forms of power wielded by, 141, 145, 149
  limits of power wielded by, 149–50, 152, 167
  resonances with the *kuttāb* (secretaries), 141–2
  see also Ḥabāba
Qubbāʿ, al-, 97
queens, 106, 128, 145, 148, 152–4, 167, 177
Qummī, al-, 35, 90
Quran
  as a historical source, 4, 19
  concept of humility in, 67–8
  fears of translation/mispronunciation of, 120–1
  punishment for slander in, 64–5
  verses 24:32–34 of, 24–31
  verses 33:4–6 of, 20–4
Quraysh, 50–3, 56–7, 87, 108–9, 116–18, 155–62, 166
Qurṭubī, al-, 90, 92

Rashīd, Hārūn al-, 148
Rashīd ibn ʿAbdallāh ibn Khālid, 120
Rāshidūn caliphs, 3, 124–5, 161
Rāzī, al- *see* Fakhr al-Dīn al-Rāzī
Rightly-Guided caliphs *see* Rāshidūn
Robinson, Chase, 178
Robinson, Majied, 108, 111, 125, 127
Rubin, Uri, 62, 97

Saʿd ibn Abī Waqqāṣ, 59–62
Saʿd ibn ʿUbāda, 53, 111
ṣaḥāba see Companions
sāʾiba, 54; *see also* manumission
Sālim ibn ʿAbdallāh ibn ʿUmar, 123–4
Ṣanʿānī, al- *see* ʿAbd al-Razzāq
Sarjūn ibn Manṣūr, 162–3
Sasanians, 5, 143, 158
Sawda bint Zamʿa, 62, 81
Sayeed, Asma, 80–1
Sayf ibn ʿUmar, 65
scapegoats, 12, 142, 160–2
serfdom, 8–9, 179
sexuality, 11, 29–31, 86, 141
Shia, 23, 33, 35–6, 94–5, 117, 128, 130
singing-girls *see qiyān*

sīra (biography), 81, 179
slander *see qadhf*
slave trade, 35, 85, 112
slavery
  and sexual ethics, 25
  as presented in Q 24:33, 28–31
  basic legal parameters of, 6–7
  early Christian views of, 31–2
  historical forms of, 8, 88, 142, 145
  in early Islamic Medina, 81–6
  limits of as a conceptual framework, 9
  see also unfreedom
succession, imperial, 126, 150, 152
Successors, 58, 109
Suʿdā bint ʿAbdallāh al-ʿUthmāniyya, 150–1
Suddī, al-, 86, 88–9
Sufyanids, 127, 155, 161
Sulaymān ibn ʿAbd al-Malik, 146
Sumayya, 49, 57, 62, 86, 94–6, 98
Sunni, 7, 33–5, 80, 87–91, 117, 124, 130, 148
symbolism, 56, 63–4, 67–8, 82–90, 93–4, 146–8, 176
Syria, 57, 97, 120, 122–3, 129, 154–9, 163

ṭabaqāt, 51, 54, 59, 81, 108–10, 121
tābiʿūn see Successors
Ṭabarānī, al-, 92
Ṭabarī, al-, 34, 64–5, 90–2, 120, 153–4, 178–9
tafsīr (exegesis), 22–6, 32–6, 82–94, 96–7
taḥaṣṣun (chastity-adjacent), 19, 24–31, 37
Taif, 49–51, 53, 56–8, 60, 96
ṭalīq allāh (freedman of God), 48, 51–6, 68, 77, 86
tārīkh (historiography), 57, 63–4, 68–9, 81, 86, 153–4, 178
tasyīb see *sā'iba*
Thaqif, 49–51, 54, 56, 61–3, 68
Tiflis, treaty of, 181, 183
Toledano, Ehud, 80
tribalism, 108–9, 114, 116, 125–7, 131, 160–1, 167
ṭulaqā' (late Meccan converts), 51–2
Ṭūsī, al-, 92

ʿUbaydallāh ibn Ziyād, 95, 162
ʿUmar I ibn al-Khaṭṭāb, 50, 64–7, 124
ʿUmar ibn Hubayra, 151
ʿUmar II ibn ʿAbd al-ʿAzīz, 146–8, 165, 179
Umayma, 89–90
Umayyads
  and Arabness 58, 61, 107, 118–19, 123–4, 143–4
  bureaucratic practices of, 154–67
  downfall of, 120–1
  in Abbasid memory, 148
  political reforms of, 107, 140, 145–53, 158, 162, 193–4
  reproductive practices of, 106–19, 125–7, 167
  see also names of individual Umayyad caliphs
Umm al-Ḥajjāj, 150
Umm Ḥujr, 120
Umm Saʿīd al-ʿUthmāniyya 150
umm walads (concubine-mothers)
  as distinct from prostitutes, 77–8
  average birthrates of, 114–15
  caliphs born to, 125–31
  children of, 9, 106–8, 110–36
  compared to free wives, 113–15
  famous scholars born to, 123–4
  in Islamic law, 7, 116–17
  non-canonical forms of, 119–20
  political rhetoric about, 123–4, 128–31
  'various', in Ibn Sa'd's Tabaqat, 111
unfreedom, 8–9, 163, 177–84
ʿUqayshir, 97
ʿUṣfūrī, al- *see* Khalīfa ibn Khayyāṭ
ʿUtba ibn Abī Waqqāṣ, 59, 62
ʿUthmān ibn Affān, 53, 120–2, 161–2, 165

Wāḥidī, al-, 92
walad lil-firāsh, al-, 62–3, 97
Walīd II ibn Yazīd, al-, 126, 147, 150
Wāqidī, al-, 53–4, 65–6
Webb, Peter, 4–5, 180, 183
w-l-y (Arabic root), 21–4

Yaman, 126, 166
Yaʿqūbī, al-, 128, 179
Yāqūt al-Ḥamawī, 96
Yazīd I ibn Muʿāwiya, 126, 162
Yazīd II ibn ʿAbd al-Malik, 144–52, 167
Yazīd III ibn al-Walīd, 126, 128

Zādhān Farrūkh, 163
Zamakhsharī, al-, 34–5, 90–1
Zayd ibn ʿAlī, 128–30
Zayd ibn Ḥaritha, 32–3

Zayn al-ʿĀbidīn *see* ʿAlī ibn al-Ḥusayn
zinā (fornication), 31, 82–4
Ziyād ibn Abīhi, 49–50, 56–68, 94–5, 162, 164
Zubayrī, al-, 180
Zubayrids, 65, 164
Zuhrī, al-, Ibn Shihāb, 87, 90
Ẓulayma, 94

EU representative:
Easy Access System Europe
Mustamäe tee 50, 10621 Tallinn, Estonia
Gpsr.requests@easproject.com

www.ingramcontent.com/pod-product-compliance
Lightning Source LLC
Chambersburg PA
CBHW070351240426
43671CB00013BA/2462
9781474491792